CENSORING HISTORY

ASIA AND THE PACIFIC

Series Editor: Mark Selden, Binghamton University

Exploring one of the most dynamic and contested regions of the world, this series includes contributions on political, economic, cultural, and social changes in modern and contemporary Asia and the Pacific.

ASIA'S ENVIRONMENTAL MOVEMENTS
Comparative Perspectives
Yok-shiu F. Lee and Alvin Y. So, editors

CENSORING HISTORY
Citizenship and Memory in Japan, Germany, and the United States
Laura Hein and Mark Selden, editors

CHINA'S RETREAT FROM EQUALITY
Income Distribution and Economic Transition
Carl Riskin, Zhao Renwei, and Li Shih, editors

CHINA'S WORKERS UNDER ASSAULT
Anita Chan

THE CONTENTIOUS CHINESE
Elizabeth J. Perry

THE POLITICAL ECONOMY OF UNEVEN DEVELOPMENT
The Case of China
Shaoguang Wang and Angang Hu

THEATER AND SOCIETY
An Anthology of Contemporary Chinese Drama
Haiping Yan, editor

WHAT IF CHINA DOESN'T DEMOCRATIZE?
Implications for War and Peace
Edward Friedman and Barrett L. McCormick, editors

WOMEN IN REPUBLICAN CHINA
A Sourcebook
Hua R. Lan and Vanessa L. Fong, editors

CENSORING HISTORY

CITIZENSHIP AND MEMORY IN JAPAN, GERMANY, AND THE UNITED STATES

LAURA HEIN AND **MARK SELDEN**
EDITORS

AN EAST GATE BOOK

M.E.Sharpe
Armonk, New York
London, England

An East Gate Book

Copyright © 2000 by *Bulletin of Concerned Asian Scholars*

Library of Congress Cataloging-in-Publication Data

Censoring history : citizenship and memory in Japan, Germany and the United States /
edited by Laura Hein and Mark Selden.
    p.   c.m. — (Asia and the Pacific)
"An east gate book."
Includes bibliographical references and index.
ISBN 0-7656-0446-9 (hc. : alk. paper) — ISBN 0-7656-0447-7-(pbk. : alk. paper)
1. History, Modern—20th century—Historiography. 2. History, Modern—20th
century—Study and teaching. I. Hein, Laura Elizabeth. II. Selden, Mark. III. Asia and
the Pacific (Armonk, N.Y.)

D413.5.C43 1999
909-82′072—dc21   99-044612
                                     CIP

Printed in the United States of America

For our teachers—formal and informal

Contents

Acknowledgments   ix

Part I: Introduction

1. The Lessons of War, Global Power, and Social Change
   Laura Hein and Mark Selden   3

Part II: Textbooks and Historical Memory

2. The Japanese Movement to "Correct" History
   Gavan McCormack   53

3. Consuming Asia, Consuming Japan: The New Neonationalistic
   Revisionism in Japan
   Aaron Gerow   74

4. Japanese Education, Nationalism, and Ienaga Saburō's
   Textbook Lawsuits
   Nozaki Yoshiko and Inokuchi Hiromitsu   96

5. Identity and Transnationalization in German School Textbooks
   Yasemin Nuhoglu Soysal   127

6. The Vietnam War in High School American History
   James W. Loewen   150

7. War Crimes and the Vietnamese People: American Representations and Silences
David Hunt   173

Part III: Politics of the Classroom

8. The Continuing Legacy of Japanese Colonialism: The Japan–South Korea Joint Study Group on History Textbooks
Kimijima Kazuhiko   203

9. The Power of Selective Tradition: Buchenwald Concentration Camp and Holocaust Education for Youth in the New Germany
Gregory Wegner   226

10. Teaching Democracy, Teaching War: American and Japanese Educators Teach the Pacific War
Kathleen Woods Masalski   258

Contributors   289

Index   291

Acknowledgments

Many people helped bring this book to publication. Peter Katzenstein, James Loewen, Gavan McCormack, Gary Okihiro, Michael Sherry, and Marilyn Young provided thoughtful and challenging comments on earlier drafts of the introduction. Koseki Shoichi, Asanuma Shigeru, Akiko Hashimoto, Lane Fenrich, and John Bushnell gave helpful advice. Yuehim Tam, Steven Potts, and Kathleen Woods Masalski provided critical, engaged commentary at the 1988 meetings of the Association for Asian Studies in Washington, DC. Jennifer Rogers assisted with both ideas and dozens of trips to the library. Vinca Merriman made it clear that nine-year-olds care about the issues raised here. Nakamura Masanori first alerted us to the significance of the Orthodox History Group. Kristine Dennehy ably translated his ideas in our first project on this topic, published as "Textbook Nationalism, Citizenship, and War: Comparative Perspectives," a special issue of the *Bulletin of Concerned Asian Scholars*, 30.2 (April–June 1998). Tom Fenton, the *Bulletin*'s managing editor, contributed far more than his title would suggest.

Gathering the visual images was an especially time-consuming task even though many of the contributors helped, especially Hiro Inokuchi. The Office of Research and Sponsored Projects at Northwestern University provided indispensable funds. Christopher Tassava found many of the images, negotiated for permission to use them, and created the maps. Peter Hayes cleared the way to use the images of Buchenwald. Tom Fenton prepared the images for publication. Turning to the prose, Alice Colwell gave the book elegant and learned copyediting and Angela Piliouras marched it through production with her customary efficiency.

One of the pleasures of writing this book was rediscovering how many teachers see education as the essential process by which a democratic polity is created and sustained. Educators around the world share that radical vision. They take on the task of empowering young people to participate in the larger political and social world. Both challenge and encouragement, their willingness to shoulder that burden remains an inspiration. This book is dedicated to them.

Part I

Introduction

1
The Lessons of War, Global Power, and Social Change

Laura Hein and Mark Selden

Education, Citizenship, and War: What's At Stake?

Schools and textbooks are important vehicles through which contemporary societies transmit ideas of citizenship and both the idealized past and the promised future of the community. They provide authoritative narratives of the nation, delimit proper behavior of citizens, and sketch the parameters of the national imagination. Narratives of nationhood, like textbooks themselves, are always unfinished projects, requiring revision and reinterpretation to remain relevant in ever-changing times.

Controversies over textbook content often break out when prevailing domestic assumptions about national unity are challenged and when international relations change rapidly, as in many parts of the contemporary post–Cold War world. Major wars are defining moments in forging and sustaining national identities. Textbook controversies reveal one important way that societies negotiate, institutionalize, and renegotiate nationalist narratives. This volume examines and compares controversies over textbook depictions of recent wars in Japan, Germany, and the United States.[1]

History and civics textbooks in most societies present an "official" story highlighting narratives that shape contemporary patriotism. Education helps articulate relations between state and society and sets the boundaries and terms of citizenship. People fight over textbook content because education is so obviously about the future, reaches so deeply into society, and is directed by the state. As Michael Apple and Linda Christian-Smith put it, texts "participate in creating what a society has recognized as legitimate and truthful."[2] Because textbooks are carried into neighborhood schools and homes, and because, directly or indirectly, they carry the imprimatur of the state, they have enormous authority. Some ideas about the past derive from other sources, such as monuments, museums, movies, popular fiction, and family stories, yet formal education carries a special weight. Given their authoritative character, texts are particularly important "sites of memory."[3] Although controversies over textbooks are often based on the assumption that texts fulfill Gramscian expectations about hegemonic institutions, we argue here that the existence of the disputes themselves signal challenges to hegemony.

Nationalism is a multidimensional phenomenon expressed in many forms, including school curricula. Stein Tonnesson and Hans Antlov succinctly describe nationalism as "an ideological movement for attaining or maintaining a nation-state."[4] Building on this approach, we emphasize two interrelated themes of nationalism that run through history lessons everywhere. The first is the relationship between citizens and the state, often centering on recognition (or denial) of ethnic, linguistic, and religious differences. The second is foreign relations, especially the conduct of one's own nation in war. History lessons not only model behavior for citizens within their own society but also chronicle relations with others. The stories chosen or invented about the national past are invariably prescriptive—instructing people how to think and act as national subjects and how to view relations with outsiders.

Textbook authors and teachers face a daunting task when confronted with the history of a discredited war. When the subject is World War II in Japan or Germany, or the Vietnam War in the United States, it is impossible to discuss either the actions of citizens or the treatment of outsiders in ways that satisfy everyone.[5] Should teachers defend the least objectionable goals of the wartime state while acknowledging the brutality with which those aims were carried out? Or should they condemn the nation's war goals and practices? And if so, on what grounds? As an aggressive war? An imperialist war? A war that violated human rights? An irrational, that is, unwinnable war? Should teachers and texts stress changes since defeat or focus on national continuities? How should they teach about dissent during the war? Were defeat and perhaps even military occupation by foreigners a blessing in disguise in that they stopped the nation from carrying out cruel and self-destructive actions? These questions are deeply divisive because they cut to the heart of ideas about nation and citizenship. More than half a century after World War II, they still spark acrimonious debate both across the original battle lines and within each country.

Grappling with the issues of citizenship and war responsibility necessarily reveals assumptions about the purpose of education, assumptions that immediately affect the lesson plans. Teaching students to debate controversial issues and question basic premises implies a very different concept of citizens' rights and responsibilities than does memorization of a sacred text. Education models citizenship through its form as well as its content. Teachers' stances toward both the texts and their students, moreover, shape what and how students learn. Debates over education are always in part about defining citizenship and training children to meet that ideal.

Many educators in the United States, Germany, and Japan see the task of creating an informed and active citizenry through education as the bedrock of political democracy. This concept has a very long history in the United States. After World War II, many Japanese and Germans blamed their educational systems for contributing to the war by teaching them blindly to accept authority. Democratic education for them is itself a clear repudiation of the war. In that spirit, postwar educators in both nations pledged to equip young citizens with the tools to question their own government and "keep it honest." As Nozaki Yoshiko and Inokuchi Hiromitsu point out in chapter 4, Ienaga Saburō, an author of Japan's very first postwar history text, has kept government censorship of textbooks on the public agenda for thirty-five years out of a commitment to precisely this vision of a democratically engaged citizenry. The German curriculum on the Holocaust Gregory Wegner describes in chapter 3 sends the similar message that students have the civic and moral responsibility to prevent anything like Nazism from developing in the future. Some American educators also have drawn a variety of critical lessons from the Vietnam War and other wars, but their analyses have not had nearly as great a political or social impact as in Germany or Japan.

Yet in all three countries the vision of education as a tool of democratic citizenship has coexisted uneasily with other models: notably, education to compete in the global marketplace, to conform to officially sanctioned ideals of homogeneity, and to sacrifice for national security goals.[6] That tension over defining the fundamental rights and responsibilities of citizens is at the heart of the most important controversies over textbook content. The essays gathered here take a stand on this question—they all assume that education should teach students how to judge for themselves when to support and when to oppose the policies of their own states.

One of the main reasons people challenge hegemonic nationalist narratives is that they find unacceptable the depiction (or lack of depiction) of people like themselves. Social movements demanding equality, compensa-

1.1 *Hitler* comic book

This comic book was designed for use in German schools as a tool to explain and criticize Nazism. Anti-Semitism was first pursued legally—for example, a 1935 law, discussed in this image, deprived German Jews of legal rights and another law named the swastika as the national symbol. But some worried that introducing Nazism to a new generation, even to critique it, could serve to justify it. Friedemann Bedurftig and Dieter Kalenbach, *Hitler* (Hamburg: Carlsen Verlag GmbH, 1992). Used by permission.

tory benefits, and an end to discriminatory practices against women and ethnic minorities have transformed nationalist narratives since World War II in many parts of the globe. We use the ongoing debates over Japan's wartime exploitation of "military comfort women" as sex slaves for the military, German treatments of the Holocaust, and U.S. wartime internment of Japanese Americans to spotlight changing concepts of citizenship. When any group wins a larger measure of civic or political rights or even the most basic recognition as human beings, their victory compels renegotiation of the accepted definitions of the citizen and/or national subject.

In Japan, publicly acknowledging the human dignity of the ex–comfort women not only constituted criticism of wartime leaders who saw nothing wrong with enslaving them but also forced reevaluation of the implicit gendered and racial assumptions of the national narrative. Confronting the corrosive effects of racism in both international and domestic contexts is also critical to reassessment of the Holocaust in West and unified German educational materials and of Japanese American internment in American ones. By contrast, national patterns of remembrance of the Vietnam War in the United States have not yet provoked comparable textbook challenges.

Although the primary audience for nationalist narratives in general, and textbooks in particular, is domestic, controversies repeatedly spill across national borders. They do so most often when the subject is an international event such as a war or when it involves the treatment of racially, ethnically, or religiously distinctive social groups who live both within and beyond national borders. International conflicts also have their own histories. In postwar Germany and Japan, for example, criticism of World War II was imposed by occupation authorities, who made eradication of nationalism in textbooks a key part of demilitarization and democratization policy, thereby not only politicizing but also internationalizing the issue from the start. Yet all countries must regularly negotiate narratives of their past within the mutually constitutive frameworks of international relations and domestic social change and contend with the increasing interconnection between foreign and domestic pressures.

International scrutiny of national textbooks is clearly increasing. Educators across the globe now critique the textbooks of other nations and respond to criticism of their own texts in international forums. In this volume, Kimijima Kazuhiko (chapter 8) and Kathleen Woods Masalski (chapter 10) describe binational discussions in which teachers have embarked on the difficult task of finding a language that bridges two very different national perspectives on World War II. Kimijima's account of discussions between Koreans and Japanese, Masalski's of Japanese and Americans, and Yasemin Nuhoglu Soysal's of Germans and Poles (in chapter 5) suggest that pressure will grow on educators in many countries to rewrite their nationalist narratives in ways acceptable to outsiders.

Domestic demands to institutionalize social change and international pressures explain most of the controversy over textbooks in all three countries, but the intensity and focus of the debates vary considerably. German and Japanese educators have fought among themselves over textbook depictions of wartime society and specifically over treatment of both citizens and outsiders. Yet as these essays show, debate over textbooks in Germany seems to have been resolved far more amicably than in Japan.

In contrast, Americans have fought over textbook treatments of Americans during World War II but have paid scant attention to their depiction of foreigners. Of course, a major reason for that contrast is the difference between defeat and victory, but there is also very little controversy among Americans over U.S. textbook depictions of the Vietnam War, despite defeat there. American conduct in World War II has generated considerable domestic debate. African Americans and women, for example, have demanded that textbooks recognize their contributions during World War II as part of their larger struggle for greater civic inclusion. But Americans have faced very little sustained *foreign* criticism of U.S. conduct in World War II, with the notable exception of the atomic bombing of Hiroshima and Nagasaki. Nor has the United States faced foreign criticism of its retrospective analyses of its intervention in Vietnam.

One reason that textbooks have been more controversial in Japan than in Germany or the United States is the different structure of control over their content. Because Japan's national government has directly supervised and censored textbooks since the late nineteenth century, textbooks provide authoritative statements of national policy and ideology. In postwar West Germany, and subsequently in united Germany, publishers have developed textbooks along guidelines established by local states, but no mechanism of central control exists.[7] In the United States, where state review boards determine adoptions in some states, notably Texas and California, and where local school boards, principals, or individual teachers freely choose books in others, textbooks do not have the same close association with national authority as in countries where national agencies monitor, censor, and authorize texts (as in Japan) or where government officials actually write them (as in China, Taiwan, and the Republic of Korea).[8] Decentralization changes the terms of the debate, although "the market" may restrict textbook writers and publishers as much as does direct state regulation.

In addition, Japan has experienced particularly intense international pressure to acknowledge the brutality of the presurrender empire. Japa-

1.2 and 1.3 War orphans

Japanese texts often depict orphaned and repatriated Japanese children, emphasizing civilian hardship and glossing over the suffering the Japanese inflicted on others. These 33 orphaned children returned from Manchuria on December 5, 1946. The older girl in front, Hosoda Ishiko, carries the cremated remains of her parents in the white box around her neck for burial in Japan. American texts are far more likely to show children orphaned by the Axis, such as this world-famous picture of a baby, taken on August 28, 1937, after a Japanese air raid on the South Shanghai train station. Satō Akira, ed., *Asahi Rekishi Shashin Riburarii—Sensō to Shomin, 1940–49* (Asahi's photographic history collection—the war and the people, 1940–49), vol. 4. Tokyo: Asahi Shinbunsha, 1995, 201. Used by permission. NARA, NWDNS-208–AA-132N(2) War and Conflict no. 1131.

nese officials brought overseas scrutiny of textbooks down on their own heads in 1982, when Asian governments expressed outrage at press reports that the Ministry of Education had ordered Ienaga Saburō and other textbook authors to alter their accounts of the war, most famously by substituting the term "invasion" of China to "advance into" China. The Japanese government also ordered authors to sanitize their discussion of colonial policy in Korea and Taiwan, the Nanjing massacre, and the treatment of the military comfort women, prompting greater efforts by the governments of South Korea, North Korea, the Republic of China on Taiwan, and the People's Republic of China to challenge Japanese textbook content on war and colonialism.

Finally, the response to foreign criticism has differed. For reasons discussed below, since the 1960s West German officials have publicly accepted and acted on foreign criticism of textbooks. They have been far more conciliatory in their stance toward other governments that complained about textbook content than have Japanese officials, at least on the subject of the Holocaust. Germans are still divided over how to remember the war, but they have greater incentive than their Japanese counterparts to satisfy neighboring countries. This is not because the Germans feel guilt whereas the Japanese feel only shame. Nor are Germans more remorseful by nature than Japanese. Some Germans feel guilt, shame, and remorse for their wartime actions as do some Japanese. Others in both countries do not. Rather, larger numbers of Germans than Japanese currently believe that teaching their children positive accounts of Nazism and the war will cost them too much in the future. Germans, notably political leaders, recognize that they have more to lose by clinging to their wartime claims than do Japanese. Their consensus is that the problems created by officially repudiating the Nazi war are less serious than those created by continuing to defend it.[9]

By contrast, public statements about the war by Japanese officials have been far more ambivalent. Although several prime ministers have issued apologies for Japan's wartime conduct, the government has yet to reject unambiguously either the wartime polity or wartime aims. It has, however, sought to implement damage control ever since the 1982 international contretemps over textbooks. For example, the Ministry of Foreign Affairs treats textbook controversies as an important aspect of Japan's international relations. It staffs a large Tokyo office that prepares dual-language versions of widely used Japanese textbooks; maintains a library of older textbooks; provides curricular materials about Japan in such languages as English, Chinese, Thai, and Malay; and fields questions from overseas teachers who wish to develop their own curricula about Japan.[10]

More important, Japanese officials in the 1990s responded in a number of ways to international criticisms. Current high school and middle school textbooks contain information critical of the war, and nearly all of them mention harsh colonial policies, the Nanjing massacre, and the military comfort women. The discussion is typically elliptical, however. For example, one middle school text explains the Nanjing massacre as follows: "The Japanese army on the Chinese continent occupied cities such as Shanghai, Nanjing, and Canton. When they occupied Nanjing, many Chinese people were massacred (the Nanjing massacre incident), but people in Japan were not informed." A footnote elaborates further: "The number of victims of this incident, including both POWs and ordinary civilians, has been estimated at 100,000. The Tokyo War Crimes Trial used the figure of 200,000, and the Chinese government puts it at above 300,000."[11] Like the official commentary about them, the textbooks themselves seem to seek an elusive middle ground that avoids explicit evaluation of the wartime past. Their enigmatic comments can be used either to open debate about wartime attitudes and postwar responsibility or to dismiss the events in question as regrettable but unimportant facts, depending on the stance of the classroom teacher.

Ironically, one reason Japanese are stalemated over how to remember the recent past is that postwar occupation policies permitted far more continuity of personnel and rules in Japan than in Germany. The Allied victors demanded that the postwar German government eliminate Nazi leadership, yet they kept the Japanese emperor and many of his advisers in power to ensure stability. Cold War priorities were another reason the United States protected Japan from Asian demands for reparations and punishment during and after the occupation. In some ways, Japan avoided overseas pressure until the post–Cold War era to rethink its wartime actions; Germany faced and responded to similar pressures earlier. The end of the Cold War also has meant greater international pressure on the United States to revise its official story of twentieth-century international relations but not yet enough to force changes in the American debate.

Disputes over remembrance of wartime behavior can and do explode in areas other than textbooks. Both Germany and the United States have experienced internationally inflected fights over public policy and official commemoration of war in museum exhibits, war memorials, and other public art. The 1995 Smithsonian Institution's *Enola Gay* exhibit about the bombings of Hiroshima and Nagasaki produced far more international controversy than has the content of any American textbook. Similarly, public monuments commemorating the Holocaust in Poland, Germany,

1.4 Popular support for the war
Japanese textbooks avoid pictures such as this one of naval recruits leaving from Tokyo station on December 9, 1943, who appear thrilled to join the war. Textbooks skirt the enormous popularity of the war in the early years. Satō, ed., *Asahi Rekishi Shashin Riburarii*, vol. 2, 226–27. Used by permission.

and Austria have been far more bitterly contested than have textbook descriptions.[12] Attention to these different forms of war remembrance raises two different cautions about the argument we make here.

First, the contrast between Japanese and German remembrance of World War II is greater in policy toward textbooks than in some other areas. For example, the plans for two memorials to the war in Berlin and Tokyo, both opened in the 1990s, show similar strategies for remembering the war. Both memorials discourage self-criticism and deflect attention away from German or Japanese responsibility for the war. Critics have noted that in 1993 the German government rededicated a Berlin museum opened in 1816, the Neue Wache, as the "Central Memorial of the Federal Republic of Germany for the Victims of War and Tyranny." The concept, Chancellor Helmut Kohl made clear, was to "keep alive the memory and remembrance of the victims of war and tyranny in reunified Germany," referring to victims of both National Socialism and Communism.[13]

As Siobhan Kattago observes, "In the Neue Wache, German guilt is displaced by creating an imagined community of victims, and by blurring the building's original military function with national honor and sacrificial loss." The result is to conflate the experiences of Nazism and Communism and to efface the distinction between the hardships faced by victims of the Nazis and by German civilians during the war. Moreover, that sense of shared victimhood is proposed as the foundation for a shared identity in a unified Germany. In short, Kattago finds, "By casting German victimhood in universal terms such as war, tyranny and maternal mourning, German aggression and complicity are downplayed and forgotten."

This is precisely the sleight of hand presented to Japanese visitors at the new Showakan Museum in Tokyo, which also blurs war and postwar and presents victimization as an experience shared equally by Japanese and other Asians.[14] That perspective is likely to resonate with Japanese and German civilians, who did suffer greatly under Allied bombing and invasion in the final months of the war. Surely the German ability to resolve memory of the wartime past in textbooks in ways that satisfy other nations is important, but these forms of institutionalization of memory outside the classroom may pull Germans in a far different and more disturbing direction.

In contrast, all parties to the Goldhagen debate (briefly summarized by Wegner in this volume) accept the Nazi leaders' guilt for crimes against humanity as uncontroversial and differ only on the extent of culpability of the general German population.[15] Similar debates exist in Japan, but on a much smaller scale. From this angle, comparisons of the larger cultural context of war remembrance in Japan and Germany look much like the one revealed through the narrower prism of debate over textbooks.

A second caveat about our argument in this book is that the lack of overt international conflict in some places may well mean a problem deferred rather than resolved, as we suggest in the case of American memories of the Vietnam War. Americans have never been compelled to reevaluate their actions or their defeat in Vietnam. Although the scale of destruction and the numbers of dead were not as great in Vietnam as in either the European or Pacific theaters of World War II, the United States did face fierce international criticism of the war at the time. Americans have never acknowledged that criticism—or the criticisms that surfaced in many parts of the world in the 1980s, reframed to protest U.S.-financed wars in Nicaragua and El Salvador, and again in the 1990s, in response to the two U.S.-led bombing campaigns in Iraq and the former Yugoslavia. In the future, Americans may find that others demand the kind of reflection on the Vietnam War that is today being exacted from Germans and Japanese for World War II.

The next section explains why international pressure to revise textbook accounts is more easily accepted in Germany than in Japan, where leaders are as yet unable to achieve consensus on a coherent strategy for the future. It also analyzes the reasons why there is at present far less international pressure on the United States to revise its official story. The third section examines the ways that domestic demands for social change have transformed textbook narratives in all three countries. The final section notes how national and international pressures combine today to heighten controversy in Japan more than in Germany or the United States.

After the Cold War: Nationalism, Regionalism, and War Memories in the 1990s

The collapse of the Cold War system opened possibilities for new political, economic, and security alignments at the regional level in both Europe and Asia. The reunification of Germany, the collapse of the Soviet Union and Yugoslavia, the extension of NATO membership to several former Warsaw Pact nations, the uncontested handover of Hong Kong to China, and the growth of China-Taiwan trade and cultural relations all exemplify the profound shifts that marked the end of the Cold War—and now require reconceptualizing both past and present. Those realignments led people everywhere to adapt national narratives to the new arrangement, or at least to grapple with the implications of competing narratives.

The 1990s witnessed economic and political reintegration across old Cold War lines. One consequence of the new regional configurations is that small nations and semisovereign states have been able to command greater international attention and exercise greater leverage than during the era of two blocs and two superpowers. Another is that places formerly on Cold War front lines could afford to act with far greater autonomy than in earlier years. This held true for clients of the United States, such as Taiwan and South Korea, and for those of the Soviet Union, notably Eastern Europe and Vietnam.[16] The waning of the Cold War also created opportunities for domestic critics of authoritarian regimes in many places, including Taiwan, South Korea, and much of Eastern Europe, to demand political concessions and more democratic practices.

The collapse of Cold War structures and ideology, by laying bare or even dismantling arrangements that had been in place since World War II, turned world attention to earlier patterns of power and behavior. Historical memory of World War II suddenly gained new potency. Suppressed but not forgotten, old conflicts born of colonialism and war took on new urgency. This was particularly pertinent for the former Axis powers, which then had to bring to all future international negotiations not only the long-neglected baggage they had accumulated during World War II but also that of the Cold War. As Germany and Japan moved from decades of political subordination to the United States (or, in the case of East Germany, to the Soviet Union), they also lost the protection they had enjoyed from accepting full responsibility for their wartime acts. Grievances once swept under the rug by expensive American brooms in the name of anti-Communist unity (or by less expensive Soviet brooms in the name of Communist unity) were exposed to public view once again. In short, in the 1990s other Europeans and Asians gained new leverage to insist on recognition of their perspectives in German and Japanese historical memory, and specifically in textbook narratives of history.

Since the collapse of the Soviet Union, pressure on Japan and Germany to confront their wartime relations with other nations has become a major precondition for negotiating a common future. Officials of both nations have struggled with the issue of how far to go; at times leaning toward forthright apology and substantial compensation to the wartime victims and at others extending begrudging apologies, evading official responsibility, and offering minimal compensation.[17] Yet German leaders have chosen the former approach far more consistently than have their Japanese counterparts.

Germans fight over memories of the war as bitterly as do Japanese, but they have moved farther toward embracing a new vision of their future and thus a coherently revised story of their past. West German leaders long ago decided that the key to Germany's future lay in full commitment to regional integration in the European Union. West (and now unified) Germany adopted an internationalist narrative appropriate to that strategy, one that appears in government statements, public discourse, and the content and tone of textbooks. As Soysal shows here, Germans have created a postwar narrative of a nation without enemies. They have done this not by concealing the history of Nazism and World War II but precisely by publicizing, critically assessing, and accepting responsibility for that history in order to make a clean break with the Nazi legacy. The task is necessarily both domestic and international. One official Soysal inter-

1.5 Made visible or invisible by the Cold War

The vagaries of the Cold War made some displaced Koreans visible to Americans and their allies, such as this woman scavaging in the ruins of Seoul during the Korean War. In contrast, Koreans who were forced by the Japanese to work in the Sakhalin coal mines during World War II were stranded without passports throughout the Cold War era because the island reverted to the USSR in 1945, even though Japanese were repatriated in the late 1940s. National Archives Records Administration (hereafter, NARA), NWDNS-111-SC-351700.

viewed made the links between those two changes very clear: "You cannot preach a European Union and at the same time continue to produce textbooks with all the national prejudices of the nineteenth century."

Reframing the story of the past, including rewriting textbooks, means changing the definition of the good German citizens and their relation to the state as well as to the European and international communities. Although Germans have not yet fully come to terms with the Nazi and Holocaust experiences, German leaders have adopted a "tamed" national identity that celebrates regional diversity within Germany at the same time as integration—political, military, economic, and cultural—within the European Union. Germany's new place in a united Europe is not definitively resolved by any means, but far more of the institutional and narrative elements of accommodation are in place than are those for Japan and the Asia-Pacific region. As Peter Katzenstein puts it, "The Germanization of Europe is indissolubly linked to the Europeanization of Germany."[18] A crucial element of that Europeanization is explicit rejection of the Nazi past. That has meant substantial reparations payments. By 1997 Germany had provided $58 billion in reparations, and since then many new lawsuits have been filed against both the national government and German firms.[19]

In the realm of textbooks, German officials have participated with the Polish government in crossnational discussions sponsored by the United Nations Educational, Scientific, and Cultural Organization (UNESCO) aiming to develop mutually acceptable textbooks. They have also taken part in programs to write common European Union textbooks. German education officials have been highly responsive to international criticism. As Wegner mentions, one curriculum on Hitler for high school students was rewritten after the Israeli government protested that it was insufficiently critical of the Third Reich. German texts now sharply downplay nationalist in favor of internationalist themes. This practice, which aspires to a shared regional narrative on such contentious issues as the two world wars, Nazism, and colonialism, has helped diminish the antagonisms of other Europeans toward Germans and create a foundation of common values for the European Union.[20] Equally important, other Europeans want to build the European Union too. They have hardly forgotten the German invasions of either 1914 or 1939 but are willing to look beyond them because they share many goals with Germans today, feel reassured by this new German narrative, and, crucially, see a common European framework as the best prospect for taming German power. German success in repudiating the aggressive past is one important reason why political, social, and economic integration have proceeded so much further in the European Union than in Asia. But if Germans have clearly repudiated the Holocaust, other legacies of the war, for example, German support of Croatia after the breakup of Yugoslavia, may endure.

Japanese leaders have had greater difficulty settling on a post–Cold

War vision of Japan's place in the world. Japanese have failed to reach consensus on a new international strategy either in the realm of official policy or in public consciousness. They cannot decide whether to promote a regional Asian federation building on the experience of the European Union or to retain the U.S. alliance as the main determinant of Japanese foreign policy. Neither Japanese leaders nor the general public has ever been fully satisfied with Japan's position in the U.S. alliance system. The presence of a network of U.S. military bases more than half a century after Japan's wartime defeat is particularly unpopular. Yet the concept of an "Asian Union" faces huge obstacles. The biggest one is the deep mistrust potential member states feel toward one another. Without clear incentives for regional reconciliation, many Japanese are reluctant to take on the domestic battles inherent in rethinking their World War II actions. Frustration with those facts helps explain much of the intensity of the Japanese debate, not just over imagining the future but also over remembering the past.

The Cold War system established in the late 1940s channeled nearly all Asian political, economic, and strategic relations through bilateral relationships either with the United States or the Soviet Union. In the early postwar decades, the United States was by far the most important economic and strategic power in Asia and the Pacific. American aid and trade systems served as a hub through which most Asian nations within the U.S. sphere interacted, with few multilateral political or economic ties. For Japan, the central reality of that system was subordination to U.S. strategic policy as a quid pro quo for designation as the regional engine of economic growth. Since the 1980s, however, economic growth and intraregional economic links in East and Southeast Asia have shifted that power balance. Not only has Japanese economic power grown tremendously, but trade, investment, and technology transfers within the Asian region have transformed East Asia from a minor outpost of the world economy, with 4 percent of world GNP in 1960, to a region comparable in importance to Europe and North America, each with 30 percent of GNP. For three decades, Asia grew far more rapidly than other regions and remains strong, even after factoring in Japan's protracted stagnation in the 1990s and the Asian financial and currency crisis from 1997.[21] As a result of these changes, the United States, though still powerful, lacks the unilateral strategic and economic leverage of the early Cold War decades.

Japanese nationalists hoped that the end of the Cold War would free Japan from a half-century of subordination to the United States. Yet the new era has not led to a substantially more independent Japanese role in international affairs. Many Japanese expressed shock during the Persian Gulf War when Americans derided Japan's enormous ($13 billion) contribution to the U.S.-led effort against Iraq because Japan (whose American-imposed constitution prohibits war making) did not also send soldiers. Fujioka Nobukatsu, the leading nationalist figure in the 1990s textbook controversy covered in detail by Gavan McCormack (chapter 2) and Aaron Gerow (chapter 3), has said that this humiliating experience transformed his worldview and political orientation. He has tapped into a sense shared by many Japanese that they were cheated by history: for all the great changes in international relations of the twentieth century, and for all Japan's achievements, the one constant Fujioka and some other Japanese see is widespread global mistrust of Japan.[22]

Some Japanese have explored Asian regionalism and an appropriate companion narrative in which Japan's place in Asia is defined as an alternative to Cold War subordination to American power. Other Asians, too, have urged stronger regional integration. Malaysia's Mahathir Mohamad and Singapore's Lee Kwan Yew, for example, have stressed a commitment to "Asian values" and proposed an East Asian Economic Caucus to serve as a unified Asian regional voice, independent of the United States.

Yet Asian regionalism poses huge contemporary problems for Japan as well. In contrast to Europe, far-reaching economic and financial integration has not brought institutional unification, security alliance, political union, or a single currency. This is in part a result of the continuing legacy of the Cold War in Asia, most clearly symbolized by the divisions between two Chinas and two Koreas. But other factors are equally decisive. Social as well as geographic distances are far greater in Asia than in Europe. Europeans can travel freely and work anywhere in the Union. They entrust governance to a European Parliament and they have begun to use a common currency. Of course, the United States and NATO, a quintessentially Cold War organization, still remain powerful forces in Europe, as the 1999 war in Kosovo made brutally clear. Nevertheless, comparable levels of institutional and political cooperation are not even on the horizon for Asia despite eased Cold War tensions and substantial economic integration.

Another obstacle to institutional integration in Asia may be the scale of intraregional economic inequality. Japan enjoys two-thirds of Asia's GNP, and despite rapid economic growth in many Asian nations, the distance between rich and poor countries is vastly greater than in Europe. That interstate disparity, though, serves as a powerful barrier to regional political integration. For example, Japanese and other prosperous Asians are uneasy at the prospect that Chinese or Vietnamese workers, with incomes less than one-tenth their own, could move freely through the region as European workers do. The decision to preserve barriers to the flow of labor after Hong Kong's 1997 reversion to China is indicative of the divisions that continue to undergird the emerging Asian regional economy.

Perhaps the largest obstacles, however, are political. Japan would have to share leadership of an integrated Asian region with China. Neither the Japanese nor the Chinese government appears willing to accept that outcome. German government and business leaders support European integration in part because they know Germany will play a crucial role. Neither Japanese nor Chinese can confidently anticipate wielding comparable political or strategic leadership in Asia, and each fears domination by the other. When Japan proposed its own bailout of financially troubled regions of Southeast Asia in the 1997 crisis, for example, Chinese (and American) officials blocked it in favor of a U.S.-dominated IMF bailout. Japanese- and Chinese-centered business networks have, moreover, long competed to build and integrate the Asian economies. Under the circumstances, Japanese leaders remain reluctant to exchange their close ties with the United States for the higher risks of regional integration.

Instead, Japanese imagination continues to be dominated by a modified version of the old U.S.-centered Pacific alliance, despite its diminished value to Japan. The 1997 U.S.-Japan security agreement reaffirmed the Cold War alliance by extending the scope of joint military exercises and implicitly targeting China as the most dangerous enemy, thereby undercutting possibilities for regional alliance in Asia. The United States also continues to be the single largest market, a major investor, and the economic and strategic arbiter for Asia, as demonstrated by American leadership (for better or worse) in response to the collapse of the South Korean, Indonesian, and Thai currencies in December 1997 and in negotiations concerning Chinese entry into the World Trade Organization. Nonetheless, in the post–Cold War Pacific, the United States can no longer fully protect Japan from Asian criticisms, nor do Japanese value that protection as much as in the past. Although many Japanese are uncomfortably aware of the need for both a new strategy and a new narrative appropriate to their international future, they are uncertain what form it should take.[23]

Japanese do not yet have a compelling vision of the future that offers them either the inspiration for a unified strategy or a clear international reward for remembering the past. Other Asian nations will keep war memories on the negotiating table because, like Europeans negotiating with

Germans, they, too, want reassurances that Japanese today will not behave as did Japanese before. Moreover, they hope to construct an international framework that will "tame" Japanese economic and strategic power in the future. They also see this issue as a way to gain concessions from Japan. Even though Japanese leaders have so far retained the U.S. alliance as Japan's main foreign policy, the demise of the Cold War logic in which anti-Communism trumped all other concerns means that pressure on Japanese to repudiate their colonial and wartime past will only grow.

The United States has not yet had to respond to sustained foreign criticism for its conduct during any of its many twentieth-century wars. It has not even had to acknowledge the importance of its Allies, especially the USSR, in winning World War II. Asians who have mobilized to protest past Japanese military occupation have not mounted a similarly effective critique of American wars in Asia because of Cold War politics and, above all, because of the continued primacy of U.S. power. China, North Korea, and North Vietnam were isolated behind the iron curtain until the strategic reorientations of the 1970s. Since then, all three nations have struggled for international legitimacy, a course that has led them to seek international markets, technology, and foreign investment as well as U.S. recognition and assistance. Meanwhile, the governments of Taiwan, South Korea, Indonesia, and Thailand, among others, continue to depend to varying degrees on American markets, security, and legitimization. Likewise, Japanese postwar subordination to U.S. strategic designs, together with Japanese vulnerability to criticism of its activities during the Pacific War, has muted official Japanese criticism of the United States.[24] In short, the continued reliance of Asian nations on U.S. economic and military power silences potential critics of American wars in Asia.

This silence is most surprising for the Vietnam War because U.S. conduct there was bitterly criticized at the time, not just by Vietnam and its Communist allies but also by some of America's principal European allies. Many Japanese citizens as well protested both the war and their government's support of it. Yet there has been no sustained international debate on either U.S. actions during the war or the terms of the postwar settlement. In striking contrast to growing demands for apology and compensation from Japan by Chinese, Koreans, and others, the Vietnamese have not renewed their claims on the United States. They did ask the United States to apologize and pay restitution in the immediate aftermath of the war but quickly dropped those demands. The reasons on the Vietnamese side have everything to do with the still considerable power of the United States to shape economic, political, and strategic outcomes in the Pacific and the perception by Vietnamese leaders that their nation's future hinges on the international market, a realm for which the United States holds the keys to entry and prosperity. The United States has not only rejected all charges of war crimes but has issued no apology for any aspect of its conduct in the war and has paid no reparations.

Likewise, neither Vietnamese nor other foreigners have protested American textbook depictions of the Vietnam War. As James Loewen shows in chapter 6, few American school texts have even begun to engage Vietnamese perspectives on the war. Nor have they assessed the consequences of the war for the Vietnamese people. Some college texts, reviewed in chapter 7 by David Hunt, do better on this score, but they essentially ignore Vietnamese society and the Vietnamese people. Like the school texts, most skirt the issues that are most sensitive for Americans, such as the My Lai massacre, the tiger cages, the devastating bombing campaigns, and the environmental destruction of much of North and South Vietnam. More fundamentally, as Hunt shows, most American histories—the few exceptions are significant—avoid drawing the conclusion that "'war crimes' were in the logic of the Vietnam War."

The United States has yet to face its history of brutality and state-led aggression in Vietnam, either in textbook treatments of the war or at other sites of memory. The contrast with Germany and Japan is stark. A quarter century after its defeat in Vietnam, Americans have barely begun to come to terms with the Vietnam War in self-critical ways comparable to those by which Germans and, to a lesser extent, Japanese, have reflected on their nation's conduct in World War II. Loewen finds nothing in U.S. high school texts on the Vietnam War that is as potentially challenging to celebratory narratives as is mention of the military comfort women in Japanese texts. Of course, a considerable scholarship exists that could provide the substance for a celebratory self-portrait in U.S. textbooks. This comparative lack of self-criticism is particularly striking because there is no national censorship system in the United States; American texts conform to the official nationalist story without direct state control. The contrast between American assessments of defeat on one hand and German and Japanese on the other in part resides in differences in their experiences of defeat. The Vietnam War was not fought on American soil; millions of Americans did not die, and Vietnam rather than the United States was left in ruins. No Vietnamese forces occupied the United States following the American defeat. Nor did any international force ever compel Americans to consider the human consequences of military actions beyond their borders, in textbooks or elsewhere.

Since textbooks are an important venue in which narratives about the nation's relationship to the rest of the world are articulated, international controversies over their content signal competing models for nationhood and citizenship in the international community. The three nations examined here experienced very disparate outcomes of that process of international renegotiation. Germans have achieved a relatively high degree of agreement with their neighbors on building a unified Germany subordinated to an emerging European Union. Asians, including Japanese, are currently deadlocked over reimagining Japan, whether as junior partner to America, leader of the Asian region, or perhaps eventually an active participant in a more mutually respectful Asia-Pacific. In contrast, there has been no serious challenge to the United States' hegemonic position. The American example, unlike the German one, suggests that Japanese nationalists have a point when they complain that other nations gloss over their own dark chapters while Japan is singled out for attack. At present, the greatest pressures to scrutinize American history come not from other nations but from American citizens reclaiming their domestic history.

Citizenship in History Textbook Controversies

Textbooks frequently are the site of domestic controversies over the relationship of citizens to their state. One of the most sensitive issues is the conduct of one's own side during war. Paralleling the international debates, the Japanese are currently engaged in fierce domestic battles over depictions of the wartime treatment of both Japanese citizens and colonial subjects, whereas the Germans have come closer to consensus. In the United States, the efforts of domestic constituencies have led to a transformed textbook narrative of the treatment of racial minorities during the war, notably of Japanese Americans but also African Americans and women. There has been no comparable reassessment of the Vietnam War, however, either from the perspective of foreigners or of domestic critics of the war in school texts.

Japan's War and the Military Comfort Women

Textbooks have been the site of domestic as well as international debate in Japan since the end of World War II. Most of the battles have pitted government officials, who insisted that the Pacific War and the colonial era be portrayed in ways that flattered the wartime state, against Japanese citizens, who sought to repudiate the war and distance postwar Japan

1.6 Japanese Americans and World War II
U.S. textbooks now condemn the internment policy because it treated some Americans like hostile outsiders. In this photo from April 1942, by Dorothea Lange, Japanese family heads and persons living alone line up in San Francisco under the watchful eye of an armed guard. NARA, NWDNS-210–G2A-531.

from wartime values and actions. Those citizens see history education as a crucial battleground over democracy in Japan. Ienaga Saburō and his three decades of court challenges to Ministry of Education censorship is only the most famous example. Other scholars have painstakingly collected evidence of wartime Japanese crimes, creating a tidal wave of documentation to sweep away claims that Chinese, Koreans, Filipinos, and other victims were inventing tales of Japanese brutality. The Japan Teachers Union developed extensive peace education curricula to help teachers of all grades supplement nationally approved lessons. Both the union and citizens' groups such as the PTA organized unsuccessfully against mandated use of the rising sun flag and the anthem, "Kimigayo," because of their close associations with the presurrender imperial state. In 1999 the Diet finally approved official status for the rising sun flag and "Kimigayo" as the national anthem.

In the 1990s, Japanese began discussing the war far more frankly than in earlier decades. There was wide media coverage of such Asian grievances as the military comfort women, the Nanjing massacre, Chinese and Korean slave labor, and the grisly experiments of biowar Unit 731. In the years after the fall of the Berlin Wall, and particularly after the December 1989 death of the Showa emperor, Japanese produced stacks of testimony, including books, documentary films, and archival research, on previously suppressed or ignored aspects of the war.[25] That testimony has also clarified how difficult the war years were for most Japanese, so that memory of Japanese suffering has grown along with knowledge of the suffering of others at their hands.

The stance of government leaders has changed significantly as a result of those efforts as well as pressure from overseas. In the 1990s, several prime ministers apologized for Japan's war crimes; the government established a "private" fund to compensate former comfort women; and in 1996 Education Ministry officials approved brief mention of the military comfort women in junior high school social studies texts. One text reads "Many young Korean women and others were sent to the front lines as 'comfort women.'" Another states that "there were also some women from Korea and Taiwan and other places who were made to work in battle-front comfort facilities."[26] Many high school textbooks already included similar statements.

Those important changes have, however, been checkmated in part by countervailing ones. Government leaders have apologized, but they also hedged and prevaricated. The Japanese government explicitly rejected the UNESCO model of government-to-government negotiation over textbook content used by Germany and Poland, for example. Few Japanese politicians have been willing to stake out clear positions critical of the Pacific War and colonialism for fear of losing the most passionately nationalist segments of their constituency. In contrast to the German government, which compensated individual victims of the Holocaust directly, the Japanese government has insisted that all reparations claims were resolved by treaties with other Asian states (North Korea is a notable exception) in the 1960s and early 1970s. Moreover, Japanese compensation to Asians who had endured forced labor was, through 1997, only a tiny fraction of that provided by Germany to its victims, and none went directly to individuals.

In 1997, domestic controversy over textbooks flared again when Fujioka Nobukatsu's first two volumes of *History Not Taught in Textbooks* became two of Japan's top ten best-sellers. Since then, the third and fourth volumes, also composed of short articles first serialized in the business daily *Sankei shinbun,* have sold well, too. Charging that current textbooks demean the nation, Fujioka and his colleagues demanded more positive views of Japanese history and society, particularly with respect to World War II. In July 1996 Fujioka organized a small group of public figures and intellectuals, notably Nishio Kanji, a specialist on Germany and author of books on Nietzsche, German education, and the *Gastarbeiter* policy, and Hata Ikuhiko, a prominent military historian, into the Jiyūshugi Shikan Kenkyūkai (Liberal View of History Study Group). The group wanted all criticism of official Japanese policy and actions to be cut from textbooks. Six months later, responding to criticisms that their movement was entirely negative, they organized the Atarashii Rekishi kyōkasho o Tsukuru Kai to write their own textbook. Although a literal translation of this second group's name would be "Committee to Write New History Textbooks," its official English name, given on the copyright page of a 1997 book, is the Japanese Institute for Orthodox History Education (which we hereafter call the Orthodox History Group).[27]

The movement can best be understood as a rear-guard reaction to Japanese and international critics, who had forced the government to acknowledge culpability, apologize, and authorize significant changes in textbook accounts of the war. The Orthodox History Group hoped to influence public policy and debate by staunchly rejecting any need for official acknowledgment of Japanese wartime atrocities, let alone apologize or pay reparations. Distinctive features of the campaign include an innovative use of popular media; intense resentment of Japan's low prestige in the world; insistence that any Japanese who expressed alienation from the state was psychologically sick; and a focus on textbooks as a critical battleground for creating the new Japan. Fujioka baldly states that educational goals should be defined by the needs of the state and that if "Japanese are not proud of their own country, they will not be respected in the world."[28]

The Orthodox History Group attempts to control the debate by discrediting Japanese who criticize any aspect of Japan's war. Their logic criminalizes dissent, much as did the presurrender state. They define discussion of World War II as permitting only two points of view: the "Tokyo Trials" view of history, which blames Japan for all aspects of the Pacific War and glorifies the victor, and a "Japanese" perspective, which takes pride in the nation and the Japanese state. The group members dismiss Japanese criticism of wartime policy and praxis as "self-flagellation" *(jigyaku),* that is, not just psychological sickness but treason.[29] They reject the possibility that any Japanese could adopt an alternative view, for example, one based on humanist or internationalist principles. Such perspectives on the wartime Japanese state are likely to be damning, as Fujioka tacitly admits when he argues that incorporating information about wartime Japanese brutality in textbooks will "destroy Japan as a state for the twenty-first century. This is the real battle."[30]

The Orthodox History Group reserves special venom for textbook recognition of the system of institutionalized rape and military sexual slave labor established during the Asia-Pacific War and euphemistically called the "comfort woman" system. Until the 1990s, it was possible to maintain official silence on this subject. That position has steadily eroded since the first few elderly Koreans and Filipinas bravely came forward in 1991 and 1992 to testify about their personal experiences as slaves, and Japanese researchers then unearthed official documentation showing direct involvement of the wartime state. The Japanese government has been forced, step by step, to acknowledge that the wartime state and the military were the chief architects of their misery.[31] Critics sympathetic to the comfort women have censured the new textbook descriptions as inadequate for their failure to discuss, still less condemn, the system. But the Orthodox History Group decried these modest mentions of the comfort women as a dangerous blow to Japan's moral and political foundations.

The Orthodox History Group is right to treat discussion of the military comfort women as a crucial issue in defining Japanese nationalism and citizenship. This sordid story is central to current controversies because the treatment of these women, if actually discussed in classroom and society, would require citizens of all ages to reexamine their own relationship to the state, gender relations among citizens, and relations between Japan and Asia.[32] It falsifies precisely the assumptions that the Orthodox History Group strives to protect: the identity of interests between Japanese citizens and the state (both in the 1940s and since) and the claim that there is nothing to criticize in wartime Japan's treatment of others.

It undermines the right-wing critique of a "Tokyo Trials" view of history because the misery of the military comfort women was completely ignored at the Tokyo War Crimes Trials.[33] Later, in a revealing prosecutorial decision, Japanese who had been stationed in the Netherlands East Indies were charged in B- and C- Class tribunals with confining a small number of Dutch women in "comfort stations" but not with impressing the many Javanese and Sumatran women who labored there as well.[34] Rather than exemplifying "victor's justice," the experience of the comfort women suggests that the war crimes trials may have been insufficiently attentive to Japanese crimes against female humanity.

The plight of comfort women also spotlights both overtly racist aspects of Japanese colonialism and the deliberate evasion of international law by the presurrender government. Japanese military planners saw Koreans, who may have accounted for 80 percent of the comfort women, as ideal candidates for sexual slavery precisely because they thought of them as second-class citizens—half assimilated and racially inferior. They assumed that unmarried Korean women would be free of venereal disease because of Confucian emphasis on female chastity. Japanese leaders thought that Koreans—as colonial subjects and (until 1952) as Japanese citizens rather than enemy nationals—owed allegiance to the emperor and also that, unlike foreigners, harsh treatment of them was not covered by international law. Far from preventing Japan from taking its rightful place at the head of the Asian table, the "Tokyo Trials" view of history in this instance not only protected Japan from facing these long-standing Asian grievances but also implicated Japan in a global racial hierarchy that considered the suffering of colonized people less important than that of the colonizers.

Finally, the comfort women's stories refute the nationalist claim that the interests of the state are identical with those of its citizens, notably Japan's female citizens. The Orthodox History Group argues, in startlingly contemptuous language, the now abandoned Japanese government position that the comfort women were ordinary licensed prostitutes who were paid for their services, just like prostitutes serving other armies. The Orthodox History Group insists further that the conditions of work for the comfort women, albeit primitive, closely resembled those of legal prostitution at home.

One problem for proponents of this view is that the last point contains important elements of truth. Some prewar Japanese women were sold into sexual servitude by their impoverished families, and those transactions were enforced by state power. Their working conditions were frequently based on coercion, debt peonage, stigmatization, wretched physical circumstances, and the general social and legal assumption that sexual servitude is both a natural and appropriate service that women owe men. War and racism meant that Asian comfort women endured even more onerous conditions than Japanese prostitutes, but the commonalty of their experience is hard to ignore, and Japanese feminists have drawn the connection in order to criticize and discredit this fundamental hierarchy of prewar state and society, not just its ugliest wartime incarnation.

Careful attention to the comfort women thus undercuts ultranationalist assertions about the national subject, the state, and the proper relationship between them. It also brings to mind the huge political battles required to include even those skimpy phrases in the textbooks. Japanese textbooks, as in most countries, are written in a single, omniscient voice. Breaks in that voice are few, far between, and usually reflect deep social and political divisions. In this case, the very mention of the comfort women subverts the heroic narrative of the war and leads the reader to consider two separate, dual perspectives: Japanese versus colonial subject and (male) soldier versus comfort woman. It reminds Japanese that their nation not long ago included Koreans, Taiwanese, and other colonized people who were treated as racially inferior by nearly all Japanese. The comfort woman saga evokes the rigid gender hierarchy and sexual double standard of presurrender Japan, in which women's happiness and health were routinely sacrificed for men and the state. Thus, the appearance of comfort women in Japanese textbooks, both as colonial subjects and as women, disrupts the narrative of "100 million hearts beating as one," as the wartime slogan had it, and spotlights the complicity of millions of ordinary Japanese men in their torture.[35]

Official acknowledgment of the military comfort women in texts also ratifies the huge social transformation of Japanese society since 1945 and the imaginative distance Japanese have already traveled from the assumptions many took for granted during the war, particularly in their attitudes toward the duties of national subjects, gender relations, and women's sexuality. Coming to terms with that transformation is at the heart of the current Japanese controversy. This is why nationalists who want Japanese unquestioningly to identify their own interests with the state are so upset by the brief mention of comfort women in school texts.

Nonetheless, the bland references to comfort women (or to the Nanjing massacre or colonial repression) in school texts will not alter the celebratory narrative of the national patrimony unless they are actively discussed in schools and society. No matter what the textbook says, teaching the contested past is no easy task, as Kimijima thoughtfully explains in chapter 8. For example, many Japanese textbooks now mention the special burdens imposed on Koreans and Taiwanese in the form of forced labor, including the sexual labor of the comfort women, and mandatory cultural assimilation policies. Yet even teachers sympathetic to the former colonial subjects fear that if they stress only Japanese repression, their students will conclude that good relations with Koreans are now impossible. If they teach about the handful of Japanese who supported Korean desires for independence, however, they risk overemphasizing their historical importance and skewing the reality of presurrender colonial relations. The most educationally effective choice, even for teachers who have chosen a critical stance toward the past, is hardly obvious.

Germany's War and the Holocaust

The brutality of the Third Reich's program to exterminate European Jews is the most difficult aspect of World War II for many Germans to confront.

As have the Japanese, Germans have since 1945 debated how to remember and teach their own actions during the war. At first West Germans under Konrad Adenauer, chancellor from 1949 to 1963, avoided reflection on the past by arguing that their still fragile democracy could not withstand honest remembrance of the Nazi era. (Adenauer combined that policy with the partially contradictory one of supporting financial restitution to the state of Israel.) Discussion of the war in schools varied from state to state but was nearly nonexistent in some parts of Germany. Peter Schneider, a German novelist who grew up in Freiburg, recalled that his high school curriculum allocated more time to the Trojan War of Homer, read in the original Greek, than to the war that had ended only a decade earlier.[36]

In the 1960s, that stance gave way to the belief that both democracy and justice required not only remembrance but also criticism of the German war. Germans then fought some of the same battles over remembering the past that Japanese grappled with in the 1990s. Since then, the West German state, and since reunification the German state, in its education system and public commemoration, has collectively committed to a far more self-critical stance about the Holocaust than have Japan's governmental leaders about their wartime cruelty. The extensive Holocaust education programs described by Soysal and Wegner exemplify that position. And as Soysal observes, German teachers and textbooks now not only "reflect a consensus over the condemnation of the Nazi past" but also spend an unusually large amount of the school year discussing recent history.

Akiko Hashimoto argues that Germans and Japanese have chosen different strategies toward "moral recovery—the recovery of national dignity, national honor, and 'good standing' in the world" and that the Germans have achieved greater agreement on repudiation of World War II. The concept of moral recovery embodies moral rehabilitation in one's own eyes, not just those of others. She finds that Germans have chosen to confront the past directly as their strategy for moral recovery, in part because, for them, the very act of self-examination is praiseworthy and evidence of moral responsibility. For Germany, then, "confronting the past—in itself—adds significantly to one's symbolic capital." In the realm of education, this means teaching students that blindly following authority is unacceptable in a democratic society. The practice of individual reflection and critical assessment of state policy has not only been defined as crucial to the future but has also become inextricably linked to a critique of the wartime citizenry.[37]

The history of the German Democratic Republic shows that the contrast between Japan and the Federal Republic of Germany is political rather than cultural, as does the fact that many Japanese have long urged both state and society to confront their past. The issues are clarified by contrasting the East and West German approaches to war and Holocaust memory. East German leaders more closely resembled their Japanese counterparts than their West German ones in their preference to focus on the future (a glorious socialist one) rather than reflect on their culpability for the past. Indeed, East Germans did not see themselves as implicated in the Nazi past. Defining Nazi power as the result of monopoly capitalism, they saw themselves as representatives of the proletariat that had been oppressed by capitalists and Nazis alike. Until shortly before reunification, the East German state emphasized the fascism and downplayed the anti-Semitism of the Nazi era.[38] As Wegner explains, this view of the past was laid out quite explicitly in East German textbooks, which described the inmates of the concentration camps as Communists, labor leaders, antifascists, and Russians, not as Jews. Moreover, as Klaus Neumann points out, Germans presented Buchenwald, located less than 10 kilometers from Weimar, as the site of "self-liberation," celebrating the takeover of the camp by a group of armed political prisoners prior to the entry of U.S. forces; they downplayed the postwar brutalization and death of its inmates.[39] Unification has meant that East German interpretations of the war have been subsumed into West German ones.

Educators in unified Germany have explicitly harnessed horror at the Holocaust to their lessons on contemporary German society, particularly in their celebration of multiculturalism. They have stressed the social distance Germans have traveled since 1945 and encouraged faster progress down that path. Problems of racism and ethnocentrism have not disappeared, although the scale of racial violence is far, far smaller. There are very few Jews in Germany today, but xenophobia haunts contemporary German relations with Turkish, African, and Roma (Gypsy) immigrants. Hate crimes by Germans against immigrants are perceived by victims, perpetrators, and bystanders alike as vivid reminders of the Final Solution. German textbooks now laud ethnic diversity as crucial to German democracy and paint Neo-Nazis as the real danger to the German national future because they threaten to drag Germany back into the shameful past.

Most of the German curricula on the Holocaust are designed so that German students will not only view the past from a victim's perspective but also will use that lesson to learn respect for religious and ethnic minorities within Germany today, without seeing them as threats to national unity. Repudiation of the Holocaust has thus become a central pillar in the efforts of German educators to transform the meaning of citizenship into a multicultural enterprise within the narrative of their nation.

The memory of the Holocaust has made postwar Germans far more wary of open celebration of ethnic purity than are postwar Japanese. Currently, as part of the Europeanization process, Germans are in the midst of refashioning their concept of nation to dissolve the link between ethnicity and citizenship. Both West German and Japanese governments retained the presurrender jus sanguinis as opposed to the jus soli concept of citizenship, that is, they have defined citizenship by blood rather than (as in the United States) by place of birth. The most important practical consequence was to deny citizenship to the hundreds of thousands of German-born Turkish and Japanese-born Korean residents. The question of who could move to Germany legally and who could become a citizen reached crisis proportions in Germany in 1992 when both asylum seekers and resettlers (people of German origins) from the former Communist bloc flooded into Germany. Their arrival was followed by an explosion of xenophobic violence. German officials responded by relaxing the requirements for citizenship. They were also motivated by European Union policies that provided for free migration beginning in 1993. Germany subsequently accepted tens of thousands of Bosnian and Kosovar refugees.[40]

Yet the debate is far from over in Germany, where integration of the east still poses major economic and political difficulties. As in Japan, a revamped nationalist, right-wing critique emerged in the 1990s. According to Jacob Heilbrunn, "The new right calls itself the generation of 1989, and its main foe is the leftist generation of 1968," which, in its view, dwells masochistically on wartime deeds.[41] Like the Orthodox History Group, the New Right has made resentment at the way older Germans kowtowed to American power the heart of their critique; they reject any multicultural element in German identity and internationalism in German policy. And like their Japanese counterparts, they are particularly unsympathetic to outsiders—in the German case recent immigrants. The new right argues that granting them citizenship would harm the German polity. Textbooks have not become the flashpoint of debate for these battles, but in every other way the complaints of the contemporary German right mirror those of Japan's Orthodox History Group.

In Germany the most sensitive lesson of the war does not concern the plight of Germany's victims so much as the complicity of the general population in their victimization. The question of complicity raises many painful questions: how central were atrocities to wartime society? How widespread was knowledge of the deportations and death camps? What responsibility did ordinary citizens bear for allowing or participating directly in persecution and mass death? And most important, what do the

1.7 Social responsibility for war
Germans have been compelled to confront their collective responsibility since 1945, when the Allied forces made local civilians tour the death camps. NARA, NWDNS-111–SC-264895 War and Conflict no. 1124.

war and Holocaust teach about what people must do to safeguard a democratic future? For example, Peter Schneider, writing on Holocaust remembrance in 1995, praised the schools for giving young Germans an awareness of the Holocaust they do not learn at home. But he ended his essay with a complaint that teenagers fail to learn the most crucial lesson of all, that

> refusal to obey did not always entail risking one's life. Students learn about the Wehrmacht officers' attempt to assassinate Hitler on July 20, 1944, about heroic resistance groups like the Kreisau circle and the "White Rose." Stories of less dramatic but successful acts of resistance—the protest against the removal of crosses in Bavarian churches, the daylong demonstration in 1943 of

"Aryan" women demanding that the Government release their Jewish husbands, who had already been rounded up for transport to the camps—have not been passed on to the generation now growing into adulthood. . . . How to account for the persistence of this exculpatory myth? The answer is obvious: Every person who resisted cast a shadow over the great majority of compliant and obedient men and women who didn't.[42]

For Schneider, the Holocaust curriculum can never adequately prepare young Germans to take responsibility for peace and democracy in their own time unless it fully explores war complicity in the past.

Even when all parties agree that the goal of history lessons on the Third Reich is to discredit Nazi doctrine, they struggle over how best to do so. Wegner describes a controversy in which some German curriculum writers wanted to explain Hitler's aims in detail so that their students would develop a more informed and sophisticated critique. Others feared that greater understanding of Hitler's actions would lead a minority of students to identify with the Nazi program. Just as with Japanese curriculum on colonized Korea, there is no obvious solution to the concerns posed in this debate.

America's Wars: Japanese American Internment in World War II and the Vietnam War

Victors and neutral nations in World War II have also faced domestic pressure to reexamine their official narratives and conduct. Many nations have expressed regret for their own wartime judgments that some of their citizens were unworthy of legal protection. In 1997, France, Switzerland, the French Catholic Church, and the Red Cross all apologized for their complicity in the mass killing of Europe's Jews after historians and journalists publicized long-suppressed information on their wartime stances. Vocal critics demanded a narrative that acknowledged ubiquitous European anti-Semitism in order to make space for a less bigoted common European future.[43]

Americans, too, under pressure from minorities and women, have modified their World War II victory stories to recognize the contributions of domestic groups largely omitted from earlier heroic narratives.[44] Most Americans agree that World War II was fundamentally a "good war," fought against dangerous enemies for the right reasons. Precisely this consensus, however, makes it difficult to recognize and repudiate American actions that were widely accepted then but now are seen as unjust. Many Americans fear that to acknowledge the special obstacles to citizenship faced by

1.8 African Americans and World War II
The U.S. military and many civilian employers celebrated national unity while practicing racial segregation during World War II. Most U.S. textbooks now present the war as generally helpful to good race relations by contributing to African American gains in American society. NARA, NWDNS-44–PA-370.

some Americans would diminish the value and righteousness of the wartime victory. Like their Japanese counterparts, they worry that repudiating some wartime actions would lead to a rejection of the entire war effort—an anxiety apparently unaffected by the fact of victory or defeat.

As Frances FitzGerald and others have documented for the United States, one of the major sites of those battles for remembering the past was textbook content. In recent decades, this aspect of the project for greater civic inclusion has been very successful, and many textbooks have changed a great deal. Recent American textbooks, for example, are careful to mention the wartime contributions of African Americans under conditions of racial segregation and of women both in the military and in war industries (although fewer discuss the reversal of wartime gains for both groups once the war was over).[45]

One of the most dramatic changes in textbooks is in depictions of the U.S. government's internment of the 110,000 Japanese Americans who lived on the West Coast. Early postwar textbooks presented internment as a military necessity conducted without bloodshed. They were oblivious to the fact that two-thirds of the internees were U.S. citizens who were deprived of their constitutional rights. Eugene Barker and Henry Steele Commager, for example, concluded in an influential 1949 text, that "the civil liberties record was one of which every American can be proud. There was no hysteria, no persecution of dissenters. . . . The presence on the Pacific coast of some 100,000 Japanese posed a special problem. Because, in the emergency after Pearl Harbor, the army could not take time to investigate every Japanese, it worked out instead a rough-and-ready solution . . . relocation camps."[46]

Two decades later, the racism and uncritical acceptance of military-driven national policy exemplified by that passage were no longer acceptable. In the 1970s and 1980s, the leading high school texts described the internment as "shameful," "tragic," "war hysteria," "a grave injustice," and "disgraceful." Newer textbooks added heart-tugging photos of well-dressed and tagged Japanese American women and children en route to relocation camps, at once inviting students to consider the issue from the internees' perspective and visually recalling images of European Jews in transit to death camps.[47]

The changes clearly originated with demands by Japanese Americans that their incarceration be understood as a transgression of constitutional rights and a racist act. That position challenged other Americans to reflect on their own wartime complicity in depriving Japanese Americans of their land and liberty. Japanese Americans framed their challenge as a plea for a common stake in a more democratic and multicultural American future. A sea change also occurred in American public opinion on the subject. It is not clear whether the new perspective in textbooks led to the changes in public opinion or the reverse, but the shift to a new consensus in the textbooks definitely preceded the change in official U.S. policy in 1987, when the government apologized for the internment and began offering financial restitution. (The Canadian government apologized and offered token compensation to Japanese Canadians the following year.)[48]

At least some American teachers supplement the textbook treatment of wartime internment in ways that further emphasize the issues of morality, citizenship, and racism. Michael Romanowski found that all six of the rural midwestern high school teachers whose classes he visited thought their textbooks' discussion of Japanese American internment was inadequate.[49] Remarkably, all of them took the time to develop compensatory curriculum of some kind that problematized the internment and invited students to make critical moral judgments about this aspect of national defense policy. These teachers clearly saw their educational responsibility as affirming the ideals of just and equitable treatment of citizens and condemning racism rather than defending this particular government action. They, too, believed that highlighting the social distance Americans had traveled since the war was important in helping their students negotiate the multicultural American future.

The Vietnam War, in contrast, continues to be treated very gingerly in U.S. textbooks despite widespread criticism of the war among adult Americans. Although the central concern in high school texts is the domestic American implications of the conflict, the attitudes and policies that divided Americans during the Vietnam War are rarely spelled out in these accounts. As Loewen shows, most textbook treatments of the war seek to avoid all controversy—which not only makes it hard to discuss important issues but also fails to convey why the Vietnam War mattered so deeply to Americans at the time.[50] For example, few of the texts assess the U.S. antiwar movement, leaving the impression that the war was divisive without explaining how or why. "Having excluded the sights, the sounds, and feelings of the Vietnam era," Loewen notes, "the authors of the twelve textbooks in my original sample proceeded to muddy or exclude the issues." He finds that that such evasiveness makes textbooks boring to students.

During the Vietnam War, Americans fought over precisely the same issues of racism, justice, and the responsibility of citizens in a democracy that are at the heart of the German debate on the Holocaust. The antiwar movement questioned official interpretations of the American democratic tradition, arguing that principled resistance to unjust laws and politics is the touchstone of American democracy and responsible citizenship. The American "winter soldiers" carried that logic farthest. Their testimony to American war crimes was an act of patriotism and courage—the kind of

1.9 and 1.10 Internment presented as injustice now overcome
This photo of a Japanese American girl waiting to be shipped to an assembly
center in spring 1942 appears in many U.S. textbooks. The portrait is disturb-
ingly reminiscent of photos of refugees fleeing repression. The photo by Dorothea
Lange of a Japanese American veteran of World War I reporting for internment
was censored during the war. NARA, NWDNS-210–G-2A-6 and NARA,
NWDNS-210–G-B424.

resistance that Peter Schneider lamented has been excised from German textbook accounts of World War II. The winter soldiers eloquently argued that in treating the Vietnamese inhumanely, even committing war crimes against them, Americans debased their own nation's finest traditions.

A quarter century after the U.S. defeat, high school and most college texts still evade discussion of either political controversy or moral responsibility regarding American conduct during the Vietnam War. And in contrast to Japan, where large and well-organized domestic groups continue to pressure the government to repudiate its discredited war, and to Germany, where the war and the Holocaust are routinely criticized, few Americans today insist that reevaluation of the ways Americans fought the war in Vietnam is a crucial task toward a democratic future at home.

Loewen finds that even teachers who have no doubt that the war was wrong fear that expressing such views in class may cost them their jobs. Their anxiety persists even though public opinion polls consistently show that two-thirds of adult Americans think the Vietnam War was both morally wrong and poorly conducted. The contrast to contemporary practice in teaching about the World War II internment of Japanese Americans is striking. It may be that there is now so little support for the once dominant view that all Japanese Americans should be locked up that this subject is easier to negotiate than the many unresolved legacies of the Vietnam War. The great shift in public opinion itself means that the newer textbooks can present internment as an exceptional error rather than a symptom of a racist polity. The implicit national narrative tells the story of Japanese Americans who have overcome hardship to complete the process of becoming full citizens. It also focuses on the act of redress, allowing Americans to congratulate themselves, however belatedly, on making amends. The extent to which racism shaped other aspects of wartime strategy remains largely unexplored in textbooks.[51] Precisely because the injustice of internment is no longer controversial, it is a safe, even celebratory, way to reiterate the ideology of democratic dissent.

The Lessons of War

In important ways, current textbook versions of the history of World War II in all three countries repudiate at least some wartime visions of the nation. German leaders have rejected the Nazi vision of Aryan hegemony over Europe and have recast Germany's future within the parameters of the European Union. That stance has required not only harsh criticism of Nazi policies but, at least in theory, the advocacy of multiculturalism. Nearly all the major Japanese school texts now recognize Japan's aggression in the

1.11 Vietnam Veterans Against the War occupy the Statue of Liberty
The Vietnam Veterans Against the War (VVAW) argued that protest against the U.S. government's actions in Vietnam was the most patriotic course for all citizens, especially soldiers. Although some textbooks show antiwar activity, few explore the moral and political convictions that explain actions like this one. Source: VVAW, Inc. Used by permission.

Pacific War and mention crimes against the comfort women and the Nanjing massacre. None defends Japan's aggression either in China or from the attacks at Pearl Harbor through the end of the war. Some important issues nevertheless remain untouched. For example, none of the texts we examined even alludes to the responsibility of the emperor, as Japan's supreme leader, for either colonialism or war. The texts do, however, provide teachers and students an opportunity to explore significant critical perspectives on the war. U.S. textbooks sharply criticize the "shameful" internment of Japanese Americans and did so long before the U.S. government's 1987 apology for that policy. Recent texts also honor the wartime achievements of women, African Americans, Native Americans, and Japanese Americans, about which earlier texts were virtually silent. Those are significant markers of the social evolution in each country since 1945.

Yet textbook depictions of World War II differ in important ways in the three countries. The German story is distinctive for the internationalism fundamental to the contemporary vision of the nation expressed in school textbooks. Unified Germany gives the impression of having moved farthest toward a coherent internationalist stance appropriate to a twenty-first-century vision of a united Europe. German textbooks and public pronouncements have stressed European identity and underplayed national ambitions. They also have accepted foreign participation in the creation of a new narrative of the German nation, illustrated by receptiveness to Israeli criticism of their school curriculum on the Holocaust. Of course, one reason for that acquiescence is that in the absence of a significant postwar German Jewish constituency, the gesture of repudiating the Holocaust would have had no relevance for the future and therefore no credibility abroad without an international component. Yet there are limits to internationalist goodwill in Germany today. Economic hardship and high unemployment contribute to the attractiveness of a counternarrative of continuous twentieth-century German suffering, as Wegner notes. Nationalist sentiment may be growing again as well. Andre S. Markovits and Simon Reich argue that since the mid-1990s Europeanization is gradually being replaced by nationalism.[52] German educators' fears that they may inadvertently train a new generation of Neo-Nazis rest on the knowledge that some young Germans already see the world much as did the Nazis themselves.

The recent changes in Japanese textbooks carry a similar, though less fully developed implication of accepting foreign participation in assessments of Japan's war. Mention of the comfort women in officially sanctioned textbooks was a direct response to foreign as well as domestic critics of Japan's war and colonial rule. It not only implies official recognition that charges of brutality toward the comfort women are true but also accepts a dialogue within the Asian region about the war, as does official apology for Japan's wartime behavior. Moreover, the dialogue over the comfort women is as much or more with groups advocating contemporary women's and foreign workers' rights as it is with Asian governments, since social activists in Japan and elsewhere denounced wartime and postwar coercive prostitution of Asian women far earlier and more powerfully than did their governments, and these individuals have led the demands for apology and reparations.[53]

This vision of a shared future is, of course, precisely what the Orthodox History Group rejects when its proponents argue that textbooks are strictly for domestic consumption; that each nation must have its own distinctive, even biased views; and that Japanese ought not heed what others think. At issue is whether the Japanese state should seem properly impervious or properly sensitive to foreign criticism. Despite the efforts of the Orthodox History Group, many Japanese citizens have already accepted the latter interpretation of Japan's place in the world. Even the Japanese government has inched its way quite far toward acquiescing in the right of foreigners to insist on a national narrative that they can accept. Nonetheless, the fear of Asia Gerow sees in recent popular Japanese cinema is a warning sign that the outcome of this debate is still undecided.

In the United States, school texts have been a battleground for competing visions of gender, race, and class with enormous implications for visions of the nation, as the transformation in attitudes toward Japanese Americans since 1945 suggests. Americans now generally agree that the U.S. government was wrong to treat its residents and citizens of Japanese ancestry (now perceived by many Americans as a "model minority") as if they were hostile foreigners. The national stance toward racial segregation in the armed services and civilian life has been transformed in textbooks as in law and custom. Yet in contrast to Japan and Germany, the United States has barely acknowledged foreign perspectives in debates over reassessments of World War II or subsequent American wars. Nor have any of the school texts, including most of those written for college students, fully confronted U.S. brutality against the Vietnamese people in the Vietnam War. Americans as yet feel little pressure from domestic or foreign critics to depict foreigners as human beings. In this way, American hegemony translates into isolation from any imagined community in concert with the rest of the world.

Although current German, Japanese, and American debates over how to envision their respective places in their regional and global communities have wide-ranging implications for other nations and peoples, so do foreign perspectives on them. Many of the postwar governments in Europe built hatred of Germans into the foundational narratives of their states, just as Asian governments did with hatred of Japan. The political legitimacy of the People's Republic of China is built on the national memory of the war of liberation against relentless Japanese savagery.[54] The Polish Communist government presented Germany in textbooks and elsewhere as a permanent threat to Poland, rooted in an intrinsic German desire to take land away from Poles and Slavs. World War II, in that scenario, was only the most recent and bloodiest chapter in a very long horror story. By 1985, Polish historians had begun to move away from that interpretation toward one that saw 1939 to 1945 as a moment of discontinuity in a mainly peaceful history. Textbooks, however, still reflected the older interpretation. In the 1990s, after the collapse of the Communist government, the textbook accounts of Germans had softened to the point where one researcher described them as "enigmatic," but opinion polls in 1990 still showed that 70 percent of Poles feared unified Germany and agreed that "as long as the world exists, the German will never be a brother to the Pole."[55]

The most recent South Korean texts, discussed by Kimijima here, similarly depict Japan as the eternal aggressor and view World War II as the moment when the underlying Japanese aggressiveness against Korea was most fully revealed. They also reconceptualize World War II as beginning in 1895, when modern Japan first deployed troops to Korea, and escalating with the formal colonization of Korea in 1910. The Polish and Korean textbook narratives continue to assume the existence of threatening German and Japanese nations. (By contrast, Japanese and German texts carry virtually no criticism of the United States.) The importance of Germany in Polish history and Japan in Korean history is also much greater than the reverse. From one perspective, the longevity of suspicions in Poland and Korea keeps the Germans and the Japanese working toward rapprochement. Yet any truly integrated international future will also require change on the part of Koreans and Poles. This is unlikely to happen soon.

Narratives of the nation, in textbooks as elsewhere, must change over time to accommodate both global shifts of power and domestic social transformations. In the service of that task, past actions are continually reinterpreted, making old justifications obsolete. One key issue is how to imagine peaceful, cooperative links with former enemy nations. A second involves representing the relationship between citizen and state. Textbook depictions of World War II in all three countries repudiate old attitudes hostile to the civic inclusion of women and racial and religious minorities. Finally, to realize a newly imagined international future, governments often must take into consideration the views of the citizens of other nations as well as their own.

Here the contrast among the three countries is striking. Americans are insulated from foreign criticism to a degree unimaginable in either Germany or Japan. This luxury—actually an obstacle to engaging history—will not last forever. The ferocity of textbook and curricular debates in Japan can instruct the rest of us: the issues they wrestle with—nationalism, citizenship, regional and global cooperation, and social change—confront citizens of all nations in the contemporary world. Education is one of the key fronts where those battles will be fought. Indeed, they are already under way.

Notes

We thank Akiko Hashimoto, Peter Katzenstein, James Loewen, Gavan McCormack, Gary Okihiro, Jennifer Rogers, Michael Sherry, and Marilyn Young for astute comments and suggestions. Christopher Tassava found many of the visual images.

1. John Meyer, David Kamens, and Aaron Benavot, with Yun-Kyung Cha and Suk-Ying Wong, show convincingly the broad common ground and increasing global standardization among primary school textbooks, curricula, and educational systems across nations that differ in wealth, political and economic systems, and culture. Standardization is surely even greater at the high school level. *School Knowledge for the Masses: World Models and National Primary Curricular Categories in the Twentieth Century* (London: Falmer Press, 1992).

2. Michael Apple and Linda Christian-Smith, *The Politics of the Textbook* (London: Routledge, 1991), 4.

3. Suzanne de Castell, Allan Luke, and Carmen Luke, *Language, Authority and Criticism: Readings on the School Textbook* (London: Falmer Press, 1989); Pierre Nora, *Realms of Memory,* 3 vols. (New York: Columbia University Press, 1996–1998).

4. Stein Tonnesson and Hans Antlov, *Asian Forms of the Nation* (Richmond, Surrey, U.K.: Curzon Press, 1996), 2.

5. Discredited wars are not identical to defeats. Sometimes defeat can be associated with moral righteousness, as the defeat to the Turks in 1389 clearly is for Serbian nationalists. Barbara Ehrenreich, *Blood Rites: Origins and History of the Passions of War* (New York: Henry Holt, 1997), 204–24, analyzes the three cases examined here—Japan, Germany, and the United States—tracing the links between war and what she calls "institutionalized religious nationalism" in each to modern revivals of primordial religious passions.

6. On occupation policy in Japan, see Toshio Nishi, *Unconditional Democracy and Politics in Occupied Japan 1945–1952* (Stanford, CA: Hoover Institution Press, 1982); Yoko Thakur, "Textbook Reform in Allied Occupied Japan, 1945–1952," Ph.D. thesis, University of Maryland College Park, 1990; John Dower, *Embracing Defeat: Japan in the Wake of World War II* (New York: W.W. Norton/New Press, 1999), 245–50. For occupation policy in Germany, see James F. Tent, *Mission on the Rhine: Reeducation and Denazification in American-Occupied Germany* (Chicago: University of Chicago Press,

1982). For a discussion of the tension between views of education for the market versus the democratic polity in the United States, see Robert B. Westbrook, "Public Schooling and American Democracy," in Roger Soder, ed., *Democracy, Education, and the Schools* (San Francisco: Jossey-Bass, 1996), 125–50.

7. Ministry of Education review, censorship, and certification processes are described in detail by Lawrence Beer, *Freedom of Expression in Japan: A Study in Comparative Law, Politics and Society* (New York: Harper & Row, 1984), 260–62. See also Horio Teruhisa, *Educational Thought and Ideology in Modern Japan: State Authority and Intellectual Freedom*, ed. and trans. Steven Platzer (Tokyo: University of Tokyo Press, 1988). German textbook discussions of World War II are also limited by national laws criminalizing denials of the Holocaust.

8. A 1997 textbook debate that began in Taiwan quickly moved across the Taiwan Strait. It centered on the treatment of Japanese colonialism in a junior high social studies text used in all schools. See Julian Baum, "Schools of Thought: Long Overdue Textbook Recast Runs into Controversy," *Far Eastern Economic Review*, August 14, 1997. Critics of the text, including Yang Yizhou, writing in *People's Daily*, October 27, 1997, attacked the text for negating Taiwan's close historical relationship to China and the Chinese people as well as for whitewashing the record of Japanese colonialism. The richly illustrated social studies text, *Renshi Taiwan* (Understand Taiwan), which was test-taught in 1997–1998, is an introduction to historical and contemporary Taiwan that is attentive to aboriginal life and the mix of peoples that compose the Taiwan population. It also addresses a range of social problems, such as income inequality and gender, and—for the first time in a school text—grasps the biggest nettle by introducing the February 28, 1947 Guomindang massacre of Taiwanese.

9. Jill Stephenson, "Anniversaries, Memory, and the Neighbours: The 'German Question' in Recent History," *German Politics* 5, 1 (April 1996): 43–58; Thomas Banchoff, "German Policy Toward the European Union: The Effects of Historical Memory," *German Politics* 6, 1 (April 1997): 60–76; Ian Buruma, *The Wages of Guilt: Memories of War in Germany and Japan* (New York: Farrar, Straus, and Giroux, 1994) compares Germany and Japan. Buruma concludes that Germans had gone farther in repudiating the war but offers no consistent explanation for this.

10. The International Society for Educational Information, an arm of the Foreign Ministry, also collects foreign textbooks about Japan and texts from the former colonies. No other government sustains a textbook center of comparable scale.

11. *Nihon no Ayumi to Sekai* (Japan's path and the world). (Tokyo: Nihon Bunkyō, 1996–1997), 244.

12. Laura Hein and Mark Selden, eds., *Living with the Bomb: American and Japanese Cultural Conflicts in the Nuclear Age* (Armonk, NY: M.E. Sharpe, 1996); Edward Linenthal and Thomas Engelhardt, eds., *History Wars: The Enola Gay Controversy and Other Battles for the American Past* (New York: Metropolitan Books, 1996); James E. Young, *The Texture of Memory: Holocaust Memorials and Meaning* (New Haven, CT: Yale University Press, 1993); G. Kurt Piehler, *Remembering War the American Way* (Washington, DC: Smithsonian Institution Press, 1995); Diane Barthel, *Historic Preservation: Collective Memory and Historical Identity* (New Brunswick, NJ: Rutgers University Press, 1996).

13. Siobhan Kattago, "Representing German Victimhood and Guilt: The Neue Wache and Unified Germany Memory," *German Politics and Society* 16, 3 (Fall 1998): 86–104. The quotes are from 91. Debate in Japan on the responsibility of ordinary citizens for the war (as opposed to the culpability of the state, the emperor, or the military) has not reached the scale or received the publicity of the Goldhagen debate, which has exercised and divided German intellectuals.

14. Ibid., 100. The Tokyo museum opened in 1999. See Ellen Hammond, "Commemo-

ration Controversies: The War, the Peace, and Democracy in Japan," in Hein and Selden, *Living with the Bomb,* 100–21.

15. Robert Shandley, ed., *Unwilling Germans? The Goldhagen Debate* (Minneapolis: University of Minnesota Press, 1998); Daniel Goldhagen, *Hitler's Willing Executioners: Ordinary Germany and the Holocaust* (New York: Knopf, 1996).

16. Mark Selden, "China, Japan and the Regional Political Economy of East Asia, 1945–1995," in Peter Katzenstein and Takashi Shiraishi, eds., *Network Power: Japan in Asia* (Ithaca, NY: Cornell University Press, 1997), 306–40.

17. Buruma, *The Wages of Guilt*; R.J.R. Bosworth, *Explaining Auschwitz and Hiroshima: History Writing and the Second World War* (London: Routledge, 1993). Jeffrey Herf, *Divided Memory: The Nazi Past in the Two Germanys* (Cambridge: Harvard University Press, 1997) makes the important point that reparations were made by the West German government but not its East German counterpart. West Germany also recognized Israel early on.

18. Peter Katzenstein, ed., *Tamed Power: Germany in Europe* (Ithaca, NY: Cornell University Press, 1997), xiii. For more on memories of war in Germany, see Thomas Berger, "The Past in the Present: Historical Memory and German National Security Policy," *German Politics* 6, 1 (April 1997): 38–59; Manfred Kuechler, "Germans and 'Others': Racism, Xenophobia or 'Legitimate Conservatism?'" *German Politics* 3, 1 (April 1994): 47–74; J. David Case, "The Politics of Memorial Representation: The Controversies over the German Resistance Museum in 1994," *German Politics* 16, 1 (Spring 1998): 58–81.

19. For the $58 billion figure, Alan Cowell, "Germany the Unloved Just Wants to Be Normal," *New York Times,* November 23, 1997.

20. For German-Polish discussion, see Wlodzimierz Borodziej, "The Eighteenth Schoolbook Conference, 28 May–1 June 1985," *Acta Poloniae Historica* 54 (1986): 298–302. An exemplar of the new Pan-European approach to a common history is Frédéric Delouche, ed., *Illustrated History of Europe: A Unique Portrait of Europe's Common History*, trans. Richard Moyne (New York: Henry Holt, 1992). Not all western European nations have responded to the prospect of regional integration with equal enthusiasm. In particular, Britain's 1988 Education Reform Act instituted a "national curriculum" to stave off any loss of British identity and sovereignty. British historical textbook trends and conflicts are briefly surveyed in Stephan Shakespeare, "Old Britain, New History," *Spectator*, October 11, 1997, 11–12. In other parts of Europe, moreover, nationalism is currently a fighting matter. In addition to the former Yugoslavia, clashes continue in the former Soviet Union and in areas claimed by Basque separatists and by Irish nationalists.

21. Peter Katzenstein, "Introduction: Asian Regionalism in Comparative Perspective," in Katzenstein and Shiraishi, *Network Power*, 12.

22. Fujioka Nobukatsu and Yoshida Yutaka, "Koko ga okashii: rekishi kyōkasho ronsō" (This is strange: the history textbook debate), *This Is Yomiuri*, vol. 3 (1997), 34–73.

23. For more on the Asia debate and its relation to the U.S. alliance in Japanese thinking, see Laura Hein and Ellen Hammond, "Homing in on Asia: Renovating Identity in Contemporary Japan," *Bulletin of Concerned Asian Scholars* 27, 3 (1995): 3–17; Michael Yahuda, *The International Politics of the Asia-Pacific, 1945–1995* (London: Routledge, 1996), 229–54; Katzenstein and Shiraishi, *Network Power.*

24. By contrast, Japanese from all points on the political spectrum have argued that the U.S. wartime bombing of civilians, notably the atomic bombs, was morally indefensible, but as yet they have had only small impact on the American or international discussion. One of the most active figures in the Japanese textbook debate in the late 1990s has made this argument, using it to justify a rejection of Japanese reconsideration of their own wartime conduct. Nishio Kanji, "Acknowledge U.S. War Crimes," *Sankei shinbun,* August 9, 1997, translated in *Japan Times,* August 26, 1997.

25. Many Asian and American critics of Japanese knowledge of the war pound away at

the theme of an unrepentant Japan whose apologies are insincere and insufficient, ignoring the achievements of Japanese researchers whose painstaking work over many years provides the most compelling information base for critical movements in Japan and abroad. An excellent example of this myopia is Iris Chang's best-seller *The Rape of Nanjing* (New York: Basic Books, 1997). By contrast, the alliance of feminist groups in Korea, the Philippines, and other countries together with Japanese feminist researcher-activists has mounted an effective campaign around the sexual exploitation of Asian women.

26. Fujioka Nobukatsu, "'Jūgun ianfu' o chūgakusei ni oshieru na" (Don't teach middle school students about the military comfort women), in Rekishi Kyōkasho o tsukuru kai, ed., *Atarashii Nihon no rekishi ga hajimaru* (A new Japanese history is beginning) (Tokyo: Gentosha, 1997), 78, quotes seven textbooks.

27. A 1999 pamphlet gives the English name as the "Japanese Society for History Textbook Reform." Fujioka Nobukatsu and Jiyūshugi Shikan Kenkyūkai, eds., *Kyōkasho ga oshienai rekishi*, (History not taught in textbooks), 4 vols. (Tokyo: Sankei Shinbun Nyūsu Sabisu, 1996–1998), Fujioka Nobukatsu, *Ojoku no kin-gendai shi* (Shameful modern history) (Tokyo: Tokuma Shoten, 1996).

28. Fujioka and Jiyūshugi, *Kyōkasho ga oshienai rekishi*, vol. 2, 11.

29. Fujioka Nobukatsu, "Hi-nichi rekishi kyōiku o haisu" (Expelling anti-Japanese history education), in *Ojoku no kin-gendai shi*, 81–84. Also Fujioka and Jiyūshugi, *Kyōkasho ga oshienai rekishi*, vol. 2, 11.

30. Fujioka Nobukatsu, "Nihonjin wa jōshiki ni okure," in *Atarashii Nihon no rekishi gahajimaru*, 122.

31. Yoshimi Yoshiaki, *Jūgun ianfu* (Military comfort women) (Tokyo: Iwanami Shoten, 1995). See also the special issue of *positions. east asia cultures critique* 5, 1 (1997), on *The Comfort Women: Colonialism, War, and Sex;* Maria Rosa Henson, *Comfort Woman: Slave of Destiny* (Boulder, CO: Rowman & Littlefield, 1999); Keith Howard, ed., *True Stories of the Korean Comfort Women*, trans. Young Joo Lee (London: Cassell, 1995); Watanabe Kazuko, "Militarism, Colonialism, and the Trafficking of Women: "'Comfort Women' Forced into Sexual Labor for Japanese Soldiers," *Bulletin of Concerned Asian Scholars* 26, 4 (1994): 3–16. For a booklength compendium of public statements on depictions of the military comfort women in textbooks, see Tawara Yoshifumi, *"Ianfu" mondai to kyōkasho kōgeki* (The "comfort woman" issue and the textbook controversy) (Tokyo: Tōbunken, 1997).

32. For a longer discussion, see Laura Hein, "Savage Irony: The Imaginative Power of the Military Comfort Women in the 1990s," *Gender and History* 11, 2 (July 1999): 336–72.

33. There obviously was no general horror at enforced prostitution, since U.S. occupying forces cooperated with the postwar Japanese government to create an official prostitution system for the Allied forces using lower-class Japanese women. Yuki Tanaka, *Japan's Comfort Women: Prostitution, Exploitation and the U.S. Cover Up* (London: Routledge, forthcoming); Dower, *Embracing Defeat*, 123–29.

34. Chin Sung Chung, "The Origins and Development of the Military Sexual Slavery Problem in Imperial Japan," *positions: east asia cultures critique* 5, 1 (1997): 232–33. See also Tanaka, *Japan's Comfort Women*. Similarly, Japan was held accountable at the trials for the several thousand Western POWs forced to work on the Burma-Thai railroad but not for the vastly larger number of Southeast Asian forced laborers. Gavan McCormack and Hank Nelson, eds., *The Burma-Thailand Railway: Memory and History* (St. Leonards, Australia: Allen and Unwin, 1993).

35. Texts that mention forced labor and compulsory assimilation policies include *Sekaishi B* (World History B) (Tokyo: Sanseido, 1998), 288–89, a high school geography text; *Shinkei Nihon shi* (New Japanese history) (Tokyo: Sanseido, 1994), 310–11, a high school history text; *Nihon no rekishi* (Japanese history) (Tokyo: Yamakawa Shuppan, 1994), 336–37, a high school history text; *Shin Nihon Shi B* (New Japanese History B)

(Tokyo: Kirihara Shoten, 1998), 317, a high school geography and history text; *Nihon shi* (Japanese history) (Tokyo: Nihon Shoseki, 1994–95), 304, a high school history text. The most common adjective for Japanese policies toward colonized and occupied territories in these texts was "merciless" *(kakoku)*. *Shin sekaishi B* (New world history B) (Tokyo: Yamakawa Shuppan, 1994), a high school text, did not mention these colonial policies. See also the texts reprinted bilingually in *Japan in Modern History: Junior High Schools* (Tokyo: International Society for Educational Information, 1994), and *Japan in Modern History: High Schools*, 2 vols. (Tokyo: International Society for Educational Information, 1995, 1996).

36. Peter Schneider, "The Sins of the Grandfathers," *New York Times*, December 3, 1995, 75.

37. Akiko Hashimoto, *Japanese and German Projects of Moral Recovery: Toward a New Understanding of War Memories in Defeated Nations*, Occasional Papers in Japanese Studies (Cambridge: Edwin O. Reischauer Institute of Japanese Studies, 1999).

38. Herf, *Divided Memory;* see 362–65 for comments on the last East German government in 1990. Claudia Koonz, "Between Memory and Oblivion: Concentration Camps in German Memory," in John R. Gillis, ed., *Commemorations: The Politics of National Identity* (Princeton, NJ: Princeton University Press, 1994), 258–80.

39. Klaus Neumann, "Goethe, Buchenwald, and the New Germany," *German Politics and Society* 17, 1 (Spring 1999): 55–83. The liberation/uprising was memorialized in cement sculpture in a 1958 Buchenwald memorial to "the liberated prisoners" more than a kilometer from the camp.

40. Kuechler, "Germans and 'Others'; Andreas Staab, "Xenophobia, Ethnicity and National Identity in Eastern Germany," *German Politics* 7, 2 (August 1998): 31–46; Penny Henson and Nisha Malhan, "Endeavours to Export a Migration Crisis: Policy Making and the Europeanisation in the German Migration Dilemma," *German Politics* 4, 3 (December 1995): 128–44; Diethelm Prowe, "National Identity and Racial Nationalism in the New Germany: Nazism vs. the Contemporary Radical Right," *German Politics and Society* 15, 1 (Spring 1997): 1–21.

41. Jacob Heilbrunn, "Germany's New Right," *Foreign Affairs*, November/December 1996, 80–98. Quote from p. 82.

42. Schneider, "The Sins of the Grandfathers."

43. Daniel Singer, "France on Trial, *Nation*, November 19, 1997, 5; Alan Cowell, "Swiss Bank Reports Finding $11 Million More in Unclaimed Accounts from Wartime," *New York Times*, July 24, 1997; "Red Cross Admits Failing to Condemn Holocaust," *New York Times*, October 8, 1997.

44. See Elliot Converse III et al., *The Exclusion of Black Soldiers from the Medal of Honor in World War II: The Study Commissioned by the United States Army to Investigate Racial Bias in the Awarding of the Nation's Highest Military Decoration* (Jefferson, NC: McFarland, 1997); Ronald Takaki, *Strangers from a Different Shore: A History of Asian Americans* (Boston: Little, Brown, 1989). For belated attention to the wartime contributions of women, see Judy Litoff and David Smith, eds., *American Women in a World at War: Contemporary Accounts from World War II* (Wilmington, DE: Scholarly Resources, 1997); Ronald Takaki, *A Different Mirror: A History of Multicultural America* (Boston: Little, Brown, 1993).

45. Frances FitzGerald, *America Revised: History Schoolbooks in the Twentieth Century* (Boston: Little, Brown, 1979). For the debate on multiculturalism, see Arthur M. Schlesinger Jr., *The Disuniting of America* (New York: Norton, 1992); Henry Louis Gates Jr., *Loose Canons: Notes on the Culture Wars* (New York: Oxford University Press, 1992); Joan Scott, "The Campaign Against Political Correctness: What's Really at Stake?" and other contributions to *Radical History Review* 5, 4 (1992).

46. Eugene Barker and Henry Steele Commager, *Our Nation* (Evanston, IL: Row, Peterson, 1949), 948.

47. For example, Henry Graff and John Knout, *The Adventure of the American People: A History of the United States from 1876* (Chicago: Rand McNally, 1973), "shameful episode," 453; Lewis Todd and Merle Curti, *Rise of the American Nation,* 3rd ed. (New York: Harcourt, Brace, Jovanovich, 1972) "unjustified actions," 736; Frank Freidel and Henry Drewry, *America: A Modern History of the United States* (Lexington, MA; D.C. Heath, 1970), "war hysteria," 683; Leonard Wood, Ralph Gabriel, and Edward Biller, *America: Its People and Values* (New York: Harcourt, Brace, Jovanovich, 1985), "grave injustice," 692; Daniel Boorstin and Brooks Mather Kelley, *A History of the United States* (Lexington, MA: Ginn and Company, 1981), "disgraceful treatment," 557. Some critics still see the textbook discussion of internment as inadequate. Like Japanese textbook treatments of colonial policy in Korea and the military comfort women, the subject is often presented in a very brief factual form that forecloses rather than opens discussion of powerful controversies. Michael Romanowski, "In Textbooks We Trust," *Executive Educator* (May 1995): 38–41.

48. This discussion has benefited from Gary Okihiro's personal communication, May 6, 1999. See Gary Okihiro, *Whispered Silences: Japanese-Americans and World War II* (Seattle: University of Washington Press, 1996); Roger Daniels, *Concentration Camps: North America, Japanese in the United States and Canada During World War II* (Malabar, FL: R.E. Krieger, 1981); Gordon Chang, ed., *Morning Glory or Evening Shadow: Yamato Ichihashi and His Internment Writings, 1942–1945* (Stanford, CA: Stanford University Press, 1997); Keibo Oiwa, ed., *Stone Voices: Wartime Writings of Japanese Canadian Issei* (Montreal: Véhicule Press, 1991).

49. Michael Romanowski, "Beyond History Textbooks: Teachers, Students and the Japanese Internment," *Journal of Social Studies Research* 19, 2 (1995): 35–43.

50. In addition to the chapters by Loewen and Hunt in this volume, see James Loewen, *Lies My Teacher Told Me: Everything Your American History Textbook Got Wrong* (New York: New Press, 1995).

51. See the pioneering work of John W. Dower, *War Without Mercy* (New York: Pantheon, 1986); George Roeder, *The Censored War* (New Haven CT: Yale University Press, 1993).

52. Andre S. Markovits and Simon Reich, *The German Predicament: Memory and Power in the New Europe* (Ithaca, NY: Cornell University Press, 1997).

53. On social movements for redress, see Tanaka Hiroshi, *Zainichi Gaikokujin* (Foreigners in Japan) (Tokyo: Iwanami, 1995). Hyun Sook Kim notes that a 1992 South Korean junior high school text discusses the comfort women much as do the Japanese ones, simply including it in a list of Japanese colonial practices such as forcing Koreans to worship at Japanese shrines, adopt Japanese names, and engage in forced labor: "even women became the object of sacrifice for the war under the name *chongsindae.*" Kim argues that this bland approach reflects the interest of the Korean state in reinforcing patriarchy. "History and Memory: The 'Comfort Woman' Controversy," *positions. east asia cultures critique* 5, 1 (1997): 91.

54. We are not challenging the fundamental stance of the Chinese nationalist narrative or that of others whose anticolonial wars provided the basis of national independence. Cf. Mark Selden, *China in Revolution. The Yenan Way Revisited* (Armonk, NY: M.E. Sharpe, 1995). We note, however, that Chinese officials reify the image of an ultranationalistic and unrepentant Japan, which allows them to reenact—in textbooks and elsewhere—the great victory that originally legitimized their rule. This does not mean that no changes have taken place. PRC texts have, for example, significantly reassessed the wartime Guomindang. Until the 1990s, the PRC painted the Guomindang as enemies, but when it shifted to a policy of better relations with the Republic of China on Taiwan, it presented a

far more laudatory history of the role of Guomindang forces in the anti-Japanese resistance half a century earlier.

55. Richard P. Sander, "The Contribution of Post–World War II Schools in Poland in Forging a Negative Image of the Germans," *East European Quarterly* 29, 2 (1995): 169–87. See also Ewa Nasalska, "Ethnocentrism in the Image of Germans and Poles in German and Polish Textbooks of Recent History," *Revue des études sud-est européennes* 33, 1–2 (1995): 53–64; Borodziej, "The Eighteenth Schoolbook Conference."

Part II

Textbooks and Historical Memory

2
The Japanese Movement to "Correct" History

Gavan McCormack

"Nothing is more idiotic than to deny today the truth of what
one did yesterday."

—Ooka Shohei, *Horyoki (1948)¹*

"It is precisely its way of teaching its modern history that is
the crucial determinant of the constitution of a people as a
nation. The people that does not have a history to be proud
of cannot constitute itself as a nation."

—Fujioka Nobukatsu, *Ojoku no kin-gendai shi²*

"Liberal Historiography" and "Correct History"

The question of responsibility for the war that ended a half century ago
becomes more pressing for Japan as the war itself recedes in memory.
Social and political rifts over the issue deepen, and the international
ramifications grow more serious. Since the beginning of the 1990s, dozens of lawsuits claiming apology and compensation have been lodged
with Tokyo courts on behalf of the many victims of Japan's colonialism
and aggression, including the former "comfort women," the victims of
Nanjing and other massacres, survivors of wartime forced labor programs, and the victims of bacteriological (plague) or chemical attacks
on wartime China. Of all the issues, that of the comfort women may be
the most intractable.

The Geneva-based International Commission of Jurists issued a report on the comfort women in 1994 that referred to large numbers of women and girls having been held captive, beaten, tortured, and repeatedly raped in wartime Japanese military installations. In February 1996 a report for the Human Rights Committee of the United Nations described the comfort women as "sex slaves" and their treatment as a "crime against humanity." It called upon Japan to compensate victims, punish those responsible without regard to limitation of time, and ensure that educational curricula included the historical facts.

In Seoul, Manila, Jakarta, and the other cities of the old "Co-Prosperity Sphere" large numbers of angry women began to speak about what had happened to them fifty years ago. By early 1997 some 23,000 women in Korea (North and South), the Philippines, China, Thailand, Indonesia, and elsewhere had come forward by name to give either silent or vocal testimony to their experiences. The focus of war reflections has therefore shifted. Where men—politicians, soldiers, scholars—had always defined and debated the issues, women in the 1990s began to intervene, confronting Japan with immense moral, political, and cultural questions.

In December 1996 the U.S. Justice Department's Criminal Division announced that it had drawn up an immigration "ban list" of Japanese believed to be responsible for war crimes; three of the twelve (unidentified) people on that list were thought to be associated with the comfort women system, the others being former members of the Harbin-based Unit 731 responsible for bacteriological warfare in China and many horrific crimes against prisoners.[3] In other words, fifty years after the event, Washington had decided to place Japanese on the same level as Nazi war crimes, so uniquely heinous that suspected perpetrators should not enjoy any protection because of the lapse of time.[4]

Within Japan, after decades of government procrastination and intense effort by various popular organizations, from the early 1990s officials began to make attempts to grapple with these problems. In 1993, when the long Liberal Democratic Party (LDP) hegemony over Japanese politics was broken for the first time, the war was described by the prime minister as aggressive and colonial, and in 1995 the Diet adopted a resolution expressing formal regret over it. The government admitted official involvement in establishing and managing "comfort houses" for Japanese soldiers, and conceded that many of the women working in them had been forced to do so (*sojite kyosei datta*). A fund, nominally private but with strong official backing, was established to compensate surviving comfort women, and specific letters of apology from the prime minister,

2.1 Surrender of American troops at Corregidor, Philippines
Harsh Japanese treatment of POWs is one of the enduring reasons for international criticism
of Japan's war. It is also discussed in most American textbooks and briefly in some Japanese
ones. NARA, NWDNS-208–AA-80B-1, War and Conflict No. 1142.

accompanying solatium payments, were issued to the first of the former victims during 1996.

However, these modest advances also served to excite fierce opposition. Inside the national Diet, LDP members who insisted on the justice of the war's cause and firmly opposed any apologies formed a Diet Members League for the Fiftieth Anniversary of the End of the War (headed by former minister of education Okuno Seisuke) in December 1994. Under this name various events were conducted in August 1995, including the "Celebration of Asian Togetherness," which invited representatives of various Asian countries to "thank the war dead and praise Japan for its contribution to the independence of Asian countries."[5] In April 1996 the group changed its name to the Diet Members League for a Bright Japan. Opposition Shinshinto Party members (conservatives, led by Ozawa Ichiro, who had been in the LDP until the split in 1993) in February 1995 formed another group, Diet Members League for the Passing on of a Correct History (headed by Ozawa Tatsuo).

Outside the Diet, both of these groups were closely linked to the Citizens' Association for the Defense of Japan, founded in 1981 and headed in the 1990s by the composer Mayuzumi Toshiro. Nationalist organizations inside and outside of the national Diet could usually draw on the support of a range of other more or less traditional rightist or nationalist groups, including the National Shrine Association (*Jinja Honcho*), War Bereaved Families Association (*Nihon Izokukai*), the Unification Church (the "Moonies") and its Professors for Peace Academy, the World Anti-Communist League, and religious groups such as Seicho No Ie.[6]

New in the mid-1990s were the national organizations formed by the Tokyo University professor Fujioka Nobukatsu: the Liberal View of History Study Group (Jiyūshugi Shikan Kenkyūkai) and the Society for the Making of New School Textbooks in History (Atarashii Rekishi kyōkasho O Tsukuru Kai). They were new in both content and orientation; formerly rightist and nationalist ideas were for the first time presented as "liberal" and directed in particular at the constituency of students, teachers, and academics. If these elements were to be successfully integrated in a front alongside the established parliamentary and extraparliamentary forces of right-wing nationalism, the significance would be considerable.

Although Fujioka is the central figure, he and his cause are supported by a wide-ranging group of literary, media, academic, and business personalities, with a particularly prominent role being played by the cartoonist Kobayashi Yoshinori and the German literature scholar Nishio Kanji (of Electro-Communications University). Their movement is committed to a far-reaching reappraisal of national history, and in particular to securing the deletion of all reference to comfort women from middle school history texts. They have already issued a series of books, with titles such as *Kyōkasho ga oshienai rekishi* (The history the textbooks do not teach) and *Ojoku no kin-gendai shi* (Shameful modern history), which have become best-sellers, and they intend to produce and promote their own textbooks.[7] Popular magazines regularly feature their analysis and activities, and the national daily *Sankei shinbun* vigorously promotes them. Kobayashi Yoshinori's cartoons, published in the magazine *Sapio*, are widely read among youth. An all-night debate on the issues of war memory, textbooks, and especially comfort women on Asahi Television on February 1, 1997, pitted Fujioka and his associates against prominent historians and representatives of the many groups struggling for causes that these new nationalists oppose. It became one of the outstanding media events of the time.

By choosing the term "liberal," Fujioka and his colleagues seek to represent their position as a breakthrough from the stale and unresolved polarities of postwar discourse into something fresh and new. Some might argue that precisely such a breakthrough was occurring anyway in the mid-1990s and that Fujioka's intervention was either unnecessary or obstructive. They would point to a national consensus slowly taking shape around the acceptance of responsibility and commitment to appropriate compensation, the position stated by Prime Minister Hosokawa Morihiro in 1993 and maintained since then in its essentials even by the current LDP prime minister, Hashimoto Ryūtarō. But Fujioka will have nothing of this. He believes historical thinking is still locked within left-right dualism that only his "liberalism" can resolve. Using an expression borrowed from the popular novelist Shiba Ryotaro, he describes the dichotomy in terms of "*zendama*" and "*akudama*" ("goodies" and "baddies"). On the one hand is the so-called "Tokyo Trials view of history," the orthodoxy imposed on Japan by the occupation, which saw prewar and wartime Japan as *akudama* to the United States' *zendama*. Fujioka claims this view then became internalized in Japanese society—thanks primarily to the efforts of left-wing historians and educators—to the extent that eventually even the LDP itself became subverted and the fundamentally misguided 1990s politics of apology became established. The opposing view is the one commonly known as the "affirmation of the Greater East Asian War" view, one perhaps most famously expressed in 1969 in the work of the historian Hayashi Fusao, who insisted above all on the primacy of the Japanese role in achieving the liberation of Asia.

2.2 Bright Japan poster
This graphic, which encouraged children to see imperial Japan as "the brightest nation in the world," is reproduced from a 1941 textbook. Kuboi Norio, *Nihon no shinryaku sensō to Ajia no kodomo (Japan's war of invasion and Asian children)* (Tokyo: Akashi Shoten, 1996), 15. Used by permission.

Although Fujioka announced his rejection of both of these views, in practice his fire has been concentrated exclusively on the former, and he and his colleagues have moved ever closer to precisely the sort of affirmation that Hayashi proclaimed. In moving to try to appropriate the word "liberal" to his cause, Fujioka was implicitly recognizing that his cause would not go far if seen purely in traditional nationalist terms. But he has not practiced "liberalism" as it is commonly understood, involving a commitment to high levels of objectivity and the exploration of a relativistic, multiple causal framework.

Yet the level of support that greeted Fujioka's message suggests that in some sense he was right: many people are fed up with what they perceive to be a fifty-year-long stalemate that shows no sign of resolution and are tired of ongoing discussions of responsibility and compensation for things that happened more than a half-century ago. Many seem also to be seeking a positive identity and role in the world appropriate to the global economic superpower Japan has become.

Despite the "liberal" label and claims to superior objectivity, at the core of Fujioka and his colleagues' message is a view of history centered upon the lament for the loss of a "distinctive Japanese historical consciousness" (*Nihon jishin no rekishi ishiki*). What they describe as the postwar, orthodox, "masochistic" *(jigyakuteki)* view of history is to blame for this.[8] Although they claim objectivity and open-minded commitment to multiple causality, in practice they wish to "inculcate a sense of pride in the history of our nation."[9] For them, history lacks those intrinsic standards (of truth or evidence) that might make possible the resolution of conflicting interpretations; rather, it is subject to the ultimate moral imperative of whether or not it serves to fix a sense of pride in being Japanese.[10] They take particularly strong exception to school history texts approved for use from April 1997 that refer to the "forcible abduction of comfort women" (but also to accounts of the Nanjing massacre and other atrocities). To include such material in school texts amounts, they believe, to the loss of "our own" *(dokuji no)* historical sense; textbooks should instead restore "*correct* history" (emphasis added: *seishi*).[11]

It is a mark of how out of sync with the outside world is the discourse in Japan that Fujioka should make his case for political "correctness" under the banner of its opposite, postmodern relativism, apparently oblivious to the contradiction, and that he should be acclaimed, at least by the national media, as a serious and important thinker for doing so. By affirming the idea of a "correct history," to be given official status and promotion, Fujioka clearly implies that there is also an "incorrect history" that should be suppressed. He thereby reinstates the very *zendama-akudama* dualism that he claims to oppose, and he locates himself within the lineage of those guardians of political correctness who know the truth and are intolerant of all else. By these standards, the prewar bureaucrats dedicated to rooting out "dangerous thoughts" and the imposition of the true and glorious history of the Japanese empire were all "liberals."

The Challenge of the Comfort Women: Japan as "Grotesque Sex-Crime State"

In practice nothing is negated by the "liberals" with more vehemence than the comfort women—their existence, their servile status under the imperial Japanese army, their suffering, and their entitlement to any apology or compensation from the Japanese state. Because the story they tell does not function to increase the sense of "pride in the history of our nation," it should not be told, and those who tell it are bad *(akudama)* for doing so. Furthermore, the basis of the negation appears to be essentially a priori rather than empiricist, in the sense that it rests on the passionate belief that the Japanese state *could not possibly have been* involved in the crime of abduction and slavery on a large scale; therefore that claim is utterly false and abhorrent, and the recounting of the material in school textbooks amounts to "anti-Japanese" and "masochistic" behavior, which can only serve to "corrode, pulverize, melt, and disintegrate" Japan.[12] Schools that teach "false history" of comfort women become like a giant "Kamikuishikimura [the headquarters of the Aum sect], a mind control center staining the entire nation with anti-Japanese ideology."[13] For Fujioka, the comfort women issue is "an unfounded scandal created in the 1990s for the political purpose of bashing Japan."[14] It is even "a grand conspiracy for the destruction of Japan, in collaboration with foreign elements."[15] If such a falsehood were to be included in school texts Japan would come to be seen as "a lewd, foolish and rabid race without peer in the world."[16]

However emotional the deep commitment indicated by such formulations of its position, the Liberal View of History Group does also try to cast its appeal in scientific and empiricist terms, and for this it relies heavily on the services of a professional historian well known and respected for his work on war history, Hata Ikuhiko. In addressing the complex issues of the wartime comfort women, the case as constructed by Hata and Fujioka is that the comfort women were professional prostitutes, earning more than a general in the imperial Japanese army, or as much as 100 times the pay of their soldier customers.[17] Hata describes the work as "high risk, high return."[18] In launching their suits for compensation now, the women are described as motivated by greed and desire for money, seeing their suits as a chance to "win the lottery."[19] Hata and Fujioka insist there is no documentary evidence of compulsion or official responsibility, and they reject the evidence of the women themselves as not on oath or subject to constraints of perjury laws. They propose an analogy to illustrate the relationship between the privately run comfort stations and the *(ianjo)* imperial Japanese army, seeing the comfort stations as akin to the restaurants within the Ministry of Education building, physically within the premises and subject to certain constraints of payment of rent, health controls, and the like but fundamentally independent in terms of management and treatment of their staff. As the Ministry of Education is not responsible for the services or the labor relations in restaurants housed within its building, so, they argue, the Japanese army cannot be held responsible for the conduct of the sex business in the old Japanese empire at a time when prostitution was legal anyway and standards and values were very different from what they are today.[20]

Hata also advances an argument on financial grounds: that if responsi-

2.3 and 2.4 Colonial subjugation

I Jyon-suk, who was drafted into factory work at age 13, just after this photo was taken. In 1992, she holds a bank book recording her wages, most of which she never received. Korean girls were treated particularly harshly and many were forced into sex work. Ito Takashi, "Shogen," *Jugun Ianfu-Joshi Kinro Teishintai* ("Testimony," the military comfort women and Women's Labor Service Corps) (Nagoya: Fubaisha Publishers, 1992). Used by permission.

bility to compensate the women were officially recognized, meeting the claims might cripple the Japanese state. At a figure of, say, 3 million yen for each act of rape to which they were subjected, and taking account of the number of such acts of rape over the years, he estimates that each woman could be entitled to payments of up to 70 billion yen, in which case the overall claim would soon rival the Japanese national debt.[21] It is bizarre that the argument should here shift ground from principle and truth to financial considerations and convenience, but such swings are characteristic of a discourse only thinly grounded in logic or moral principle.

Underlying these protestations about the women is the question of how to characterize the Japanese state. Fujioka and his colleague Nishio Kanji in particular argue that, although Japan may be compared with other modern states, all of which have committed various crimes or excesses, it is fundamentally different from Nazi Germany.[22] Nishio goes to great lengths to protest that, even if what he describes as "Japan's theocratic state under the emperor as high priest" may have fought "a slightly high-handed patriotic war" (*sukoshi*

2.5 Southeast Asian and POW forced labor
Local residents forced to labor for the Japanese war effort óften endured conditions even worse than those of Western POWs. In this picture the two groups work together on building a railroad bridge, either at Songkurai in Thailand or Ronsi in Burma around 1943. Australian War Memorial, negative no. P0406/40/22. Used by permission.

omoiagatta aikoku sensō), it certainly did not commit "crimes against humanity" such as would warrant its inclusion with Nazi Germany in the category of "historically unprecedented terror state."[23] Fujioka adds that it was neither terror state nor a "grotesque sex-crime state."[24]

The difficulty with this claim is that although genocidal intent as such was unique to the Nazis, the casualties and destruction in the Asian war overall matched and even exceeded those on the European front. The crimes were also as abhorrent, particularly in regard to the comfort women but also to the crimes of the Japanese medical and scientific elites (most shockingly known from the record of Unit 731), and there were similarities in racial ideology and the "science" of eugenics, and more generally in relation to wartime "forced labor" (*kyōsei renko*).[25] In many respects Nazi and Japanese ideology and practice were similar, and indeed in some respects Japan was guilty of crimes that even the Nazis did not commit—bacteriological and gas warfare, trading in opium to finance the activities of its puppet governments, and (also in China) the forced evacuation of vast areas of all population *(mujin chitaika)*.[26]

Unlike the former Nazi and present German governments, which are divided by a historical chasm, however, the present Japanese state enjoys a high measure of continuity with its wartime predecessor; indeed its wartime head of state, all suggestion of possible war crimes charges against him having been dismissed on political grounds, continued in office until 1989. If the analogy is pursued, it becomes clear that the sort of views upheld by Fujioka and his colleagues—denying the comfort women, denying Nanjing, and denying other atrocities associated with Unit 731—are generically one with those that in the German (and French) case would be proscribed under the legislation forbidding Holocaust denial.

Man and Movement

Who, then, is Fujioka? And in what context is his movement and its lineage to be understood? Born in 1943, Fujioka was given the personal name "Nobukatsu," literally, "Faith in Victory," at just that moment when the tides of war were turning toward defeat. As a young man, he was by his own account a believer in "one-country pacifism," associated with leftist groups, and as a junior academic in Hokkaido University enjoyed a modest reputation as a scholar specializing in educational teaching methodology.[27] He moved to Tokyo University in the early 1980s but remained relatively unknown until he returned in 1992 from a year of studying cultural anthropology at Rutgers University.[28] During that year he underwent the sort of crisis that is commonly referred to as a *tenkō*. He experienced a sense of humiliation at the Japanese response to the Gulf War and was profoundly influenced by reading books such as Michael Walzer's *Just and Unjust Wars* and Richard Minear's *Victor's Justice*.[29] "The scales fell from my eyes," he said, after reading Minear.[30] He came to see Japan as lacking in the "will as state to protect its security" and to view the "Greater East Asian War" as a "just war" and the postwar Japanese peace constitution as a fetter on the Japanese state and an inhibition preventing the emergence of a proper Japanese sense of nationalism.

Since he describes as much an emotional (or even "religious") experience as an intellectual one, there is no necessary logical consistency to it. Indeed eclecticism is characteristic. Of the influences upon him, he at-

taches the greatest importance to newspaper editor, politician, and re-
nowned interwar liberal Ishibashi Tanzan (1884–1973) and the postwar
novelist Shiba Ryōtarō (1923–1995), who specialized in historical themes.
What Fujioka does not recognize is that Ishibashi's "liberalism" made
him in the 1920s a profound critic of the state, an advocate of complete
Japanese withdrawal from its colonial possessions, and a proponent of
"small Japanism," whereas Shiba, for all his vivid evocation of the drama
of the Meiji period, even in the book Fujioka professes most to admire,
Saka no ue no kumo (Cloud over the hill) was withering in his portrayal
of the great nationalist hero of the Russo-Japanese War, General Nogi
Maresuke. He had no sympathy at all for twentieth-century imperialist
Japan, especially for the war of the 1930s with China, which he denounced
as "unjust and meaningless," an "aggressive war" or a colonial war fought
for oil and resources.[31] It would seem to be in some abstract, spiritual
sense that he wishes to appropriate Ishibashi and Shiba, not the actual
ideas or politics they espoused.

The left-right trajectory Fujioka describes is a common enough historical pattern; what is unusual is his representation of the switch in terms
of a transcendence of the historical stalemate of left-right opposition. In
practice, he is uncritical in his affirmation of the wars of the prewar Japanese state. Save in his use of the label "liberal," it is difficult to distinguish his views from those of traditional rightists. Despite the theoretical
incoherence, it is no new liberal view of history that he propagates but the
old imperial one, the *kokoku shikan*.[32] What is most puzzling and para-
doxical, however, is the curious reticence of Fujioka and his colleagues
to address the question of the emperor himself or the imperial institution
around which the imperial view of history traditionally has cohered. Furthermore, like earlier *tenkōsha* (ideological converts), Fujioka retains much
of the structure and "agitprop" style of his "leftist" days in his reborn
rightist state. The same priority to structure that once inclined him to seek
solace in the formulas of the Japan Communist Party appears to have
survived his conversion intact and to be driving him to construct a new,
no less dogmatic and even more self-righteous version of "correctness."

While the "intellectual" foundations of the new "liberalism" were thus
constructed by Fujioka, Nishio, and others, the campaign in the provinces and the streets kept pace. It was characterized by the sort of intimidation and violence familiar from pre- and postwar rightist and
ultranationalist groups rather than by anything distinctively "liberal."
Demands accompanied by threats were issued to publishers of textbooks,
and convoys of rightist trucks blaring martial music and uttering intimi-

datory slogans circled the offending publishing company offices. The names of publishers and the authors of the offending texts have featured prominently in books and pamphlets issued by the Liberal View of History Group, and blown-up photographs of the private homes of the textbook authors have been circulated with obviously threatening intent. Leaflets praising as a patriotic hero the right-wing fanatic who assassinated Socialist Party leader Asanuma Inejiro in 1960 are pointedly delivered to publishing offices, and violent and fascist organizations such as the Sekihotai, which was responsible for the 1987 attack on the office of *Asahi shinbun* (which left one journalist dead), come to lend Fujioka their support.[33] In all of this, it is hard to detect anything new, harder to detect anything liberal.

Although Fujioka and his colleagues blitzed the media with their exhortations and protestations and applied direct political pressure to the minister of education, their campaign has been signally unsuccessful. After intensive efforts to get local governing bodies to bombard Tokyo with requests to revise the textbooks, one prefecture (Okayama) and eleven lesser local government bodies did submit various resolutions to Tokyo, but many others simply shelved the draft resolutions.[34] Furthermore, the Okayama outcome so surprised and shocked local residents, especially women, that a nationwide movement intent on blocking the attempted campaign elsewhere quickly emerged.[35]

Apart from pursuing the immediate war- and memory-related causes, other issues on which this new front is active include opposition to sex education in schools (stressing chaste education, or *junketsu kyōiku*), opposition to married women's retention of their original family name, and other "family" causes. It has yet to declare its hand on the fundamental question of constitutional reform. In sum, Fujioka's movement rests upon a formidable social base, and his successful coalition around the issue of comfort women, moral and family issues, and the project to create a "bright" history and national identity point to the emergence of a new configuration, with unpredictable consequences.

Toward Understanding and Interpretation

The movement at whose head Fujioka has emerged since the mid-1990s may be seen as firmly rooted in the fabric of postwar Japanese nationalism, revised and reformulated to accept to the changed circumstances of the post–Cold War period and Japan's emergence as a global economic superpower with aspirations to become a superpower *tout court*. Fujioka's personal experience of revelation during his Gulf War sojourn in the United

2.6 Demonstration of national pride
The Orthodox History Group insists that schools should teach about the past only in ways that instill pride in the nation. These schoolgirls are trained in martial arts at the Meiji Shrine in Tokyo. This wartime image can, however, also be read as a reminder of the futility of training with bamboo spears in the age of bombers and machine guns. Satō, ed., *Asahi Rekishi Shashin Riburarii,* vol. 2, 142. Used by permission.

States and his overwhelming sense of shame at Japan's inability to project its power and image to the world may be representative of his generation, ignorant of and scarcely interested in history, humiliated by what seems to be constant harping on Japan's supposed crimes and its dark history and the farcical "diplomacy of apology" conducted by those who have spoken for the Japanese government in recent years (while distributing "hard-earned" Japanese yen to an ungrateful world), and irritated by the low posture constantly required by the Cold War incorporation within the U.S. sphere (and under its umbrella) and what is seen as a mixture of U.S. condescension and Japan bashing.

The clarion call for construction of a proud, pure, and honorable history seems to call forth a strong emotional response. The sense of resentment may be seen as a kind of "victim complex" (*higaisha ishiki*). Because of the way the Fujioka movement moves to appropriate this sense, special resentment has to be directed at the claim of others to be victims, and they find it especially galling that old women should be rising up in accusation throughout the region. So seriously are their allegations taken and so gross the slur on Japan's honor that even the telling of their stories is judged to be a threat to the very survival of Japan, nothing short of "a grand conspiracy for the destruction of Japan" (as noted previously). In this grim role reversal, the women victims are turned into assailants who conspire to cast violent and threatening slurs on the honor and virtue of Japan.[36]

The parallels with European revisionism are plain. The dismissal of the comfort women issue or the Nanjing massacre as myth parallels the dismissal of the Holocaust, and in both cases the victims are recast as aggressors. Thus, for example, the 1980 words of the French literary scholar Robert Faurisson could be easily rewritten by changing only the context of the remarks from Europe to East Asia: "The alleged Hitlerian gas chambers and the so-called genocide of the Jews form a single historical lie whose principal historical beneficiaries are the state of Israel and international Zionism and whose principal victims are the German people."[37]

The conundrum at the heart of prosperous and affluent Japan is the strength of these sentiments of resentment, victim complex, and longing for purity, innocence, and solace, and the scale of commitment to the construction of a "history in which people can take pride," *as if that were the function of history*.[38] Pollution is a powerful theme in this discourse, as if a history might become polluted more by the revelation of the shameful than by the denial of truth. This group can sweep aside the researches of a generation of historians, and in some cases (on television) even proclaim proudly that they have not read the work and that it would take a kind of pervert to undertake the sort of intensive research on comfort women that has been done by the historian Yoshimi Yoshiaki.[39]

The issues raised by the phenomenon are treated with the utmost seriousness by critics and intellectuals in Japan. The historian Nakamura Masanori sees the Fujioka phenomenon in the context of an oscillation throughout modern history between nationalism and internationalism, Westernization and chauvinism. He believes the desire for a new and positive Japanese identity has reached a peak, especially on the part of the present youth and student generation who have been brought up in ignorance of history, surrounded by images and lacking in the capacity for independent thought.[40] For Satō Manabu (like Fujioka, a Tokyo University professor of education), Fujioka and his colleagues represent a postbubble, post-Aum phenomenon of "eccentric, egocentric nationalism," a nationalism that is curiously deformed in that it has (at least as yet) no outward expression but only its inward-looking dimension.[41] The political scientist Ishida Takeshi sees in the phenomenon evidence of a general crisis of Japanese intellectuals, especially at Tokyo University (where he himself spent his career before retirement). Although he supports the idea of a "liberal" view of history, he points out that that should mean in practice a movement beyond the common postwar perspective in which the world has been viewed only through the lens of the U.S.-Japanese relationship that incorporates a yearning to see, think, and feel from multiple Asian and multiple *Zainichi* (foreign residents of Japan) identities, especially from the perspective of the socially weak, the victims, and those neglected in the decadence of official academicism.[42] This is a "liberalism" directly opposed to Fujioka's insistence on finding and imposing the "correct" view. Ishida's criticism is echoed by Soh Kyong-sik, a Korean critic who lives in Japan and notes that the spaces within Japanese society for minorities such as his own *Zainichi* community are bound to shrink to the extent that Fujioka's cause advances.[43] The apprehension and astonishment of large numbers of Japanese intellectuals at the Fujioka phenomenon is captured by Kunihiro Masao, who speaks of being unable to set aside the fear that what he is witnessing is "the rush of Japanese-style fascism."[44]

Conclusion

Although Fujioka sees the "Tokyo Trials" view of history as something imposed by the United States in the course of the occupation and the root of subsequent Japanese humiliation, that is a highly ambiguous assessment. "Leftists," as a matter of fact, have been as critical as rightists of the trials, arguing that they were distorted, not only by the assumption that guilt was exclusive to the defeated—a critique long ago accepted widely outside Japan—but also because of the decision on political grounds to remove from their purview all consideration of certain crucial matters: the emperor, Unit 731, and the comfort women. The more the spotlight is directed, after more than half a century, onto the problem of the Tokyo Trials, the more obvious this must become, and the more likely that the debate will evolve in directions that true "liberals" will welcome but that Fujioka and his colleagues will find difficult to control. Ultimately, the problem of the trials is not only that of where responsibility was assigned but of where it was concealed and evaded, often by a semiconspiratorial joint U.S.-Japanese agreement.

The lament over the loss of the sense of state in an increasingly borderless world and over the loss of conservative control over the levers of power within that state is common enough throughout the world, but the passion with which Fujioka and others address these matters is extraordinary. Their fear and vulnerability is difficult to comprehend given that the Japan of which they speak is a global economic giant, claimant to a permanent seat on the United Nations Security Council, and the success story of the twentieth century. What exactly is it that they fear? Analogies may be drawn with the sort of "politics of resentment" that spreads across the industrial world as urban masses find themselves becoming victims of anonymous global forces, but in the Japanese case economic factors seem to play only a slight role. Instead, Fujioka is driven by fear of the shrinking of the authority of the state, the degradation and dissolution of its authority and symbols.

The Fujioka phenomenon highlights the dilemma facing Japanese conservative and nationalist ideologues as they struggle to come to terms with the changed global circumstances of the post–Cold War world. Moderate elements with strong links to the political and business elites have concluded that maintenance of a "hard" line on questions of the history of Japanese imperialism and militarism in Asia is blocking the path to a future great power or even hegemonic role for Japan in the twenty-first century and therefore—whether for reasons of principle or tactics or often a combination of both—have chosen the path of apology and reconciliation; others like Fujioka insist on the national virtue and purity, whatever the cost. One may go on to suggest that Fujioka's articulation of the Japanese nationalist aspiration is peculiarly vehement because it expresses the sense of desperation of those who see themselves as a shrinking and embattled minority, with the political mainstream, including the core factions of the LDP, having already shifted ground. It is that shift that should be seen as more significant than the frenzied opposition it has occasioned, although the latter, a powerful blend of intellectual incoherence and emotional force, is certainly not to be ignored.

Fujioka and his group maintain that the gap between Japan and its neighbor countries over history and memory is unbridgeable, that the depth of anti-Japanese sentiment on the part of countries such as China and Korea is so great that "if we were to try to get a mutual historical sense with our Asian neighbors it would be bound to lead to surrender on our part."[45] To quote Fujioka again, "Because we are Japanese, it is only natural that we should think of things first from the perspective of Japan and its national interests."[46] It seems hard to deny that Fujioka's plans for a positive view of Japanese history and the policies he urges on the Japanese government would, if ever adopted, set back immeasurably the process of rapprochement with Japan's Asian neighbor countries. If Japan chose to speak to the region in shrill tones of correctness and narrow Japanese pride and to adopt textbooks that would substitute for historical education the inculcation of an eclectic set of edifying stories designed to promote traditional virtues and nationalist fervor, closely akin to prewar ethics textbooks, it would also have to confront its neighbors, rejecting their histories (insofar as they chose to recount their memory of Japanese imperialism, aggression, and war) as "incorrect." The regional consequences would be unpredictable but inevitably disturbing.

Yet this late twentieth-century articulation of the Japanese nationalist aspiration neglects two key dimensions of Japanese nationalism: the emperor on the one hand and the United States on the other, the inner and outer axes of national identity, both of them subject to taboos that prevent free or open discussion. The Fujioka blend of considerations of national pride, honor, and purity suggests a rootedness in the historically privileged representations of Japanese identity built around the quintessential Japanese self—the unsullied, sublime, imperial essence. For such an essence to be sullied by the representation of Japan as a terrorist state, or a "rapist" state, is utterly abhorrent. The other crucial question for Japanese nationalists is also one they fear to express and can only repress and articulate in distorted form: the resentment over the long-continuing military and strategic dependence on the United States. One may well wonder how this new attempt to express a positive, pure Japanese identity will in due course address these two questions.

Fujioka and his colleagues have launched the debate into new waters in that they have constructed and attempted to confer respectability upon a new notion of Japan as unalloyed good, delinked (so far) from traditional formulations of Japanese identity centered upon the emperor and under the cloak of liberalism. The ideological mix looks unstable and its prospects unpredictable. Sooner or later, the nationalist forces currently supporting Fujioka in his distorted and limited evocation of nationalist themes are bound to turn to confront the contradictions and inconsistencies within it. When that happens, we will see what lies beneath the thin veneer of liberalism that covers Japanese right-wing nationalism in this, its newest guise.

It is not necessarily worrying that post–Cold War Japan should show such evidence of a strong desire to articulate a Japanese identity in which past, present, and future could be meaningfully integrated around a core that could command the loyalty of its own people and the respect of the world, for that desire is universal. What is troubling, rather, is that liberalism and rational-

2.7 The Japanese emperor and security alliance with the United States
The two key dimensions of postwar Japanese nationalism unacknowledged in recent debates over textbook content and excluded from Japanese texts are the emperor and the security alliance with the United States. Emperor Hirohito and President Richard Nixon review the troops at the arrival ceremony for the Emperor at Elmendorf Air Force Base, Alaska, in 1971. NARA, NLNP-WHPO-MPF-C7392(29).

ism are used to conceal a mode of reasoning that is both antiliberal and antirational. Equally disturbing is that a mode of politics has recently emerged as a significant national movement that echoes the violent and intolerant 1930s and not only chooses to call "antinational" or "masochistic" all with which it disagrees but also victimizes the very same women who were among the most abject victims of the militarism of a half-century ago.

Notes

1. Ooka Shoheishu, *Chikuma gendai bungaku taikei*, vol. 69 (Tokyo: Chikuma Shobo, 1975), 50.
2. Fujioka Nobukatsu, *Ojoku no kin-gendaishi* (Shameful modern history) (Tokyo: Tokuma Shoten, 1996), 30.
3. Even the former governor of Tokyo, Suzuki Shun'ichi, was rumored to be on this list. (Hasegawa Hiroshi, "Suzuki zen to-chiji mo risuto koho," *Aera*, December 30, 1996 to January 6, 1997, 10–11. See also Joji Shingo, "Kyu Nihon-gun kankeisha Bei e nyukoku kinshi," *Asahi shinbun*, December 23, 1996.

4. The question of Washington's motives is complex. Suffice it to say here that concern for the human rights of the women was unlikely to have figured high among its priorities.

5. See Gavan McCormack, *The Emptiness of Japanese Affluence* (Armonk, NY: M.E. Sharpe, 1996), 275.

6. For discussion of these details, see Inoue Sumio, "Chiho gikai o arasou 'kusanone de hoshuha' no shitsunen," *Shūkan kinyōbi*, March 28, 1997, 22–25; Suzuki Yuko, "'Jiyushugi shikan' tonaeru yokaitachi," *Shūkan kinyōbi*, January 31, 1997, 11; Nakamura Seiji, "Rekishi kyōkasho kaizan ha to uyoku jinmyaku," *Shūkan kinyōbi*, March 14,1997, 22–25.

7. Fujioka Nobukatsu and Jiyūshugi Shikan Kenyūkai, eds., *Kyōkasho ga oshienai rekishi* (History not taught in textbooks), 4 vols. (Tokyo: Nyūsu Sābisu, 1996–98); Fujioka Nobukatsu, *Ojoku no kin-gendai shi* (Shameful modern history) (Tokyo: Tokuma shoten, 1996), 83.

8. See Takahashi Shiro in *Sapio*, January 15, 1997, 97.

9. Tomoko Otake, "Row over Denial of Sex Slaves Rages," *Japan Times*, December 28, 1996.

10. Kobayashi Hideo, "Ajia to kyōchō shite koso han'ei ha aru," *Sekai*, May 1997, 205.

11. From a report of the founding meeting of the group on December 2, 1996: Kajimura Taichiro, "Yurushigatai 'Nihon yuetsu shikan,'" *Shūkan kinyōbi*, December 13, 1996, 16–17.

12. Fujioka, *Ojoku*, 30.

13. Fujioka Nobukatsu, "Han-Nichi kyōiku Satian dasshutsu no ki," *Shinchō*, July 1996, quoted in Hayashi Miyayuki, "'Jiyūshugi shikan' tojo no haikei to sono keifu," *Tsukuru*, March 1997, 90.

14. Fujioka Nobukatsu, "Sex Slave Issue Is a Scandal Invented to Bash Japan," *Asahi Evening News*, January 26, 1997.

15. Fujioka Nobukatsu, "Ianfu kyōsei renko kyoko no shomei," part 1, *Gendai kyōikugaku*, November 1996, quoted in Suzuki, "'Jiyūshugi shikan' tonaeru yokaitachi," 11.

16. Fujioka, "Sex Slave Issue." The adjectives he uses repeatedly in his Japanese texts are: *kōshoku, inran, guretsu,* more directly translated as "lascivious, depraved, idiotic." Fujioka, *Ojoku*, 27.

17. Hata Ikuhiko, "Iwayuru 'sampa' ha ikanishite ianfu o seiiki to kashita no ka?" *Sapio*, January 15, 1997, 87–89.

18. Hata Ikuhiko, "Jugun ianfu mondai de kuni no hoteki sekinin ha toenai," *Sekai*, May 1997, 325. Hata, like Fujioka, seems to have undergone a transformation in his thinking, because he is on record in 1985 as holding the view that 70 to 80 percent of the women were "called up" in a way "approximating to forced labor, but without written records because they were supernumeraries." *(Nihon rikugun no hon: Sokaisetsu,* quoted in Tawara Yoshifumi, "Fujioka Nobukatsu shi no kyōkasho kogeki no sajutsu o abaku," *Shūkan kinyōbi*, May 9, 1997, 31.

19. Fujioka Nobukatsu, "Ajia no ianfu mondai no kyoko: Indonesia genchi chōsa hoka kara aburidasu," *Sapio,* December 11, 1996, 104.

20. Fujioka, *Ojoku*, 25–26; also his "Monbu daijin e no kokai shokan," *Voice*, October 1996, 76. The analogy is repeated in Hata Ikuhiko, "Ianfu 'minouebanashi' o tettei kenshō suru," in *Shokun*, December 1996, 55.

21. Hata, "Iwayuru 'sampa' ha."

22. Nishio Kanji and Fujioka Nobukatsu, *Kokumin no yudan* (Tokyo: PHP, 1996), 150.

23. Nishio Kanji, "Waitsuzekka wa seija janai," *Ronza*, November 1995, and "Kotonaru higeki," *Bungei shunju*, 1994, quoted in Kajimura Taichiro, "Rekishi kaizanshugi ha chisei e no botoku de aru," *Sekai*, July 1997, 80.

24. Fujioka Nobukatsu, *Sankei shinbun*, September 27, 1996, quoted in Suzuki, "'Jiyūshugi shikan' tonaeru yokaitachi," 11.

25. On eugenics, see Kaneko-Martin, "Nazi Doitsu to tennosei Nihon ga kokuji suru chi no shinwa to kokka shisō," *Shūkan kinyōbi,* February 14, 1997, 26–29.

26. Kajimura, "Rekishi kaizanshugi ha chisei e no botoku de aru," 80.

27. He had links to the Communist Party-affiliated Minsei, not the New Left. See Fujioka, *Ojoku,* 91. For more on his young adulthood, see Fujioka Nobukatsu, "Ikkoku heiwashugi no moto de sodatta watashi ga . . . genba no tondemonai kiki ni ki ga shimasu," *Sapio,* October 9, 1996, 104–7.

28. For interesting comments on Fujioka's career by his Tokyo University *sempai* (student in an older cohort) and by Horio Teruhisa, current president of the Nihon Kyōiku Gakkai, see the interview with Horio in *Shūkan kinyōbi,* January 31, 1997, 15–19.

29. Michael Walzer, *Just and Unjust Wars* (London: Allen Lane, 1978); Richard Minear, *Victor's Justice* (Princeton, NJ: Princeton University Press, 1971).

30. Fujioka, *Ojoku,* 96–97, and, for his brief discussion with Minear, 101–7.

31. Ishibashi in his journal *Tōyō Keizai,* 1921 (quoted in Sakamoto Tatsuhiko, "Meiji Taisho no shinbun ni arawareta 'shinryaku,'" *Shūkan kinyōbi,* April 4, 1997, 26); on Shiba, see Kunihiro Masao, "Nihon kareobana ron no naka de saku 'jiyūshugi shikan' to iu adabana," *Shūkan kinyōbi,* February 14, 1997, 23 (and sources cited there). Nakamura Masanori, *Kin gendai shi o dō miruka: Shiba shikan o tou* (Tokyo: Iwanami, 1997), Iwanami Bukkuretto 427, 51.

32. Horio's assessment in *Shūkan kinyōbi,* January 31, 1997, 18.

33. Satō Akira, "Kore ga uyoku no kogeki to kyōhaku no itoguchi da," *Shūkan kinyōbi,* March 21, 1997, 26.

34. "Okayama kengikai ga saitaku," *Asahi shinbun,* December 18, 1996.

35. Inoue, "Chiho gikai o," 22–25.

36. Suzuki, "'Jiyūshugi shikan' tonaeru yokaitachi," 11.

37. Quoted in Pierre Vidal-Naquet, *Assassins of Memory: Essays on the Denial of the Holocaust* (New York: Columbia University Press, 1992), xiii.

38. See the interesting discussion by the social psychologist Miyaji Shinji, "Seijuku shakai ni shinkuro dekizu kyōko no rekishi ni sugaru oyaji," *Asahi shinbun,* March 27, 1997.

39. Nishio Kanji, on "Asamade" late-night television, TV Asahi, February 1, 1997. (See comments by Nakamura Seiji, "Rekishi kyōkasho kaizanha to uyoku jinmyaku," *Shūkan kinyōbi,* March 14, 1997, 25.)

40. Nakamura Masanori, "'Nihon kaiki' yondome no nami," *Mainichi shinbun,* February 4, 1997. (English translation by Kristina Dennehy as "The History Textbook Controversy and Nationalism," *Bulletin of Concerned Asian Scholars* 30, 2 (April–June 1998): 24-29.

41. Satō Manabu, "Taiwa no kairo o tozashita rekishikan o dō kokufuku suru ka" (Zadankai discussion with various others), *Sekai,* May 1997, 186.

42. Ishida Takeshi, interviewed by Utsumi Aiko, "Ishitsu na tasha no shiten o fumaete rekishi o miru," *Gekkan Oruta,* March 1997, 15–19 (translated into English as "Looking at History Through the Eyes of the Other," *Ampo: Japan-Asia Quarterly Review* 27, 4 [1997]: 32–37).

43. Soh Kyong-sik, "Jiyūshugishi gurupu ni hangeki suru," *Shūkan kinyōbi,* February 7, 1997, 26.

44. Kunihiro, "Nihon kareobana ron," 23.

45. Foundation statement of the Society for the Making of New School Textbooks in History, December 2, 1996. See Nishio Kanji, "Atarashii rekishi kyōkasho no arasoi," *Voice,* February 1997, 110–11.

46. Quoted in John Vachon, "Text Uses Whitewash to Turn History into Propaganda," *Asahi Evening News,* December 8, 1996.

3

Consuming Asia, Consuming Japan: The New Neonationalist Revisionism in Japan

Aaron Gerow

History and the National Melodrama

When I first spotted a copy of *Kyōkasho ga oshienai rekishi* ("History Not Taught in Textbooks") prominently displayed in a bookstore, I supposed that this work written by Fujioka Nobukatsu and the Liberal View of History Study Group critiqued the Ministry of Education's textbook examination system.[1] I was thus surprised to find that this best-selling book is actually a collection of feel-good narratives about "great" men and women in modern Japanese history. Existing textbooks, the book assumes, bad-mouth Japan, promoting a history of "self-abuse "that, as Fujioka baldly states in the introduction, "originates in the interests of foreign nations."[2] History education, Fujioka argues, must benefit the Japanese state and should make Japanese "proud" of their nation again.

It is certainly possible to counter this rose-colored nationalist history by citing facts it ignores or by correcting its numerous errors. The title itself and the presumption that Japanese history textbooks are defined by a "self-abusive" view of Japan seem to warrant a rebuttal at this level. Anyone familiar with Ienaga Saburō's court case is aware that the Ministry of Education has in the past consistently opposed including any discussion of Japanese war atrocities in school texts. The very assertion that the antiseptically cleaned and excised school books have failed to present Japan in a positive light is at best disingenuous and at worse a fabrication. It is the patent absurdity of such a claim, however, that in a sense makes it immune to positivistic counterargument, since it is from the start not an assertion of fact but an evocation of certain emotions, myths, and popular narratives.

Consider the title of Fujioka's book in relation to its packaging. Next to the title, the largest lettering on the front is the book band (*obi*), which proclaims, "We really didn't know this country well. Seventy-eight stories we want to engrave into the minds of Japanese."[3] What is interesting about both of these phrases is that since their subjects are left unstated in the original Japanese, they could contextually just as possibly be "I" or "we" and refer equally to the readers or the authors. At best, the first sentence most likely designates the readers and the second the authors, but the shift of subject within a general ambiguity of subjectivity helps construct (one could say "interpolate") a community between author and reader conducive to the attempt to reconstruct a national subject (wherein "I" and "we" are inseparable: "we Japanese"). The book band thus invokes a certain linguistically generated communal/national emotion.

The evocation of national community is further enhanced in the black-and-white photo framed in red that dominates the cover. It is an old photograph (the era is unclear) of a young woman with a sleeping baby strapped onto her back. She could be the baby's mother, but given her age, she seems more likely an older sister or nursemaid. Maybe hers is the history that has not been told—that of women (there is a section in the book on "great" women)—or perhaps of the common people. Yet her face does not accusingly tell a narrative of oppression and neglect; she does not look the victim. Her visage is remarkably calm and self-assured, the image of a poor but hardworking woman, the proud figure whose story must be the one weaving its way into the hearts of the Japanese. The three sequels to the first volume all feature old photographs of boys or men, significant in both their innocence and nationalist self-confidence (one shows a proud young man with a Japanese flag).

The title, however, tells us that these photographs are not simply an evocation of innocence: these figures are supposedly untaught, unknown people who were placed on the back shelves of the historical archive and then forgotten. Perhaps Fujioka promises his readers a return to innocence, but the rhetoric of this consumer product's packaging implies that the innocence of these figures is significant only to the degree it has been lost and suppressed from the pages of school textbooks. Although they don't look like victims, perhaps it is their innocence itself that was sacrificed during the interval between when the photo was snapped and today. One would suppose the subsequent loss of innocence was a result of Japan's modern history of war, but the argument of the book lays the blame on current methods of teaching and narrating history and the authorities that supervise those methods. It does so by turning the title phrase, which could equally be a leftist accusation against a militaristic state that did not teach past truths in its approved textbooks, into indignation over a weak democratic system that ignores the good heroes of modern Japan.

The packaging of Fujioka's book engages us in narratives that are not reducible to the book's contents. It is significant, for instance, that it is a woman with a child who graces the cover of the initial volume, and not only because it perhaps provides a virginal counterpart to the comfort women who are elided inside. Looking at her face, I was reminded of the melodramatic heroines of 1950s *hahamono*, the Japanese film genre focusing on the unrecognized sacrifices of mothers. That genre, one can argue, was central in the postwar construction on a popular level of the myth of victimization that reconfigured a war of aggression as one in which it was the Japanese who suffered.[4] Although the girl in the photo may not be the child's mother and she is far younger than the middle-aged heroines of those films, that only gives her the same desexualized status as these usually widowed women who devoted their lives to their children rather than to fulfilling their own desires. All bear a purity of heart overruled by forces beyond their control and we, as readers/viewers, are meant to identify with their narrative of suffering.

Fujioka's book ties into such victimization narratives as the *hahamono* through the structures of reading and pleasure it invites as much as through its content. Each tale reads like a film narrative designed to jerk a tear or two or lift the spirits of the audience, encouraging identification between subject, reader, and author such that the ultimate victims of this historical silence about "great" Japanese become the Japanese people themselves. That is why this is not a work that simply wishes to make its readers proud they are Japanese; that would make it no different than the hagiographic biographies of illustrious Japanese one finds in any school library in Japan. Its power lies in the assertion that these stories are supposedly repressed by educational and state institutions, marked as taboo for children by bureaucratic authorities. The pleasure of reading them then lies in both the thrill of breaking taboos, flaunting a feigned oppositionality, and in identifying with these role models—not just because they are great but because they have suffered by being rendered silent. As with the pleasure of watching melodrama, the enjoyment is fundamentally masochistic, the delight in making oneself the victim of injustice so as to justify one's own existence.[5] It is reveal-

3.1 History Not Taught in Textbooks
This prewar photo of a young girl caring for a baby suggests the drama of individual fortitude in adversity and presents that scenario as the key metaphor for the Japanese nation. A very similar photo graces the cover of *Kyokasho ga oshienai rekishi*. Goto Kazuo, Matsumoto Itsuya, and Hayasaka Motooki, eds., *"Furui Shashin" Kan—Bakumatsu kara Showa made* (The "old photograph" bureau—from the late feudal to the Showa era), (Tokyo: Asahi Shinbunsha, 1986), 90.

ing that Fujioka's favorite epithet for his opponents is the charge that *they* are masochists.

History Not Taught in Textbooks is thus as much involved in narratives of victimization and melodrama as it is with an evaluation of historical facts. As such, it relies on certain desires and mythical patterns that are impervious to positivist counterargument and can best be explained only by analyzing the book as a cultural, discursive, or even literary text, one that intersects with a variety of other texts, from the historical to the fictional, from the printed to the televisual. Only then can we see how the new textbook revisionism operates as a broad narrative structure that creates and in turn is created by certain consumerist desires molded by the contemporary historical conjuncture.

National Threats in the Post–Cold War World

As a manifestation of the narrative of victimization, the textbook revisionists rely on broad-based Japanese perceptions of both real and not-so-real victimizers. Although the United States is still evoked as an oppressor, Fujioka himself largely refrains from criticism of America and the U.S.-Japan Security Treaty. More prominent in his rhetoric and that of his colleagues is the potential threat that other Asian nations pose.[6] The revisionists frequently warn about the economic rise of Asia, the growing power of the Chinese state as an international player, and Chinese and Korean aspirations with regard to islands that Japan claims as well. Revisionists make arguments such as, "Why must we teach the same view of history the Chinese have?" (i.e., of the Nanjing massacre, etc.)—as if teaching from this perspective would render Japan "weak," in effect betraying the nation in a confrontation with China. In objective terms the rest of Asia cannot now rival Japan's economic strength, but Japan's prolonged postbubble economic slump (even if it is largely due to domestic factors) has bred insecurity that inspires a search for external villains in the narrative of Japan's economic suffering. In this context the rhetoric of the neonationalist revisionists describes nothing other than a war with Asia, one that at this stage may be only economic but that eventually may put the leadership of Asia at stake.

Such a confrontation with an external threat would not seem to merit the urgency Fujioka and his followers exhibit if it were not for the fact that there is, simultaneously, a perception that Japan is not ready to meet such an enemy, in part because of Japan's weakness in the world but even more because of the increasing presence of internal threats and divisions—of the "Other" making headway on Japanese soil. The formation of the Committee to Write New History Textbooks is first and foremost a reactionary phenomenon, attempting to prevent changes believed to be damaging to Japan's national strength. The committee was formed less to create original textbooks than prevent the use of new ones referring to the darker side of Japanese modern history (though often in an abridged, undeveloped fashion).

This effort to return to the past, however, is difficult to sustain given the sense that the forces that previously unified the Japanese have weakened since the end of the Showa era. As a narrativization of this, Aoyama Shinji's

1996 film *Helpless*, a brilliant evocation of teenage alienation and loss of identity, significantly takes place in 1989, the year of Emperor Hirohito's death, and features a *yakuza* (gangster) in constant search for his "boss"— the authority figure whose death he cannot accept because it was so central to his identity.[7] The loss of narratives about Japanese group identity provided by Hirohito and Showa has been exacerbated by the breakdown of the Cold War world structure and its comforting story of good versus evil. As many have pointed out, this is a crucial intertext to the textbook debates: the loss of the East-West binary has undermined Japan's identity as the democratic front against Communism in Asia without providing new structures to supplant that.[8] The Gulf War and the Smithsonian *Enola Gay* debacle seemed to underline the fear that Japan, in spite of its role as an economic superpower, has not won respect in the international political arena and thus possesses no identity among nations. This sense of shame in being Japanese, and especially the inability to take pride in oneself in the face of others, is frequently cited in the writings of Fujioka's group and is the reason they think Japanese make matters worse by repeatedly condemning themselves.

Such resentful feelings probably existed before the Gulf War, but without the narrative of the Cold War that had channeled them into the democratic defense of anti-Communism, the new target became postwar democracy itself. The loss of Cold War restraints has given the go-ahead for the expression of nationalist thoughts that had until now been repressed as alien to Japan's aspirations to be the model democracy in Asia. War apologists such as Hayashi Fusao and the militarist right existed before, but now "normal" media figures like newscaster Sakurai Yoshiko and cartoonist Kobayashi Yoshinori air the topic of revising Japan's wartime past in a way rarely seen before. This new generation has aligned with the old right to make this a very public, media- and government-oriented revisionist campaign, quite different from the guerrilla-like tactics found in Neo-Nazi revisionism in Europe, as Ukai Tetsu points out.[9] One reason it is so public, I believe, is because the feelings on which the campaign is based were constructed in popular media, cinema, TV, and literature. Although the narratives of the *hahamono* or mythification of the suffering at Hiroshima and Nagasaki expressed those feelings, they were never before allowed to be released in the form of an articulated nationalism. Repressed by the ideal of the "peace-loving democratic country," these emotions now emerge together with a recognition of that ideal's inability to provide a strong, positive national identity in the new world order.

Much of the fear about Japan's weakness is directed at those elements

3.2 Still from *Helpless*
Aoyama Shinji's 1996 film *Helpless* takes place significantly in 1989, the year of Emperor Hirohito's death. It features a gangster in a constant search for his "boss"—the authoritarian figure whose death he cannot accept because it was central to his identity. ©WOWOW + Bandai Visual. Used by permission.

within the country that are seen as undermining the Japanese sense that they comprise a unified, homogeneous nation. In this fantasy, the Other not only encroaches on Japan's borders but is beginning to tear it apart from within, weakening its very soul. The Other assumes numerous guises in contemporary Japan. One, of course, is the large number of legal and illegal foreign workers in Japan, rendered menacing in tabloid tales of crime by foreigners and illegal immigrant smuggling rings reputedly run by the Chinese mafia. Even Koreans born and legally residing in Japan are seen by conservative groups as potential threats to the state, particularly since some local governments recently eliminated the citizenship requirement for public servants. The fear is that the identity of Japan itself is at stake when not even its official agents are Japanese. Women, too, are seen as persistent menaces, represented most recently by a proposal to allow women to keep their own family names after marriage. Conservative politicians successfully rallied to block this change in family law, charging that it would undermine the unity of the Japanese family and thus the nation. This issue is intimately related to the textbook debate: local legislatures have combined calls for the elimination of references to comfort women in the new textbooks together with statements protesting the proposed family law revisions, making them an integrated set of resolutions.[10]

Given their focus on education, the textbook debates are most directly concerned with another potential threat: the young. Japanese youth do not exhibit the political radicalism of their predecessors in the 1960s and 1970s, but in the eyes of many in the media, education, and elsewhere, their apathy and lack of adherence to any metanarratives (Marxism, democracy, or even Japan) itself bodes ill for Japan's future. Their identities as Japanese remain uncertain, as youngsters rarely choose as their role models the Japanese found in Fujioka's books. The foreign influence on youth culture is an old phenomenon, but the continuing popularity of all things American or the recent rise of black street culture or Asian culture as objects of emulation reflects a situation where identity boundaries are being crossed right and left. The inability of Japanese youth to connect not only with their country but with their compatriots was one of the central targets of criticism in Kobayashi Yoshinori's *Sensōron* (On war), a comic book that sold nearly half a million copies and became one of the main topics of intellectual debate in Japan in 1998 not only because of its effort to justify Japan's part in World War II but because it was popular among the young. Kobayashi, looking at the recent rash of juvenile crime, teenage girls engaged in "compensated dating" *(enjo kōsai),* and lonely and apathetic adolescents who

3.3 The empty center

In Kobayashi Yoshinori's *Sensoron* (On war), the empty individual gains definition through national history just as the nation relies on an empty center for its unity. Gentosha, 1998, p. 366. Used by permission.

not only lack social manners but seem unable to relate to other people in society, argues that the "individual" has run amok in contemporary Japan, leaving larger social structures such as the "public" and the "state" and the communal values they embody in threat of ruin. His solution is to reinscribe the individual in the public—which he, without any qualms, equates with the state—in part by putting forward World War II–era Japan and such specific examples as the kamikaze pilots as an ideal standard for the moral order of individuals serving society.[11]

The problems Kobayashi and others say are plaguing contemporary youth culture can be interpreted as a reflection of real social discontent among younger Japanese. Expressions of a profound sense of alienation and lack of place among young people are a common element in recent cinema, especially in Aoyama's *Helpless, An Obsession* (*Tsumetai chi*, 1997), and *Shady Grove* (1999), Yamamoto Masashi's *Junk Food* (1998), and Toyoda Toshiaki's *Porno Star* (1998). The cultural effects of this phenomenon, however, are deeply ambiguous. On the one hand, cynical disillusionment with the postwar democratic nation does bring some young people to sympathize with the neonationalist revisionists, especially when led by a popular *manga* artist like Kobayashi. Ironically, it may be the very disconnectedness of Japanese youth that lies behind Kobayashi's popularity; as Oguma Eiji argues, it is the perception that established socializing institutions such as the family and school have ceased to function that makes Kobayashi's celebration of the state attractive to his younger readers as an alternative mode of identity formation.[12] Yet when younger Japanese express this lack of belonging through school bullying and random violence, like that of the fourteen-year-old serial killer in Kōbe, these youth themselves begin to take on the aura of the non-Japanese Other. The 1997 film *Happy People* (directed by Suzuki Kōsuke and based on the popular *manga* cartoon by Sawa Hidekatsu) on the surface looks like a black-humored parody of the facade of social harmony, showing everyday people committing insane acts in the name of happiness. Nevertheless, it clearly places the blame for these acts not on those committing them but on the presence of Others in Japanese society who are forcing "normal" Japanese to become abnormal. The primary Other in this film is the young, who are portrayed as nothing more than animals.

Educating About the Threat and Building the Nation

Textbook revisionists are reacting to these threats through the ideological apparatuses of history and education. Fujioka and his followers make

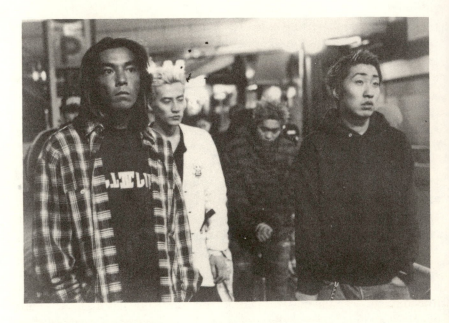

3.4 Still from *Junk Food*
Disaffected and delinquent youth in Yamamoto Masashi's *Junk Food* roam a multiethnic urban jungle, groping for new relationships and identities. Stance Company. Used by permission.

history a weapon of confrontation—or even the means by which to build proud Japanese who can win the war they imagine is imminent. Yet the revisionist textbook group cannot fully be explained by their effort to make history subject to the nationalist project. As Narita Ryūichi stresses, Fujioka is in some ways trying to protect the schoolroom from the invasion of historical research, separating education from historiography.[13] This is one reason some of his followers do not deny, for instance, that the war in China was one of "invasion" (*shinryaku*) yet still profess to support him: to them, such tragedies may be historical truth, but that does not mean they should be taught to children as a part of a national education program. Since Fujioka himself is a professor of education at Tokyo University with no credentials as a historian, and most of the members of the Liberal View of History Study Group are schoolteachers, the textbook movement must be seen primarily as an educational issue. Historians may say whatever they want, the reasoning goes, but schools are meant to develop and socialize Japanese citizens and, as such, are not places to impart knowledge that may make children question or feel ashamed of their Japanese identity. As an educational theory, then, "liberal historiography" tries to solve the nation's serious educational problems by reinterpreting students as receptacles of national ideology, to be protected from any knowledge that may prompt them to question their status as national subjects whose duty is to serve the state. Schools are seen as ideological state apparatuses devoted to the national interest that produce citizens/subjects rather than individuals with a capacity for criticism. It is not difficult to see the similarities to the prewar education system.

Education has functioned as a symbol within the narrative of the Japanese nation in other conflicts in the recent past. A few years ago, several school faculty committees released the minutes of their debates over the issue of the "national" flag. Discussions raged at the time at many schools over whether to obey the Ministry of Education's decision to require schools to fly the rising sun flag and play "Kimigayo," which the ministry described as the "national anthem." One of the oft-repeated arguments in favor was that fostering respect for the rising sun was a part of the process of internationalization (*kokusaika*).[14] This may seem curious (one would think internationalization implies the toning down of nationalism), but it is logical given two assumptions: that Japan does not have a robust national identity and that the international arena is, in Hobbesian terms, a mean and brutish place. According to this scenario, Japan would sink under the aggressive waves of other nations without a strong self; only the establishment of a firm national consciousness, as a prelude to entering the international arena, can help it keep afloat in the future. History, then, is to function like the Japanese flag to provide an ideological locus through which Japanese can be defined as Japanese, in solidarity against the world. History is merely a collection of signs in a set of myths and stories about Japan that are necessary to create a national consciousness. In this sense, the effective interrelation between the discourse of the neonationalist revisionists and mythical narratives about the nation is only an example of the role they hope historical discourse will play in the schools.

Another central myth is constructed from *Nihonjinron,* or ideologies about the essence of the Japanese people that help redefine the boundaries of the national subject. As with much *Nihonjinron* discourse, Fujioka often uses the term "we": "Because we are Japanese, it is only natural that we should think of things first from the perspective of Japan and its national interests."[15] This assertion of a "natural" logic is profoundly ideological, creating an essence to Japaneseness that dictates not only what Japanese are but what they must be if they want to be called Japanese. The creation of this tacitly coercive subject position effaces all those who are ethnically not Japanese, even if they live in Japan, as well as Japanese who do not subscribe to this logic (those, for instance, who do not side with the "national interest" as Fujioka describes it).[16] In other words, the coercive "we" divides Japanese from all others and eliminates differences among Japanese by silencing those who don't agree.

Fujioka writes that the question of what Japan must do should always be considered from both the point of view of Japan and "how that must look from the perspective of others."[17] Here he proclaims that his liberal interest takes into account the voices of others, but then his views of history and education are clearly meant to reunify the national body by effacing traces of the threatening Other from its midst. If other points of view are to be considered, it is only as a mirror of recognition for Japan, where outsiders acknowledge Japan's flag and sovereignty and respect its power. If this is internationalism, it is extremely self-centered internationalism.[18]

The treatment of the comfort women is the most revealing case of rejecting rather than talking to outsiders. To rebuild the Japanese national body and create a "healthy nationalism" (*kenzenna nashonaruizumu—* the revisionists' attractive catch phrase), the scarred bodies of comfort women themselves must be further violated by being forgotten. The violence against the Asian and female Other again renders impossible the dialogue Fujioka purportedly desires. Discourse denying the existence of comfort women cannot be conceived as part of a dialogue (no one would make such absurd comments to a Korean, for instance). "Since these are monologic words," to quote Satō Manabu on Fujioka, "communication is impossible."[19] The ideology of the textbook revision movement is thus in many ways the reproduction of the closed-society consciousness (*sakoku ishiki*) of the modern emperor system, one that denies the existence of the Other. It is a set of platitudes meant for Japanese consumption, a magical potion to cure the wounded national soul.

The Consumption of Asia and the Nation

Fujioka and the Liberal View of History Study Group must also be analyzed as a product to be consumed. I have considered the packaging of their first book, but note also their packaging of themselves. Most members take pains to distance themselves from oldtime rightists who proclaim the glories of the Greater East Asia War; many, like Sakurai Yoshiko, acknowledge the atrocities committed by Japan.[20] They call themselves "liberals" and declare themselves bound, as Fujioka writes, neither to the U.S. view of Japan represented in the Tokyo Trials nor to that of the inventors of the Greater East Asia Co-Prosperity Sphere. Ethnologist Ōtsuki

Takahiro, one of the group's younger members, wrote at length about the bankruptcy of both left and right under the Cold War structure; he declares he wants a "healthy nationalism," "which is neither 'right' nor 'left,' neither 'conservative,' nor 'reformist,' nor 'liberal,'" and which has nothing to do with the central symbol of the old right, the emperor.[21] This is a movement conscious of the post–Cold War atmosphere and the reigning disillusionment with established ideologies; it thus sells itself over the airwaves as sweeping the field clean of old ideological baggage and reconstructing an unburdened nation.

This attractive and less offensive self-packaging may have cost the movement both clarity and significance. Suga Hidemi, a commentator not unsympathetic to the revisionists, has argued that it is impossible for them to win the textbook debate because their insistence on a liberal image constitutes acceptance of the rhetorical and discursive structures with which the left defines the debate. They cannot succeed in creating an ideology of a strong Japan because, in this age, it is nearly impossible to construct a citizenry willing to die for the nation.[22] Kobayashi's "On War" hopes to change this, but (as I have analyzed elsewhere) it tries to do so by reducing the nation to an object of consumption and reducing national memory to the recollection of such popular cultural representations of history as children's *manga*.[23] The new right-wing revisionism has become part of the flow of floating signifiers that constitutes consumer culture. Its ideology enforces homogeneity and service to the state, but only within a culture of consumption that seems to infiltrate all forms of cultural, political, and intellectual production. Fujioka's group is different from the old right precisely because its location within the economy of signs differs, rendering their nationalism essentially consumerist. If textbook revisionism poses a threat, it does not do so of itself but only as part of a larger text of myths and narratives about Japan that are being consumed everyday.

To elucidate the problem of consumerist nationalism, I consider the popular film *Swallowtail Butterfly (Suwaroteiru)*, directed by Iwai Shunji and released in 1996.[24] After the success of *Love Letter* (1995; distributed in the United States as *When I Close My Eyes*), Iwai has been proclaimed by some to be the savior of Japanese cinema and, in particular, the representative of contemporary youth culture who can finally bring teenagers back to theaters for a Japanese movie. Through the use of very current, MTV-like aesthetics and popular music, *Swallowtail Butterfly* sketches less a narrative than a place: a space called Yen Town somewhere in Japan that is populated by Chinese, Americans, Iranians, and most every other ethnicity. Money rules in Yen Town as part of an international economy that stands in contrast to the "normal" face of the rest of Japan, one that is not supposedly penetrated by flows of transnational labor. Only a third of the film is in Japanese, with the rest of the dialogue in Chinese and English and the credits entirely in English. Some Japanese actors are cast as Chinese and actually speak their lines in English and Chinese.

At first glance *Swallowtail Butterfly* appears to be part of a series of films critiquing the myth of a homogeneous Japan by focusing on its ethnic minorities, Ōtomo Katsuhiro's *World Apartment Horror* (*Wārudo apātomento horā,* 1992), Sai Yōichi's *All Under the Moon* (*Tsuki wa dotchi ni dete iru,* 1994), and Yamamoto's *Junk Food* all being good examples. It can also be seen to represent both the border-crossing, fluid identities, as well as the a- or even anti-social behavior of Japanese youth that reactionary educators find so disturbing.[25] There are no model Japanese here; in fact, the purely Japanese characters are mostly villains. It appears that there is no unified, linguistic "we" with which to unite the nation. *Swallowtail Butterfly* as a phenomenon seems to embody less a nationalist than a "nationless" (*mukokuseki*) culture, one groundless and possibly even anti-Japanese.[26] Yet as I would argue, it is due first to the ambiguity of contemporary Japanese youth culture and second to the overarching nature of a consumerist nationalism able to unite the apparently contradictory positions of the film and Fujioka's book that the two ultimately share the effort to efface the Other and reconstruct the nation in a postmodern consumer culture.

Consider first the crucial scene in which the lead character, Ageha, with her friend Huan, ventures off to the opium den to visit the doctor.[27] There the aestheticization of postcolonial bricolage that reigns throughout the film gives way to a terror directed against the Chinese opium smokers they find there. On the one hand, the young couple's gaze is colonial, unmistakably viewing an Other that is both disgusting and inferior. Despite the film's linguistic (and subtitled) polyphony, the words of these Chinese are not given subtitles, something that renders them not only more alien but also without an internal soul that could raise them above the level of objects of fear. At the same time, the scene, with its distorted camera angles and abrupt cuts, reminds one of a more modern gaze: that of two tourists lost in unfamiliar territory, suddenly confronted with something not (yet) rendered consumable by the discourse of tourism. It is a scenario familiar from film genres ranging from the travelogue to the ethnographic documentary, from the science fiction film to the Indiana Jones series.[28] In a film that reduces everything to the same fetishized, consumable image, here is something not so easily swallowed: the return of the repressed, the Other making itself known.

That this Other is Asian is indicative of the film's politics. Yomota Inuhiko has argued that the marginal people in *Swallowtail Butterfly* are treated with a "tourist-like curiosity, a mix of utopia and fairy tales," and are thus devoid of any reality. On the one hand, the film's view of Asia is, to him, similar to the utopian conception found in the popular television program *Denpa shōnen* (Broadcast youth), which has featured "documentary" episodes of struggling comics forced to travel throughout Asia without money and to rely on an almost idyllic, "premodern" sense of kindness on the part of locals. On the other hand, even though Koreans are central to any consideration of Japan as a multicultural space, constituting the majority of foreign nationals living in Japan and suffering the most discrimination historically, the film features not a single Korean or word of Hangul, as if, in Yomota's words, they are "not an exotic and ideal object of tourism . . . not fashionable when narrating the cosmopolitan atmosphere of contemporary Japan."[29]

Asia is cool as long as it is commodified or utopian in its treatment of tourists in trouble. All that escapes that consumerist process, like the Chinese in the opium den, must be a threat, the Other which commodification itself aims to efface. For all its multicultural celebration of Asian intermixing, for all its polyphony of languages, *Swallowtail Butterfly* reveals a deep-seated fear of Asia and presents the Japanese subjectivity to conquer it. The film offers less a linguistic than a visual "we" for Japanese spectators, a subject position constructed by shot angles and editing through which they can identify with the terror felt by Ageha and Huan.[30] This visual point of reference is in the end the tourist/consumerist gaze, the new identity offered for young Japanese through which they can simultaneously consume and silence the Asian Other, venture abroad while never being threatened as Japanese.

Swallowtail Butterfly dovetails with Fujioka's project by constructing a gaze that effaces the Other and covers over the historical past (the sociohistorical origin of Yen Town is never explained, for instance). It markets a "liberal" acknowledgment of other voices similar to the one Fujioka proclaims, at the same time repackaging those voices for the Japanese consumer, reducing a supposed dialogue to a monologue. The postmodern desire for an exotic Asia shown in *Swallowtail* may seem far removed from the desires of the textbook group, but Iwai's consumption of Asia must be seen as the reverse side of the coin of Fujioka's consumption of Japanese history. Both reduce Japan and its Others to images and narratives that can be reshuffled to reconstruct a mythical Japan.

3.5 Still from *Swallowtail Butterfly*
Ageha (center), in an ostensibly multicultural utopia, based on excluding the unconsumable and dangerous Asian Other. Pony Canyon. Used by permission.

Consider the scene toward the end of *Swallowtail Butterfly* in which Feihong, an illegal Chinese immigrant, is brutally tortured to death by Japanese police who verbally abuse him as a "Yen Towner." His only retort to them is the exclamation: "Your *furusato* [hometown, native place] is Yen Town, too." In narrative terms, this operates as Feihong's attempt to undermine the police's (and thus the Japanese state's) division between Japan/*furusato* and Yen Town. In the ideology of *furusato*, anyone may have a hometown, but only Japanese can have a *furusato*, a rural origin that preserves their ties to traditional social and family structures against the dislocations brought on by the modernization and urbanization of Japan, allowing them to stay Japanese even amid Westernization.[31] Yen Town thus could not be a *furusato,* as the concept is too closely tied to Japanese identity. Feihong's attempt to locate the police's origins in Yen Town can thus at first glance be considered part of the film's larger effort to deconstruct Japanese identity, especially given how the effort by other characters in the film (such as Ageha) to name Yen Town as their *furusato* stretches and distorts the original meaning of the term.

Neither the film nor the characters, however, ever reject the concept of *furusato* itself or critique its narrative and the ideological role it plays in constructing the nation. In an incisive investigation of the ideology of

3.6 Still from *Swallowtail Butterfly*
Even the Chinese immigrant Feihong seeks stability in a Japanese *furusato*. He is murdered by Japanese police, suggesting the ugly underside of nostalgic longings for a nationalist hometown/homeland. Pony Canyon. Used by permission.

furusato, Jennifer Robertson underlines how *furusato*, patriarchically constructed as a nostalgia for maternal origins, is valuable to the extent it is distant, lost, and in the past, in contrast to the disruptive present. The yearning of the Yen Towners for *furusato* indicates how much they, similarly, lament their homelessness and search for their lost maternal beginnings (the film commences, in fact, with the death of Ageha's mother). *Swallowtail Butterfly* cannot properly be called a celebration of border-crossing, of hybridity and creolization, or of fluid identities, because its characters are all seeking a past wholeness promised by the ideology of *furusato* on which to ground their identities.[32]

Robertson's observation that the ideologies of internationalization and the nostalgic *furusato* are not opposites is instructive here: "Through the dominant discourse of a paternalistic nostalgia refracted as progressive internationalization, and vice versa, both Japanese and foreign historical, social, and cultural formations . . . are made available as an anodyne realm: a realm in which the status quo is reproduced, gratification offered, and profits made possible to compensate for various social, economic, and political disparities."[33]

One can argue that *Swallowtail Butterfly* is a perfect example of the coterminal nature of *furusato* and internationalization, for Iwai skillfully combines cosmopolitan hipness with conservative nostalgia (the film is narrated as a past event), in part through having foreigners yearn for the same maternal place as Japanese. Iwai's film opens up the possibility that non-Japanese can have a *furusato*, but only by constructing them as having the same desire for a secure locus against the vicissitudes of transnational border-crossing. The Other is then presented as in effect desiring to be Japanese, a representation that effectively absorbs the Other in the "Self." The constitution of Yen Town as a *furusato* is merely the reconstruction of the narrative of the Japanese nation on the lines of the consumerist elision of difference, creating a new Japan amid the detritus of the postcolonial era, a space where all can become Japanese by buying into the image of *furusato*.[34] In this respect, it shares all too much with Fujioka's effort to reconstruct the Japanese nation from a post–Cold War assemblage of consumable images of great Japanese. For Japanese youth who have lost their sense of national history and their pride in being Japanese—who in effect are the equivalent of Iwai's nationless Yen Towners—the neonationalist revisionists offer the commodified icon of Japan as the space on which to narrate the nation.

Fujioka and the textbook group have arisen, as I have argued, because of a complex historical conjuncture at the center of which is the growing fear of threats both internal (the young, etc.) and external (Asia). Others that are perceived to be weakening the national Self. This conjuncture cannot be fully understood, however, without conceiving how aspects of these threats are actually part of the same phenomenon as the neonationalist revisionists. If Fujioka's group were merely a return of the old right and if contemporary youth culture were simply an embrace of Asia and other foreign cultures, then the opposition between the two would be clear and unambiguous. As we have seen, however, the repackaging of Japanese nationalism must be viewed as a sometimes contradictory part of the same cultural phenomenon as the consumerist celebration of Asia, in a manner similar to how the ideologies of *furusato* and internationalism are connected. Consumerism offers a vision of Japan's accepting Asia, whereas nationalism creates one of Japan's accepting itself. Both sell unoffensive, consumable images of Japan, reducing the nation to a narration of commodified images and nationalism to consumption of those images, all in order to offer utopian identities to Japanese feeling the disruptions of global consumer capitalism. Fujioka and the textbook revisionists should be considered a threat, but not because they are simply the revival of the old right. It is their use of the media and the market, a use exemplified by the image of the girl and baby on the cover of "History Not Taught in Textbooks," and the narratives that book contains, that makes them share in the equally dangerous nationalism of which *Swallowtail Butterfly* is but one manifestation: consumerist nationalism.

Notes

1. Portions of this essay were originally published on the "H-Japan" Internet discussion list (h-Japan@h-net.msu.edu) on February 20, 1997, as a commentary on an article by Nakamura Masanori. At that time, it benefited from a considerable number of comments and criticisms, including ones from Abe Markus Nornes, Laura Hein, and Mark Selden. I was greatly helped as well by discussions between colleagues in the Workshop in Critical Theory (WINC) study group, particularly Ukai Tetsu, Narita Ryūichi, and Ōuchi Hirokazu, and two anonymous readers of my second draft. The positions expressed herein are ultimately my own, but I owe all of these individuals deep thanks.

2. Fujioka Nobukatsu and Jiyūshugi Shikan Kenkyūkai, eds., *Kyōkasho ga oshienai rekishi* (History not taught in textbooks) (Tokyo: Sankei Shinbun Nyūsu Sābisu, 1996): 10.

3. In Japanese, "Honto wa kono kuni no koto, yoku shiranakatta. Nihonjin no kokoro ni kizamitai 78 no monogatari."

4. Such mothers typically lost children in the war or struggled greatly in the poverty-stricken aftermath (both tragedies very real to contemporary Japanese), but their sacrifices always go unrecognized by their children or community. The masochistic pleasure involved in identifying with this suffering was a central means by which 1950s Japanese film audiences narrativized wartime and postwar history as a tale of unjust and unrecognized but still stoically endured misery. Two of the more interesting examples of the genre are Kinoshita Keisuke's *Japanese Tragedy* (*Nihon no higeki*, 1953) and Naruse Mikio's *Mother (Okāsan*, 1952).

5. There are many discussions of the relation between masochistic pleasure and melodrama in feminist film studies, with Mary Ann Doane, *The Desire to Desire: The Woman's Film of the 1940s* (Bloomington: Indiana University Press, 1987) providing a good outline.

6. The "reasianization" Laura Hein and Ellen Hammond have discussed, in which conservatives have called for Japan to rejoin Asia (as its leader), is, I believe, the other side of the same coin of the perception of Asia as a threat. "Homing in on Asia: Renovating Identity in Contemporary Japan," *Bulletin of Concerned Asian Scholars* 27, 3 (1995): 3–17.

7. Where Japanese film titles are listed exclusively in English (as *Helpless*) the film original has an English language title only.

8. This theme dominates much of the discussion among Satō Manabu, Kang Sangjung, Komori Yōichi, and Narita Ryāichi in "Taiwa no kairo o tozashita rekishikan o dō kokufukuysuru ka?" [How to overcome the view of history that has closed off the avenues of dialogue?], *Sekai* 635 (May 1997): 185–99.

9. See Ukai's comments in the discussion, "Rekishi to iu senjō kara" (From the battlefield called history), *Impaction* 102 (1997): 68–69.

10. A point made by Kano Mikiyo, "Seikimatsu kyōkasho kyōsōkyoku to sei no daburu standādo" (The Fin de Siècle Textbook Capriccio and the Sexual Double Standard), *Impaction* 102 (1997): 36.

11. Kobayashi Yoshinori, *Sensōron* (On War) (Tokyo: Gentōsha, 1998). See also Aaron Gerow, "Zuzō toshite no *Sensōron* (*Sensōron* as an Image Text), *Sekai*, 656 (December 1998): 118–23.

12. Oguma concludes that "in this sense, the prevalence of me-ism and a sense of isolation is not in opposition to this kind of nationalism, but rather is the other side of the same coin." See his contribution to the *Sekai* issue on *Sensōron*, "'Hidari' o kihi suru popyurizumu: Gendai nashonarizumu no kōzō to yuragi" (Populism that avoids the "left": the structure and vacillation of contemporary nationalism), *Sekai* 656 (December 1998): 94–105.

13. See his comments in "Taiwa no kairo o tozashita rekishikan," 194. Treating historical research as a field unconnected to mass public discourse is not new: that was why many Marxist historians could continue publishing in specialized journals well into the 1930s without severe regulation. The publicity of the discourse—and how much it appears before children—has historically been the measure of how much government oversight it earns. The history of film censorship in Japan compared to that for printed publications also reveals this double standard. Many uncensored novels were cut only when they came to the screen.

14. See, for instance, one such set of minutes printed in the *Asahi Shinbun*, March 29, 1993, 11.

15. Fujioka and Jiyūshugi, *Kyōkasho ga oshienai rekishi*, 10.

16. A point Komagome Takeshi makes in analyzing the same phrase: "Jiyushugi shikan wa watashitachi o 'jiyū' ni suru no ka?" (Will the liberal view of history "liberate" us?), *Sekai* 633 (April 1997): 64–66.

17. Fujioka Nobukatsu, *Ojoku no kin-gendai shi* (Shameful modern history) (Tokyo: Tokuma Shoten, 1996): 135, quoted in ibid., 62.

18. My use of the term "self-centered" resonates with Takahashi Tetsuya's use of *jikochū* to critique Katō Tenyō's controversial assertion that Japan must bury its dead before it can deal with the dead of Asia. See his comments in the roundtable talk "Sekinin to shutai o megutte" (On responsibility and the subject), *Hihyō kūkan* 2, 13 (1997), particularly 13–16.

19. Kang Sangjung also pointed out that the revisionists only "want to reiterate a monologue without an Other." See comments by Satō and Kang in "Taiwa no kairo o tozashita rekishikan o dō kokufuku suru ka?" 187.

20. Though, as Oguma notes, the "amorphous" nationalism of Fujioka and many of the revisionists like Kobayashi has recently drawn closer to that of traditional right-wing nationalism as the latter has joined up with the movement. Oguma, "'Hidari' o kihi suru popyurizumu," 99–100.

21. Ōtsuki Takahiro, "Boku ga 'Atarashii Rekishi Kyōkasho o Tsukuru Kai' o sukedachi suru wake" (The reason why I am backing the "Committee to Write New History Textbooks"), *Seiron*, April 1997: 56. Oguma notes the discomfort apparent in Ōtsuki's use of nationalist rhetoric (Oguma, 103–4), and this may be one reason Ōtsuki, who was one of Kobayashi's main supporters, has recently distanced himself from the *manga* artist as Kobayashi has gone even further to the right.

22. Suga Hidemi, "Kyōiku hihanron josetsu (6): Sono tame ni shiniuru 'kokka'" (An introduction to a critique of education, 6: a "state" one can die for), *Hatsugensha* 33 (January 1997): 86–91.

23. Gerow, "Zuzō toshite no *Sensōron*."

24. This discussion of *Swallowtail Butterfly* is partially a culmination of talks I gave on the film at the Feminizumi to Gendai Shisō Kenkyūkai (Feminism and Contemporary Thought

Research Group) (September 1996), the Workshop in Critical Theory (December 1996), and the Shimin Geijutsu Kōza (Citizen's Art Lectures) (November 1997). I would like to thank the participants of those sessions for their comments and suggestions.

25. The film's depictions of crime by minors, particularly drug use and counterfeiting, earned it an R rating (children under fifteen prohibited) from Eirin, the film industry's ratings board.

26. Kiyoshi Mahito reads the film positively as a *mukokuseki* attack against the culture of the yen and as a work answering in fictional terms the yearning for definition by Japanese youth who essentially lack such identity these days. See "Gendai Nihon no seishun, sono kanōsei: Iwai Shunji no eiga sekai o tōshite kangaeru" (Youth in contemporary Japan and its possibilities: contemplating this through the cinematic world of Iwai Shunji), in Kumazawa Makoto et al., eds., *Eiga mania no shakaigaku: sukurin ni mieru ningen to shakai* (A sociology of film mania: people and society visible on screen) (Tokyo: Akashi Shoten, 1997): 45–72.

27. Although Huan's name is Chinese, the film does not make it clear that he knows the language. He, like Ageha, is a parentless child searching for origins. Yet just as Yomota Inuhiko argues that Ageha, whose parentage remains ambiguous, is ultimately inscribed in the film on the side of "us" Japanese, so is Huan figured in this scene as the representative of the audience. See Yomota Inuhiko, "Stranger Than Tokyo," trans. Aaron Gerow, paper presented at "Asian Culture at the Crossroads," Hong Kong, Baptist University, November 1998, 4–8.

28. Much has been written on the relationships among travel/tourism, the gaze, and postcoloniality: how the hierarchy of vision (the seer and the seen), supported by the economics of consumption, works to reproduce colonial relations of power between the Western traveler and the Eastern native. Two recent examples are James Clifford's *Travel and Translation in the Late Twentieth Century* (Cambridge: Harvard University Press, 1997) and Nicholas Thomas's *Colonialism's Culture: Anthropology, Travel, and Government* (Princeton, NJ: Princeton University Press, 1994). Two recent books on the colonialist gaze in cinema are Matthew Bernstein and Gaylyn Studlar, eds., *Visions of the East: Orientalism in Film* (New Brunswick, NJ: Rutgers University Press, 1997), and E. Ann Kaplan, *Looking for the Other: Feminism, Film, and the Imperial Gaze* (New York: Routledge, 1997).

29. Yomota, "Stranger Than Tokyo."

30. Yet the strategic use of subtitles, silencing some and allowing others to "speak," effectively makes Japanese the linguistic locus of the film.

31. The image of *furusato* becomes more and more an object of consumption, an ideology in need of selling, as many Japanese lose any real contact with their rural hometowns. For examples of the marketing of *furusato*, see Marilyn Ivy, *Discourses of the Vanishing* (Chicago: University of Chicago Press, 1995).

32. Yomota notes how the languages used in the film are never creolized and thus themselves remain only objects of touristic fascination. Iwai, he contends, remains ignorant of the living nature of language, as well as of the difficulties of people who must live everyday with the foreignness of words. Yomota, "Stranger Than Tokyo," 7.

33. Jennifer Robertson, "It Takes a Village: Internationalization and Nostalgia in Postwar Japan," in Stephen Vlastos, ed., *Mirror of Modernity: Invented Traditions of Modern Japan* (Berkeley: University of California Press, 1998), 128.

34. This opens the way for a certain slippage: non-Japanese can buy this image, too. In fact, *Swallowtail Butterfly's* success in other East Asian countries is a matter worthy of further research. My concern in this essay, however, is how the film operates in a discursive context that also includes Fujioka's texts.

4

Japanese Education, Nationalism, and Ienaga Saburō's Textbook Lawsuits

Nozaki Yoshiko and Inokuchi Hiromitsu

> "Who controls the past," ran the Party slogan, "controls the
> future: who controls the present controls the past." And yet
> the past, though of its nature alterable, never had been
> altered. Whatever was true now was true from everlasting to
> everlasting. . . . All that was needed was an unending series
> of victories over your own memory.
>
> *George Orwell,* Nineteen Eighty-four

National Narrative and Identity

On August 15, 1945, the day Emperor Hirohito announced to his subjects
the acceptance of the Potsdam Declaration, the Suzuki cabinet resigned
en masse. Ōta Kōzō, the outgoing education minister, presented his final
instruction to the schools on that day. His message was that Japan's defeat had been brought on by the people's insufficient dedication to the
emperor, along with their failure to bring into full play the spirit nurtured
by their imperial education. Hereafter, he concluded, students and teachers ought to devote themselves wholly to their duties as imperial subjects
and to the maintenance of the *kokutai*.[1] In referring to *kokutai*, Ōta had in
mind the emperor, who in presurrender doctrine was the essence of the
nation and embodied the national identity. Ōta, like many other officials
who had promoted ultranationalistic and emperor-centered education in

the service of war, persisted in his determination to secure the imperial state even while accepting military defeat. In this way, much of the imperial system, which had committed all sorts of atrocities, remained intact at the beginning of postwar Japan.

A modern nation-state governs its people in part by creating and disseminating narratives. One important site of such efforts is school textbooks, especially history and social studies textbooks. After all, education is one of the most effective ways to promote a national narrative (official history) and to make and remake certain identities into the national identity.[2] The state, whether directly involved in textbook production and circulation or not, can readily reinforce dominant ideologies. In response, alternative and oppositional forces develop their own counternarratives and identities. For the meanings attached to a given identity—in this case the national identity—are "an unstable and 'de-centered' complex of social meanings constantly being transformed by political struggle."[3]

The ongoing battles over educational content in postwar Japan have been one of the crucial fronts in a long-running struggle over the identity of the nation itself. To be sure, struggles over the national narrative existed in Japan before and even during World War II, when official narratives such as the Imperial Rescript on Education and other "fine militarist stories" played a crucial role in Japanese identity formation.[4] Because of the state's strict, often violent oppression, counternarratives (e.g., the proletarian educational movement) were unable to redirect the nation's course. Throughout the postwar era, education would become a hotly contested arena for competing social forces and their visions of Japan's future. Ienaga Saburō has been a crucial figure in that political struggle since the end of the war.

Early Postwar Struggles over the National Narrative

The early occupation period saw substantial changes in textbook policy as U.S. officials sought to demilitarize and democratize Japan. Seeking to keep militaristic content from the sight of occupation officials or to create a favorable impression on them, Japanese bureaucrats made the first change prior to any occupation directives.[5] It was called textbook "black out" (*suminuri*), and it involved the literal blotting out of offending passages. On September 20, 1945, the Ministry of Education ordered schools to delete militaristic content in textbooks and educational materials and gave several criteria for doing so, without specifying the precise passages that were to be blacked out.[6] However, it left intact those passages that celebrated the imperial nationhood and morality.

Throughout the fall of 1945, teachers gradually began to direct students to black out parts of the textbooks. Because of the ministry's vague instructions, local officials, schools, and teachers developed their own lists for identifying items to be removed from textbooks in all subject areas. As a result, no two blacked-out textbooks were exactly alike, and the locally developed lists often included far more items than the ministry's. To some extent, a different construction of national narrative took place in each classroom.[7]

In October the Supreme Command for the Allied Powers (SCAP) issued several directives pertaining to curriculum content and textbooks, including the elimination of militarist and ultranationalist materials from schools. On December 15 SCAP ordered the abolition of any government propagation of Shinto, which included a ban of such state-authored teaching materials as *Kokutai no Hongi* (The true meaning of the *kokutai*) and *Shinmin no Michi* (The path of the imperial subject). SCAP also informally suggested a rewrite of Japanese history textbooks. Finally, on December 31, it ordered the suspension of the teaching of morals *(shūshin),* Japanese history, and geography and demanded that existing textbooks and teachers' guides in these subjects be withdrawn and new history textbooks be developed.

Following SCAP's December 31 order, some Japanese historians, including Ienaga Saburō, began to address the issues of postwar Japanese history education, textbook writing, and publishing. In fact, Ienaga, who was a historian as well as a former high school and normal school teacher, drafted his own history textbook in early 1946. His book *Shin Nihonshi* (New Japanese history) reflected his view that education should be based on verifiable facts and should convey democratic values and the desire for peace.[8] At the time it was published in 1947, all textbooks were required to be state-authored. Ienaga's *Shin Nihonshi*, therefore, was published by Fuzanbō as a general book. The lawsuits he later filed were for revised versions of this book.

The Last State-Authored History Textbooks

The Ministry of Education began writing new history textbooks in the fall of 1945. In December a committee was formed to examine the contents of existing elementary and secondary school history textbooks and to write new ones. Toyoda Takeshi, a former normal school teacher who was appointed in October 1945 to be one of the compilers of the Ministry's Textbook Bureau, was the author for the elementary/secondary school

4.1 Ienaga Saburō
Professor Ienaga sued the government three times to be allowed to include material in his textbook that he saw as crucial to understanding Japanese history. His lawsuits have helped shape the content of current textbooks, and his trials have dramatized the issue of textbook censorship. National League for Support of the School Textbook Screening Suit (NLSSTSS). Used by permission.

textbook, and Maruyama Kunio, another compiler, was appointed to develop the normal school textbook. The project was canceled in May 1946, when Toyoda had completed only the section on ancient history. SCAP then insisted that the ministry commission other historians not associated with the Textbook Bureau.[9]

The new project was launched with a plan to develop three textbooks (for elementary, secondary, and normal schools), each dividing Japanese history into four periods (ancient, medieval, early modern, and modern/contemporary). The Ministry of Education officials chose eleven historians, who began work in the cafeteria of the Historiographical Institute of Tokyo Imperial University. Each selected and organized the content, but all eleven followed three principles: no propaganda of any kind; no militarism, ultranationalism, or propagation of Shintoism; and inclusion of the accomplishments of ordinary people in the area of economics, invention, scholarship, and art, with mention of the emperor's achievements only when significant. SCAP's Japanese employees examined the manu-scripts daily, and although SCAP never actively asked the authors to in-clude specific descriptions, it did veto some passages.[10]

Ienaga was asked to write the section on ancient Japanese history for the elementary school textbook later entitled *Kuni no Ayumi* (The course of our country). Because the manuscript had to be finished in about a month, he used Toyoda's draft as a basis; however, he deleted the sec-tions on mythology, began the text with a description of Stone Age civili-zation based on archeological findings, and described the formation of Japan as a state without any mention of imperialist ideology.[11] Ōkubo Toshikane, Ienaga's coauthor, who was assigned to the section on mod-ern and contemporary history, referred to the Nanjing massacre of 1937 by noting: "Our army . . . ravaged Nanjing, the capital of the Republic of China." The line was brief but clear in signifying the event as one of Japan's wartime wrongdoings.[12]

Kuni no Ayumi, published in September 1946, was the first postwar, state-authored history textbook. It was also the first Japanese textbook to list the names of its authors. Despite the advances it made, however, *Kuni no Ayumi* was criticized by both the Japanese left and several foreign countries for failing to eradicate completely the emperor-centered view of history.[13]

The 1947 Constitution, the Fundamental Law of Education, and the Failure of State-Authored Texts

In late 1946 and early 1947, the legal framework for educational decisionmaking changed to a significant degree, as the "democratizing of Japan" under the occupation moved swiftly, at least on the surface. The new constitution, promulgated in 1946, offered a narrative of Japan's na-tionhood that differed substantially from the presurrender ultranational-ist emphasis on the imperial state. It stated that sovereign power resides with the people (the emperor's status was changed to that of a "symbol" of the nation) (article 1), guaranteed basic human rights (article 11), and renounced war (article 9). Simultaneously, the "new education" took shape, as the constitution guaranteed academic freedom (article 23) and the people's right to an education (article 26). On March 31, 1947, the Diet passed the Fundamental Law of Education and the School Education Law.

The Fundamental Law of Education articulated the principles of post-war education, including the aim of education as the "full development of personality" (article 1), and provisions for "equal opportunity in educa-tion" (article 3) and "coeducation" (article 5). Most important, it stated that "education shall not be subject to improper control, but it shall be directly responsible to the whole people" (article 10).[14] The law was, in a sense, an educational constitution. As the Ministry of Education put it at the time, it was "a declaration of new educational ideals." In essence, the law was meant to replace the Imperial Rescript on Education.[15]

By contrast, the School Education Law, which dealt with the practical operation of schools, stipulated that elementary school textbooks were to be screened, approved, and/or authored by "competent authorities" (*Kantoku-chōi*, article 21). Similar procedures were stipulated for secondary school textbooks. At first, the "competent authorities" were assumed to be not only the Ministry of Education but also the prefectural school boards that would be created. In May, however, in the School Education Law Enforcement Regulations (which was not an actual piece of legislation), the ministry restricted what was meant by "competent authorities" to the ministry itself.[16]

The new legislation and SCAP policy made it impossible for the government to insist that schools use only state-authored textbooks. In September 1947 the ministry announced that it would introduce textbook screening in 1948 (for the 1949 school year) and established several committees to develop the plan. The Japan Teachers Union (JTU) sent representatives to participate in the committee meetings.

Although it was not clear at this time who was to have the legal right to adopt textbooks, the ministry suggested that the schools, in consultation with the teachers, would select textbooks according to their own educational needs.[17] Many of those concerned with education, including teachers, scholars, and the editors at publishing houses, welcomed the ministry's position and launched numerous new textbook projects. Even the JTU initiated its own projects, which resulted in its submitting about sixty textbook manuscripts for screening.

Textbook screening during the occupation was a rather complicated, two-fold process. Publishers were required to submit both Japanese and English versions of manuscripts. First, the ministry of Education examined the Japanese manuscripts. Five commissioned examiners evaluated each manuscript, and sixteen appointed committee members made decisions. Then the Civil Information and Education Section (CIE) of SCAP screened the English versions of those the ministry approved. If the CIE requested a revision, the publishers and authors needed to resubmit the manuscript to the ministry's committee. The 1948 textbook screening was rushed, and only a small number of the manuscripts were approved. As of August 11, 418 of the 584 manuscripts submitted passed the ministry's scrutiny, but only 90 of the 418 passed the CIE's. The book publishers immediately began making sample copies for the upcoming textbook exhibitions.

Beginning on August 25, textbook exhibitions were held at local school districts, and sixty-two of the approved textbooks, including two written by the JTU, were displayed (the remaining books were still in production). Many teachers welcomed the new textbooks in an atmosphere full of excitement and enthusiasm.[18] In 1950, with teachers promoting the "nongovernmental" textbooks, the ministry of Education announced it would cease writing its own textbooks. It made one further futile attempt to reintroduce "standard textbooks" in 1952, but when this last-ditch effort failed, it gradually ceased publishing state-authored textbooks. From 1953 onward, the ministry began instead to seek ways to "write" textbooks by screening them.

The Conservative Turn in Education Policy During the 1950s and 1960s

After the introduction of textbook screening, the publisher Sanseidō asked Ienaga to write a high school history textbook; since his *Shin Nihonshi* was already out of print, he agreed. He submitted the revised text of *Shin Nihonshi* to the Ministry of Education in 1952. It was rejected because one of the five examiners gave the manuscript extremely bad marks. When Ienaga resubmitted it—with no changes—to a different group of examiners, it was approved and published (in 1953).

Some of the reasons the ministry gave Ienaga for the initial rejection disturbed him. For instance, the ministry faulted his manuscript for its portrayal of fifth-century diplomatic relationships between Japan and China, particularly the account of Japan's envoy bringing tribute to China. According to the ministry, the depiction of Japan as politically subordinate to China would cause students to suffer a sense of inferiority. The ministry also argued that too much space had been given to the Pacific War. It stated that because the students had experienced the war themselves, the entire subject should be dropped. Other perceived faults included the description of women's status during the ancient and early modern periods and descriptions of poverty and peasant rebellions in the early nineteenth century. Ienaga publicized his concerns about these criticisms in the *Asahi* newspaper.[19]

Ienaga was troubled about the future of history education—and his fears

4.2 Images of hardship

Japanese textbooks show Japanese enduring hardships during World War II but leave ambiguous the question of the forces causing the hardships. They are victims, but victims of what? Fate? The Allies? The Japanese government? For example, Japanese texts frequently include photos of some of the 400,000 children sent to the countryside with their classes to avoid bombings. Here the evacuees say good-bye to the children who are staying behind. Satō, ed., *Asahi Rekishi Shashin Riburarii* vol. 3, 24–25. Used by permission.

were justified. The recovery of the Japanese right, including ultranationalists, was under way in the early 1950s. With the victory of the Chinese revolution and the outbreak of the Korean War, occupation policy elevated anti-Communism above democratization, and many of those who had been purged because of their cooperation in carrying out Japan's war activities were depurged and appointed or elected to important posts. Educational policy took an overtly conservative turn after the Ikeda-Robertson talks of 1953, in which the United States pressed for the remilitarization of Japan.[20] Both the U.S. and Japanese governments saw it necessary to revise the narrative of a new, peaceful, democratic Japan that was fostered during the early postwar years and promoted by teachers.

Conservatives attacked peace education curricula and accused the JTU of promoting a Communist agenda. They succeeded in passing a series of new laws: one in 1953 to give the education minister the authority to screen textbooks and two in 1954 to limit the political activities of public school teachers and to ensure the "political neutrality" of compulsory education. In the general election of February 1955, the revision of the 1947 constitution—especially its renunciation of war—was at stake. Textbook policy also became one of the major issues, when Nakasone Yasuhiro of the Democratic Party *(Minshutō)* advocated a more centralized textbook publishing and adoption system—essentially a return to state-authored textbooks. The election results marked a clear political division. Out of 467 seats, and against the Democratic Party's 185 and the Liberal Party's 112, the Socialist Party *(Shakaitō* or SP) won 156. With one third of the lower house seats, the SP held enough votes to block initiation of any undesirable amendment to the 1947 constitution. The battle over the constitution was done (at least for this round), but not the one over the textbooks.

When the Diet opened in June, the first postwar textbook attack occurred, and it became a model for later attacks. The right-wingers (with members in the Liberal and the Democratic Party) launched an attack on education by inviting Ishii Kazutomo, a former disgruntled JTU official, to the Diet to testify on alleged bribery of local school officials in charge of textbook adoption. The hearing served as the occasion for mounting an attack on textbooks, since Ishii's main topic turned out to be "biased textbooks," especially the social studies textbooks, including history textbooks. Ishii later worked with the Democratic Party on its publication of brochures entitled *Ureubeki Kyōkasho no Mondai* (The Deplorable Problems of Textbooks).[21]

In 1956 the Hatoyama administration of the Liberal Democratic Party *(Jiyūminshutō,* formed in the fall of 1955, LDP) submitted three bills aimed at gaining control over education: the first was for government appointment rather than election of local school boards; the second was to establish a special council for educational reform (i.e., to change the Fundamental Law of Education); and the third was to tighten textbook screening and adoption. Protest against these proposals was immediate and strong and arose not only from intellectuals and educators but also from the general public—in what remains to date the biggest protest in postwar education history. The administration rammed the first measure through by bringing police into the Diet, but it could not save the second and third.

Meanwhile, by 1956 the ministry of Education had already tightened screening criteria and brought more conservatives into the screening committee (an action that did not require legislation). After the 1956 Diet, the LDP administration shifted its tactics to strengthen control over textbooks through "regulations" instead of legislation. This approach was far more successful. That year, the ministry rejected eight social studies textbooks as "biased" and required authors to make revisions that included eliminating negative references to Japanese wartime conduct. The ministry also pressured textbook publishers to remove some authors from their projects.[22] Although it increased the number of screening committee members and made the textbook examiners its full-time employees, the ministry stopped sharing with authors the documents listing and explaining the conditions for approval and began to give its "comments" (*iken*) concerning revisions only orally. The ministry officials apparently wanted to keep their words invisible.[23]

In the late 1950s, the ministry rejected many textbooks, especially in 1958, when it turned down 33 percent of textbook manuscripts.[24] The examiners evaluated not only for factual accuracy but also for the level of patriotism. The ministry further strengthened its hand in 1958 by making compliance with the instruction guidelines mandatory. Finally, in 1963, a bill was passed that made textbooks free to all students in grades 1–9 (i.e., compulsory education) but that also further consolidated the adoption process. In the new arrangement, county-level school boards (consisting of several local school districts) rather than local schools were to select the textbooks. In effect, teachers lost control over textbooks, and the process of monopolization of the textbook industry was established. State control over textbooks became easier and more complete because the number of textbooks shrank.

In sum, the late 1950s and 1960s saw the textbook production and adoption system becoming more and more like the state-authored textbook system that was in place during World War II.[25] History textbooks

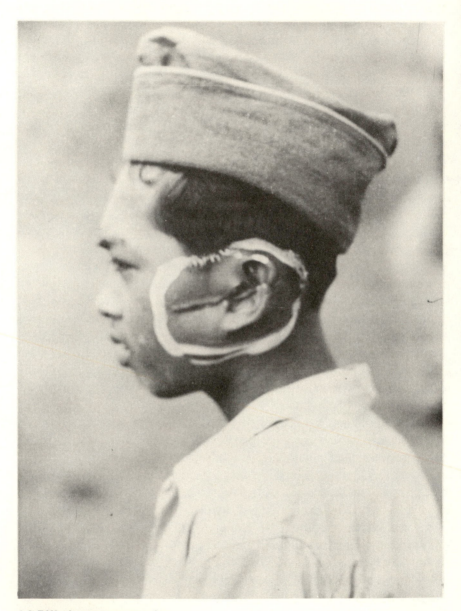

4.3 Differing war memories
The casual brutality inflicted on civilians by Japanese soldiers is a major component of war
memories in Asia but not a key theme of Japanese remembrance in textbooks. The scars on
the face of this Filipino boy, Juan Castillo, had mostly healed by September 25, 1945, when
he was photographed. NARA, NRE-338–FTL(EF)-3134(7).

that included references to the Nanjing massacre were discontinued, and those that survived the process showed the scars of their struggles to get through (e.g., the number of descriptions of atomic bomb damage was reduced and lines were added to stress "the emperor's judgment" in accepting the Potsdam Declaration). Because of the institutional arrangement developed in the postoccupation period, the Ministry of Education had the upper hand. It was Ienaga's court challenge, then, that brought a new aspect to the struggle.

Ienaga's First and Second Textbook Lawsuits

When Ienaga submitted a revised edition of *Shin Nihonshi* to the Ministry of Education in 1955, it was approved on condition that he make 216 changes. Ienaga made the changes, and the textbook was published in 1956. However, he immediately had to revise the textbook again, as the ministry issued new guidelines.[26] His book was rejected in 1957 and conditionally approved in 1958. After another revision, it was eventually published in 1959. Ienaga revised the textbook again a few years later, but when he submitted it to the ministry in 1962, it was again rejected (in 1963). This time the ministry disclosed only twenty or so of its reasons. Ienaga, who had to guess at most of the ministry's criticisms (in fact, there were 323 items altogether, a fact that became known only later, in the course of his court battle), revised the textbook yet again, and it was approved in 1964 on condition that 293 items be changed. He altered the text accordingly, and it was approved and published.

By this time, Ienaga was convinced that textbook screening was a form of censorship. Ienaga took his case to court in the belief that the ministry would not change its practice without a battle. Even though some legal scholars and publishers' union members worried that a lawsuit was risky, he filed his first suit against the national government in 1965. Many of those opposing textbook screening, especially the JTU and the Publishing Workers' Union, as well as individual teachers, scholars, and publishers' staff, supported his decision.

Although he demanded financial compensation for the psychological duress caused by the screening process, Ienaga's chief objective was to demonstrate that state screening of textbooks was unconstitutional (e.g., a violation of freedom of expression and scholarship) and contrary to the Fundamental Education Law (i.e., a violation of the principle protecting education from improper control). To succeed, he needed to prove that in requesting numerous revisions, which he listed in his suit, the ministry had violated his rights.[27] Some of those points were related to the depiction of the Asia-Pacific War. For example, Ienaga had stated that "most [Japanese] citizens were not informed of the truth of the war, and so could only enthusiastically support the reckless war." The ministry of Education had insisted that calling the war "reckless" was a value judgment and that it was inappropriate to make such value judgments about contemporary events. The ministry had also declared that the manuscript contained too many illustrations of the "dark side" of the war, such as an air raid, a city left in ruins by the atomic bomb, and disabled veterans, and so had asked that some be removed.[28]

Meanwhile, Ienaga attempted to reinstate six phrases in the 1967 edition of *Shin Nihonshi* that he had changed for the previous edition. In response, the ministry held that his desired changes could not be regarded as "improvements" (in its view, the purpose of revision). Ienaga then decided to file a second lawsuit, an administrative lawsuit asking the minister of education to revoke the ministry's decision on the ground that the rejection of Ienaga's revised version was unconstitutional and contrary to the Fundamental Law of Education. The chief objective of the second lawsuit was the same as the first, but its advantages were that (1) because it was an administrative suit, the legal procedure was less complicated than that of the earlier "damage claim" suit, and (2) it involved only six specific points. These features kept the debate focused and resulted in the lawsuit's moving more rapidly through the courts.

One of the specific points in the second suit dealt with Japan's earliest history, particularly the characterization of myths contained in two eighth-century texts, *Kojiki* and *Nihon Shoki*. Ienaga had stated that "all [of the myths] were composed after the imperial family had integrated Japan in order to justify the origin of its rule." The ministry of Education had ordered him to eliminate these lines. As a result, the textbook represented the myths as if they were facts. Another contention concerned a description of the 1941 Japan-USSR Neutrality Treaty. The ministry had ordered Ienaga to add the line "Japan entered the treaty as the USSR proposed" and suggested the elimination of a footnote that read: "After the German army invaded the Soviet Union, Japan collected its army close to the border under the name of the 'Kwantung Army special maneuvers,' and was preparing to invade Siberia in the event that the situation became advantageous to Japan." The ministry's intent seemed to be to create an impression that the Soviet Union's declaration of war against Japan in 1945 was the sole violation of the treaty.

The Court Decisions and Ienaga's Achievements in the 1970s

By the end of 1967, because of the first suit, details of the textbook screening process and the exact reasons for the rejection of Ienaga's textbook were emerging, despite government resistance. It also became known that the ministry had kept documents explaining its objections to Ienaga's textbook but that the state was refusing to submit them to the court, insisting on the need for confidentiality. Ienaga's request for a court order to hand over the documents was granted in part; however, when the state appealed the disclosure decision to the higher courts, the first suit was stalled.

Meanwhile, the second suit proceeded comparatively quickly. The Tokyo District Court, with Chief Justice Sugimoto presiding, ruled in Ienaga's favor in 1970. Recognizing the people's educational rights and freedom, the court decided that in the case of Ienaga's textbook the state had clearly exceeded its authority and that although government screening in itself could not be considered unconstitutional as long as it only corrected obvious mistakes, it could be unconstitutional when it ordered a change in educational content.[29] The minister of education appealed the Sugimoto decision to the Tokyo High Court. Five years later, with Chief Justice Azegami presiding, that court dismissed the state's appeal, while avoiding a direct judgment on the constitutionality of government screening. Although the decision was less clear-cut, Ienaga had won again. The minister appealed the decision to the Supreme Court.

The first suit began to move again in the early 1970s. After the Supreme Court dismissed the state's appeal against disclosing the ministry's documents and after considerable public pressure, the state submitted its file on the case. Although the ministry's file actually substantiated Ienaga's argument and testimony, the Tokyo District Court handed him only a partial victory in 1974. The court found some abuse of power in the requests made by the ministry on eleven specific items (out of the 293 that Ienaga had contested), but it affirmed the state's right to regulate the content of education and declared state textbook screening constitutional. Ienaga appealed to the higher court, and the state also appealed to revoke the eleven points it had lost.

The late 1970s saw indications that Ienaga's court battle would be a protracted one, yet the impact of his battle inside and outside the court was already apparent. From the beginning, Ienaga's lawsuit attracted strong public interest. The two suits focused attention on the textbook screening system, which had been hidden from the public. The stan-

4.4 Limits of criticism in Japanese texts
Japanese textbooks, like their American counterparts, never show soldiers who lost limbs in battle. Ienaga tried to include this image with a caption that read in part "The Horror of War: Even though the war came to an end eventually, the arms and legs of soldiers lost in battle will never return." The Ministry of Education refused permission to use the photo because "it conveys an excessively negative impression of war." *Truth in Textbooks, Freedom in Education, and Peace for Children* (Tokyo: National League for Support of the School Textbook Screening Suit, 1995), 3. Used by permission.

dards for approval, the existence of two kinds of Ministry pressure ("request" and "suggestion"), the 1,000-point scale by which textbooks were graded (800 and above was considered passing), and the existence of an official file on each textbook all became public knowledge. In particular, the state was forced to disclose the actual process by which it had censored Ienaga's textbook and to explain the reasons for its rejection, along with the names of the examiners and the committee members who had vetoed the textbook.[30] The undemocratic nature of the system had previously been known only through complaints made by textbook authors and publishers, but now the ministry's own documents revealed an arbitrary process, one rife with abuses of power.

Ienaga's victories in his second suit had an immediate influence on school textbooks. Following the Sugimoto decision of 1970, the ministry relaxed its criteria for screening, and the timing was perfect for textbook authors willing to include a wider range of material concerning Japanese wartime atrocities. Much new research on the various phases of the Asia-Pacific War, especially with respect to Japan's wrongdoing appeared in the 1970s. In 1971, for example, Honda Katsuichi began a series of reports in the *Asahi* newspaper on the Nanjing massacre and other war atrocities Japan committed in China, based on his interviews with the survivors and data gathered in China. Researchers and educators in Okinawa were collecting personal accounts of the Battle of Okinawa for the prefectural history project and other publications.

In 1973 Ienaga's revised *Shin Nihonshi* passed the screening process even though it included more detailed passages about Japan's invasion of China and Japanese colonial policy in Korea. Some history textbooks containing descriptions of the Nanjing massacre were approved, and others followed in their steps. For example, the 1978 edition of *Atarashii Shakai* (New society), a junior high history textbook published by Tokyo Shoseki, included this line: "[the Japanese army] captured Nanjing, took the lives of numerous Chinese civilians throughout China, and caused enormous damage to their daily lives."[31] Further, the line was footnoted, stating: "Immediately after entering the city of Nanjing, the Japanese army killed and wounded an enormous number of Chinese people, including women, children, and soldiers either no longer armed or wearing civilian clothes. For its actions in this incident, [Japan] met with criticism from various foreign countries denouncing [the incident] as the Nanjing massacre, but ordinary Japanese were not informed of the facts [of the event]." History textbooks also began to refer to other wartime issues, for example, to the Korean and Chinese forced laborers brought to Japan in the last years of the war. Various groups of parents, teachers, publishers' staff, and researchers who had been struggling to establish alternative and oppositional narratives in textbooks developed a new awareness of their educational rights and freedom.[32]

4.5 Nanjing massacre in texts
Many Japanese textbooks mention the Nanjing massacre, yet the accompanying images of the 1937 event are of jubilant Japanese soldiers marching into the city or celebrating at its gates. This photo shows Japanese soldiers after they defeated the Chinese at the Marco Polo Bridge on July 8, 1937, just before they moved south to Nanjing. Satō, ed., *Asahi Rekishi Shashin Riburarii* vol. 1, 29. Used by permission.

Renewed Attempts to Enforce Patriotic Textbooks in the 1980s and 1990s

In the late 1970s, the Japanese government and the LDP attempted to regain control over education, particularly by stressing nationalist (patriotic) curricula. For example, the instruction guidelines of 1977 designated "Kimigayo" as the national anthem, despite having no legal basis for the action. With LDP support, a high official of the ministry of Education simply inserted the modifier "national anthem" before "Kimigayo." That same year, the ministry rejected five high school textbooks (one in ethics/civics, two in Japanese history, and two in world history). Around the same time, it tightened its textbook screening rules again, requiring authors to follow the guidelines more closely.

Conservative politicians, especially the younger LDP hawks, attacked textbooks more vocally after the LDP won a large majority in both houses in 1980. Charging that most textbook revisions after the Sugimoto decision were inspired by Communists, they sought stricter legislation to control textbook content. A nasty campaign was launched in the LDP's weekly newspaper by Ishii Kazutomo, the same person who took part in the textbook attack of the 1950s. Ishii and the LDP attacked the authors of social studies and Japanese-language textbooks for supporting the JTU, the Communist Party, or the democratic education movements.

One of their criticisms was directed at a Russian folktale, *Ōkina Kabu* (A big turnip), which they felt promoted a Communist agenda. Originally recorded by folklorist Aleksandr N. Afanase'v (1826–1871), the story told about a couple, their granddaughter, and their household animals (dog, cat, and rat), who joined forces to pull a giant turnip out of the ground. The folktale was (and still is) popular reading material for first grade students.[33] Ishii and the LDP falsely stated that the story was a *Soviet* folk tale and Afanase'v a Soviet folklorist. They also offered an interpretation that perhaps no one had thought of—that the story was about workers, peasants, students, and intellectuals uniting to bring down capitalists. Right-wing intellectuals, economists, and big business supported these critics' demands for more patriotic curricula.

Feeling threatened by the antinuclear movement, the Science and Technology Agency (STA) joined in the right-wing criticism of junior high school civics textbooks. In 1980, it attacked textbooks for emphasizing the negative aspects of atomic power and for raising public concerns about its safety. The STA unsuccessfully pressured the Ministry of Education to change descriptions of atomic energy already in textbooks approved for the 1981 school year. The Democratic Socialist Party *(Minshatō)*, an opposition party supported by small business owners, also joined the attack, and other business groups lobbied for changes in textbook depictions of their industries.[34] Eventually, the ministry accommodated them by "suggesting" revisions to publishers.

As a result of these highly public battles, the media reported that state control over education had been strengthened and that the depiction of the Japanese wartime invasion of Asian countries had been watered down. A focal point of these reports, which received international coverage (notably in East and Southeast Asia), was the ministry's request to replace the term "aggression" (*shinryaku*) with "advancement" (*shinshutsu*).[35] In July the Republic of Korea (South Korea) and the People's Republic of China officially protested to the Japanese government. By September more than 2,000 reports on Japanese textbook screening had appeared in the press of nineteen Asian countries.[36]

In August, through an "informal talk," the chief cabinet secretary,

Miyazawa Kiichi, announced that the Japanese government would take responsibility for "correcting" the textbook descriptions.[37] From late October through November, the Ministry of Education officially announced changes in its screening policy, including a new requirement that textbooks consider modern historical relations between Japan and Asia from the perspective of international friendship and cooperation. At that point, the Japanese government unilaterally declared the controversy settled.

The Ministry of Education did not change the ideological orientation of its textbook directives, however. For example, although it now allowed use of the term "aggression," it continued to "suggest" that textbooks should report smaller numbers of victims in the massacres that took place in Nanjing, Singapore, and Okinawa during the war. Moreover, Prime Minister Nakasone Yasuhiro, who held office in the mid-1980s, was strongly interested in the nationalist reform of education and the reconstruction of a Japanese identity. Thus, once again the struggle over the narratives and identities of the nation came to the fore.

Ienaga's Third Lawsuit

When the instruction guidelines for high schools were rewritten in 1978, Ienaga revised his *Shin Nihonshi*. The revised text was approved in 1980 with 420 or so comments. The book was published after what Ienaga later described as "the longest process ever" dating back to 1957. When the Japanese government promised (in October 1982) to correct the textbook depictions of Japan's foreign relations, Ienaga asked the ministry's permission to make corrections, but his request was rejected. He submitted the revised manuscript again in 1983, and it was approved with some seventy conditions. In 1984 Ienaga filed a third lawsuit against the state, demanding compensation for the psychological damage the screening processes had caused him.

Ienaga's ultimate goal was still to demonstrate the unconstitutionality of state textbook screening. In the third suit, however, he and his counsel challenged the ministry's "abuse of power" in requesting or suggesting changes of textbook descriptions concerning specific historical events, that is, to move the court battle further into the arena of "historical truths." With this legal strategy, he and his historian counsels chose to dispute eight specific points (six Ministry requests and two of its "suggestions"). Four were related to the Japanese invasion of China, one concerned the Japanese colonization of Korea, another involved the Battle of Okinawa during the last months of World War II, and two covered domestic protests against imperial power.

4.6 Censoring peaceful postwar dissent
The Ministry of Education ordered some changes to minimize attention to peaceful postwar criticism of the government. The words "stop corrupt Diet members" on the side of this campaign box were brushed out in the screening process. *Truth in Textbooks*, 9. Used by permission.

The first point was connected to the use of the term "aggression" to describe the Japanese invasion of China. In the 1980 and 1983 negotiations, Ienaga had insisted on the appropriateness of the term, refusing to change his language despite the ministry's repeated "suggestion(s)." He also fought to include two phrases with respect to the 1937 Nanjing massacre. In the screening process, the ministry had requested that Ienaga change the line reading, "Immediately after the occupation of Nanjing, the Japanese army killed numerous Chinese soldiers and civilians" to a description stating that people died in the "confusion" around the time of the occupation. The ministry had also asked Ienaga to eliminate the mention of rape from his description of the Nanjing massacre (which read: "Not a few Japanese soldiers raped Chinese women [when occupying Nanjing]")—here the ministry argued that rape is a common wartime phenomenon not limited to the Japanese army. The ministry had requested as well that he remove the mention of Unit 731, a biowarfare unit that had conducted experiments on live human subjects.[38] It had claimed that there was no credible scholarly research on Unit 731 and that for this reason it was premature to mention it in textbooks.

The fifth point concerned Korean resistance to the Japanese invasion at the time of the Sino-Japanese War of 1894–1895. Ienaga had described the event as the beginning of a fifty-year Japanese colonization of Korea, writing that "in Korea, which was the major battlefield of the war, popular anti-Japanese resistance often took place." The ministry had objected to the phrase "anti-Japanese resistance," stating that it would confuse students.

The disagreement between Ienaga and the state rested on two radically different narratives of Japanese history. Ienaga's attempt was to critique the official narrative of Japan's conduct in World War II and the years leading up to it. He presented a different narrative of the war at home as well, at least with respect to the Battle of Okinawa, in which an estimated 160,000 civilians, including women and children, lost their lives, many at the hands of Japanese soldiers. Of the latter, Ienaga had written that "residents, both young and old, were killed," specifically pointing out that "more than a few of these civilians were killed by the Japanese army." The ministry had responded that "voluntary mass suicides" were the major cause of Okinawan civilian deaths, holding that the victims willingly gave their lives for the country (rather than being "killed" or "forced to kill" family members by the army). In short, the ministry had downplayed the massacre of Okinawans by the Japanese army.

The seventh and eighth points involved domestic events in which the righteousness of imperial power was questioned—points that the official narrative ignored. Ienaga cited two comments the ministry had given him in the screening process. The first (a suggestion for improvement) concerned a protest by Shinran (1173–1262), the founder of a major Buddhist sect, against the oppression of new Buddhist sects by the imperial court. The second (an order to change) involved the description of the volunteer army called Troop Sōmō, which had fought for the emperor during the Meiji Restoration but had then been quickly suppressed by the Meiji government because of its populist orientation.[39]

Ienaga's Court Battle from the 1980s to 1997

In the mid-1980s, Ienaga was fighting three court cases simultaneously, all of them moving toward the Supreme Court. Of the three, the second ended first—without ever properly concluding. After its appeal to the Supreme Court, the ministry of Education changed its strategy and argued that the case had "no benefit"—that it was moot—because even if Ienaga were to win, the ministry had already changed the instruction guidelines, and therefore Ienaga's 1965 textbook, following the old guidelines, would no longer be used. The Supreme Court referred the case back to the Tokyo High Court, which in 1989 dismissed the case on grounds of "no benefit," without declaring anything more specific. Ienaga decided not to appeal to the Supreme Court, since the earlier decisions, including the groundbreaking Sugimoto decision, retained their value as precedents.

The first suit, meanwhile, progressed more slowly, taking twelve years to reach a second decision. In 1986 the Tokyo High Court, with Chief Justice Suzuki presiding, overturned Ienaga's earlier partial victory at the district court. The ruling revoked the lower court's decision on eleven specific points, declaring that the ministry of Education had not been "excessively unreasonable." Ienaga appealed that decision to the Supreme Court. Seven years later, on March 16, 1993, the Supreme Court dismissed the first suit, handing Ienaga a total defeat after twenty-eight years of effort.[40]

The third suit proceeded more quickly, with decisions consistently giving partial victories to Ienaga. In its 1989 decision, the Tokyo District Court found the order to change the Troop Sōmō description unlawful, ruling that he had been wronged on this point and that the government should pay him 100,000 yen in compensation. Ienaga appealed the decision to the higher court (as did the state) because he hoped to win the main point, that state textbook screening was unconstitutional, as well as all the other specific points of contention. The latter included his arguments concerning the depictions of the Nanjing massacre, Unit 731, the Korean resistance, and the Battle of Okinawa. The account of the Battle of Okinawa had sparked the most dramatic and powerful testimony of the

4.7 The Battle of Okinawa
Textbook prose and images often allow ambiguous readings, giving teachers and students
the choice of discussing or ignoring the cruelty perpetrated by the Japanese military on
outsiders and Japanese suffering during the war. This picture of two boys in the aftermath
of the Battle of Okinawa illustrates both civilian suffering and the disproportionate burden Okinawans bore without spelling out either issue explicitly. NARA, NWDNS-127–
GR-99 (122422).

case. In 1988 Kinjō Shigeaki, a professor at Okinawa Christian Junior College, had testified that at age 16 he had participated in a "mass suicide" in which he killed his mother and younger siblings at the order of the Japanese army. Testifying for the state, Sono Ayako, who had written a documentary-fictional account of the event, stated that in her research she had found no evidence of a suicide order given by the captain himself.

In the fall of 1993, the Tokyo High Court softened the district court decision slightly. The court ruled in favor of both Ienaga's contention regarding the description of Troop Sōmō and his description of the Nanjing massacre, including mention of widespread rape, stating that on these points the ministry's screening had been excessive and thus unlawful. However, it ruled against Ienaga on Unit 731 and all other points.[41] After another appeal by Ienaga, the Supreme Court, with Chief Justice Ōno presiding, delivered the final decision of the third lawsuit on August 29, 1997. Ienaga won an additional specific point, allowing mention of Unit 731's cruel experiments. The Supreme Court ruling, though it affirmed the constitutionality of government textbook screening, agreed that the orders to change some passages of Ienaga's textbook were in violation of the law with reference to at least the four descriptions.[42] Although Ienaga lost his attempt to ban government textbook screening as unconstitutional, the court held that the ministry's requests for revision must be based on views verified or commonly accepted in the field of history studies. This decision will undoubtedly limit the scope of textbook censorship in the future.

A Conclusion: The Significance of Ienaga's Textbook Lawsuits

Ienaga's lawsuits have provided a countervailing force in the struggle over national narrative and identity construction in postwar Japan. His concern with history, history teaching, and textbooks has as much to do with the present and future as it does the past. Narratives of the past construct (and reconstruct) personal identities, and as such they "persuade [persons] to act in ways they might not otherwise act."[43] In particular, narratives of "nation" and a nation's past are powerful tools that can involve people in a shared sense of identity, clarifying who "we" are and where "we" come from.[44] In a sense, then, Orwell's insight (in the epigraph to this chapter) could hardly be more discerning. "Who controls the past controls the future" is a succinct explanation of why the Japanese government and the (ultra)nationalists have tried to alter narratives of the nation's past. (Orwell's picture of the party's total control over the present does not exactly match the Japanese case, however.)

The historical and political conditions of postwar Japan have been the context for Ienaga's struggle over the national narrative. Although most Japanese regard August 15, 1945, as the "end" of the war, for most of Japan's neighbors, including China, Korea, and Vietnam, the war entered a *new* phase on that date. In 1945 the United States exempted from prosecution in the Tokyo War Tribunal many of those responsible for Japan's war crimes, notably the emperor. Japan's acceptance of the tribunal court judgments meant not only that the pursuit of war crime issues by the occupation force ended there but also that pursuing such matters became taboo. Until recently, the Japanese government, under LDP control, ignored both the question of war responsibility, including that of accountability for colonial rule, and the voices of Asians who had suffered from Japanese actions during the war.[45]

The year 1945 did not end the struggle of Japanese seeking alternative narratives and identities.[46] They had to continue to grapple with issues of war responsibility and the meaning of such terms as "democracy" and "freedom." Ienaga was one of very few scholars who in the 1960s recognized that there were two aspects of the ordinary Japanese war experience—namely, that of assailants (externally) and that of victims (internally)—and one who unequivocally argued the need for the Japanese themselves, through their own judiciary, to pursue the issue of war crimes and responsibility.[47] He filed the textbook lawsuits, an approach totally unfamiliar to many Japanese, and fought in the name of the 1946 constitution, which guarantees the rights of citizens.

The lawsuits were, in effect, Ienaga's way of confronting Japanese war crimes and war responsibility. His suit did not pass judgment on individuals who committed crimes but made visible the operation of the imperial, ultranationalist power that had allowed such individuals to commit crimes and that now attempted to conceal them. It is no coincidence that Ienaga's position resonated with the voices of war victims in China, Korea, and other Asian countries. The immediate impact of his 1970 victory (the Sugimoto decision) was to embolden other textbook authors to document Japan's war atrocities. Ienaga's victories in his third lawsuit were partial, but they were victories nonetheless (reflecting perhaps the changed international situation in which Japan was compelled to listen to victims' voices), and his lawsuits as a whole succeeded in stimulating both research and public interest in the wartime conduct of the Japanese military. This paved the way for many Japanese to accept, or at least begin to listen to, those Asian voices demanding a hearing on unresolved issues of war and colonialism.

4.8 Demonstration following court decision
This demonstration took place after the Tokyo High Court's ruling of October 20, 1993, in Ienaga's third lawsuit. The banner announces the decision. Ienaga Saburō is in the front row, fourth from right, wearing a hat. *Truth in Textbooks*, 19. Used by permission.

Ienaga's thirty-year challenge to the state raised the question of whose knowledge ought to be represented in textbooks and taught in schools. A related question posed by Ienaga's lawsuits was that of process: who should decide the content of education and on what basis? No democratic nation has resolved these issues; the tendency, in fact, has been to ignore them. In our view, it is important to develop a democratic process through which educational content can be debated, negotiated, and selected. Textbooks need to be produced through a "free, contributive and common process of participation in the creation of meanings and values."[48] The appropriate role of the state is to ensure the fairness of such a process. The current Japanese system, which has allowed the state and the (ultra)nationalists to advance their agenda by incremental, extralegal faits accomplis should be abolished. The alternative, however, should not be a "free market" system, in which socially dominant and powerful groups decide what knowledge will be represented in school curricula.

In a society that provides universal education, school textbooks offer teachers and students "symbols to start with," "signs that some larger community exists," and as such "the possibility—indeed, the actuality— of a shared collective identity."[49] But a sifting of knowledge is always involved in the production of textbooks. This sifting is inherently problematic, since selective knowledge is given to represent a collective identity—be it a national, regional, or international identity—and so the identity constructed necessarily includes some people and excludes others. It is little wonder, therefore, that social groups compete over the symbols embodied in textbooks and that controversy accompanies the production of textbooks. This will always be the case wherever a society is committed to the democratic process. Critics who think that the problem has already been settled in their society—any society—are too optimistic, just as those who think democratic textbooks are impossible are too pessimistic. Ienaga's lawsuits suggest a possible third position, namely, that forming an oppositional narrative and identity and, simultaneously, building a consensus around it actually changes the way people see the world and themselves.

Notes

We are grateful to Mark Selden, Laura Hein, Richard Minear, Michael W. Apple, and Sylvan Esh for their suggestions and insightful criticisms on the earlier versions of this article.
    1. Yamazumi Masami, *Nihon Kyōiku Shō-shi* (A concise history of Japanese education) (Tokyo: Iwanami Shoten, 1987), 143. The term *kokutai* is often translated as "national polity," but the exact translation of the term is difficult. For further discussion, see Richard Minear, *Japanese Tradition and Western Law: Emperor, State, and Law in the Thought of Hozumi Yatsuka* (Cambridge: Harvard University Press, 1970), 56–83.
    2. Space does not permit us to elaborate on this point, but we would like to remind readers that the actual processes of identity formation through education needs to be understood as complex and flexible. See Raymond Williams, "Base and Superstructure in Marxist Cultural Theory," in *Problems in Materialism and Culture* (London: Verso, 1980), 38–40.
    3. Michael Omi and Howard Winant, *Racial Formation in the United States* (New York: Routledge, 1986), 68.
    4. The Imperial Rescript on Education was in essence the narrative of the imperial nation. See Byron K. Marshall, *Learning to Be Modern: Japanese Political Discourse on Education* (Boulder, Colo.: Westview Press, 1994), 58–62; and Horio Teruhisa, *Educational Thought and Ideology in Modern Japan* (Tokyo: University of Tokyo Press, 1988), 65–72. For presurrender textbook contents, see Nakamura Kikuji, *Kyōkasho no Shakaishi* (A social history of textbooks) (Tokyo: Iwanami Shoten, 1992); Nakauchi Toshio, *Gunkoku Bidan to Kyōkasho* (Fine militarist stories and textbooks) (Tokyo: Iwanami Shoten, 1988); and Ienaga Saburō "The Glorification of War in Japanese Education," *International Security* 18, 3 (Winter 1993/94): 113–22.
    5. See Nakamura, *Kyōkasho no Shakaishi*, 220–21; and Yoko H. Thakur, "History Textbook Reform in Allied Occupied Japan, 1945–52," *History of Education Quarterly* 35, 3 (Fall 1995): 265.
    6. The exception was the case of second-semester elementary school textbooks on the Japanese language, for which exact items (mainly war related) were specified. See Yamazumi, *Nihon Kyōiku Shō-shi*, 148–50. For the translation of a portion of the order,

see John Caiger, "Ienaga Saburō and the First Postwar Japanese History Textbook," *Modern Asian Studies* 3, 1 (1969): 2–3.

7. For further discussion on the blacked-out textbooks, see Nakamura, *Kyōkasho no Shakai shi*, 220–38; and Yamazumi Masami, *Shakaika Kyōiku no Shuppatsu* (The beginning of social studies education) (Tokyo: Nihon Tosho Sentā, 1981), 9–15. The blacked-out textbooks remained in use until July 31, 1946. In 1946 and 1947, the ministry published and distributed stopgap textbooks in certain subjects. For details, see Tokutake Toshio, *Kyōkasho no Sengo shi*, (The postwar history of textbooks) (Tokyo: Shin Nihon Shuppansha, 1995), 44–45; and Kyōiku no Sengoshi Henshū Iinkai (Committee for the Compilation of Postwar Education History), *Sengo Kyōiku Kaikaku to sono Hōkai eno Michi* (The postwar educational reform and the course of its collapse) (Tokyo: San'ichi Shoboī 1986), 131–32.

8. Ienaga Saburō, "The Historical Significance of the Japanese Textbook Lawsuit," *Bulletin of Concerned Asian Scholars* 2, 4 (1970): 8. See also Ienaga Saburō, "Sengo no Rekishi Kyōiku" (Postwar history education), in *Iwanami Kōza Nihon Rekishi* (Iwanami lecture series, Japanese history), vol. 22, *Bekkan* (special volume) 1, (Tokyo: Iwanami Shoten, 1968), 319.

9. From the beginning there was a conflict between SCAP, which thought entirely new history textbooks were necessary, and the ministry, which wanted merely to eliminate militaristic content from existing textbooks. Although Toyoda's text began with archeological findings, which pleased SCAP, it still presented as history the myths of the founding of Japan, which was quite unacceptable to SCAP. Maruyama remained as an author for the new project. See also Thakur, "History Textbook Reform in Allied Occupied Japan," 267–68; and Ienaga, "Sengo no Rekishi Kyōiku," 314–17.

10. Ienaga, "Sengo no Rekishi Kyōiku," 318–19. See also Yamazumi, *Shakaika Kyōiku no Shuppatsu*, 16–18.

11. Ienaga's specialty was ancient Japanese history. His doctoral dissertation was on eighth- to twelfth-century cultural history. According to Ienaga, most of the members were historians of "empirical tradition" (*jisshōshugi*), who were rather apolitical and who had had little experience teaching history in grade schools. See Ienaga, "Sengo no Rekishi Kyōiku," 319. For further discussion on Ienaga and *Kuni no Ayumi*, see Caiger, "Ienaga Saburō"; and Thakur, "History Textbook Reform."

12. The other two state-authored textbooks (written for the higher grades) more explicitly represented the Nanjing massacre as an atrocity committed by the Japanese army.

13. For the criticism, see Thakur, "History Textbook Reform," 270–71; Yamazumi, *Shakaika Kyōiku no Shuppatsu*, 18–19; and Kimijima Kazuhiko, *Kyōkasho no Shisō: Nihon to Kankoku no Kingendai-shi* (Textbook perspectives: modern and contemporary history in Japan and South Korea) (Tokyo: Suzusawa Shoten, 1996), 274–78. The biggest shock for those involved in the history textbook production, however, was the introduction of "social studies" as an integrated subject. The new subject denied the teaching of chronological history and so made the textbooks already developed nearly useless. For details, see Kimijima, *Kyōkasho no Shisō* 280; and Usui Kaichi et al., *Atarashii Chūtō Shakaika eno Izanai* (An invitation to new secondary social studies) (Tokyo: Chirekisha, 1992), 155–62.

14. The fear here was of state control over education—at least in a common interpretation. See Horio, *Educational Thought and Ideology in Modern Japan*, 121.

15. Ibid., 108–29. In fact, the rescript was negated by a Diet resolution in 1948. See also Yamazumi Masami, "Educational Democracy versus State Control," in Gavan McCormack and Sugimoto Yoshio, eds., *Democracy in Contemporary Japan* (Armonk, NY: M.E. Sharpe, Inc., 1986), 95.

16. This situation, which in the ministry's words was to be the case "for the time being," in fact became permanent.

17. The ministry even suggested that each classroom could adopt different textbooks.

See Nakauchi Toshio et al., *Nihon Kyōiku no Sengoshi* (The postwar history of Japanese education) (Tokyo: Sanseidō 1987), 105; and Tokutake, *Kyōkasho no Sengoshi*, 57.

18. Teachers' enthusiasm continued in the following years. See Tokutake, *Kyōkasho no Sengoshi*, 59.

19. See Ienaga Saburō *Kyōkasho Kentei* (Textbook screening) (Tokyo: Nihon Hyōronsha, 1965), 79–81; and Benjamin C. Duke, "The Textbook Controversy," *Japan Quarterly* 19, 3 (July–September 1972).

20. Ikeda Hayato was then the head of the Policy Research Committee of the Liberal Party (Jiyūtō). Walter Robertson was the U.S. assistant secretary of state.

21. According to the brochures, there were four types of "biased" descriptions: those supporting the teachers' labor union and political activities, those stressing the poverty of the Japanese workers and promoting their labor movement, those praising the Soviet Union and the People's Republic of China, and those teaching Communist ideas.

22. Two prominent academics and textbook authors, Hidaka Rokurō and Nagasu Kazuji, publicly denounced the screening and withdrew their contributions to *Akarui Shakai*, a popular social studies textbook for the elementary school level published by Chūkyō Shuppan. Around this time, Tokutake Toshio, an editorial staff member of the publisher, was inspired by Ienaga's talk to explore the possibility of bringing a court case against the screening but gave up the idea. See Kyōkasho Kentei Soshō o Shiensuru Zenkoku Renrakukai (National League for Support of the School Textbook Screening Suit, or NLSTS), ed. *Ienaga Kyōkasho Saiban Jūnenshi* (Ten-year history of Ienaga's textbook screening suit) (Tokyo: Sōdobunka, 1977), 255.

23. Almost all approvals of textbooks around that time were conditional. The ministry also created two categories of comment: "requiring modification" and "suggesting improvement." When rejecting textbooks outright, the ministry issued a brief letter and, upon the author's request, selectively explained the reasons for the rejection. In practice, this approach had the effect of making publishers and authors "self-disciplined" and sometimes caused them to alter their texts even more than the ministry would have requested. See Kyōkasho Kentei Soshō o Shiensuru Zenkoku Renrakukai (NLSTS), ed., "Tokutake Toshio Shōgen" (The testimony by Tokutake Toshio), *Ienaga Kyōkasho Saiban Chisaihen: Daiichiji Soshōhen III* (The record of Ienaga textbook lawsuits at the district court: the first suit, vol. 3) (Tokyo: Rongu Shuppan, 1991), 138–40.

24. More books were rejected in 1958 than any other year except the first, when the screening system began. The Publishing Workers' Union decided to make the rejection reasons public, publishing *Kyōkasho Repōto* (Annual report on textbooks). See Tokutake, *Kyōkasho no Sengoshi*, 103–15. For further discussion on the conservative turn of education, see Yamazumi, "Educational Democracy versus State Control," 95–97.

25. These textbook policies directly affected the elementary and junior high school textbooks, whereas the effect was less drastic in the high school textbooks (to which the free textbook policy was not applied). To date, many high school textbooks whose market share was small, including Ienaga's *Shin Nihonshi*, have been able to survive.

26. An overall, or a partial, revision and screening of textbooks usually took place every three years. The term "a tentative plan" was removed from the titles of the 1955–1956 instruction guidelines, which meant that they were now "requirements" rather than "suggested plans" for instruction. Furthermore, in 1958 the ministry began to claim that the guidelines had legal force.

27. In his first suit, he in fact disputed all the comments given by the ministry (except those requesting correction of simple mistakes, such as typos). It took his counsel more than several years to learn that, although such a strategy had certain merits, a better legal strategy would be to limit their challenge to just several points.

28. For details, see Ienaga "The Historical Significance of the Japanese Textbook Lawsuit," 8–10; Ienaga, "The Glorification of War in Japanese Education," 124–26.

29. For further discussion, see, for example, Ronald. P. Dore, "Textbook Censorship in Japan: The Ienaga Case," *Pacific Affairs* 43 (Winter 1970–71): 548–56.

30. For example, the main reason for the 1963 rejection was "flaws in both accuracy and choice of contents"; the number of "inadequate" items was 323; and the mark was 784. In 1964 the text just scraped through the screening with 73 requests and 217 suggestions.

31. The 1969 edition of the same book included only the statement "[the Japanese army] captured Nanjing."

32. For further discussion, see Mainichi Shinbunsha Kyōiku Shuzaihan, *Kyōkasho Sensō* (Textbook war) (Tokyo: San'ichi Shobō1981), 148–60; Tokutake, *Kyōkasho no Sengoshi*, 186; and Tokutake Toshio, *Kyōkasho Saiban wa Ima* (The current state of the textbook screening) (Tokyo: Azumino Shobō, 1991), 155–70.

33. This version was translated by Saigō Takehiko, a language education scholar. A different version, by Leo Tolstoy, was translated by Uchida Risako. The story has also been popular in the United States. See, for example, *Turnip: An Old Russian Folktale* (New York: Philomel Books, 1990).

34. For details of this party's attack on the textbooks, see Usui et al., *Atarashii Chūtō Shakaika eno Izanai*, 172–75. For further discussion on the textbook controversy of the 1980s, see Mainichi Shinbunsha Kyōiku Shuzaihan, *Kyōkasho Sensō*; and Yamazumi Masami, *Gakkō Kyōkasho* (School textbooks) (Tokyo: Asahi Shinbunsha, 1982).

35. The media reported it as if it were new, even though requests of this kind had been made since the 1960s.

36. Some labor unions and social action groups in Hong Kong sent a letter of complaint to the Japanese embassy; in August the official party newspaper of the Democratic Republic of Korea (North Korea) criticized the Japanese "official view" on this issue, and the Vietnamese government asked the Japanese ambassador to correct textbook remarks concerning that country.

37. The South Korean government essentially accepted the promise at this point. The Chinese government insisted that Miyazawa's word lacked concrete measures, but it eventually accepted the promise after additional explanation by the Japanese government.

38. These were mainly Chinese prisoners of war but also included people from Korea, Mongolia, European countries, and the Soviet Union. See Sheldon H. Harris, *Factories of Death: Japanese Biological Warfare, 1932–45, and the American Cover-up* (London: Routledge, 1994), 49.

39. For details, see Ienaga, "The Glorification of War in Japanese Education," 126–27; and National League for Support of the School Textbook Screening Suit, *Truth in Textbooks, Freedom in Education and Peace for Children: The Struggle Against the Censorship of School Textbooks in Japan*, (Tokyo: NLSTS, 1992), 10–19. Troop Sōmō was very popular with the peasants and played an important role in drawing peasant support for the Meiji government. Peasants felt betrayed when the government executed the members of Troop Sōmō for allegedly fabricating an official announcement about a tax cut that would have benefited peasants.

40. The court did not even notify Ienaga before handing down its ruling, a questionable legal maneuver in and of itself.

41. By this time the existence of Unit 731 had become common knowledge, mainly because of Morimura Seiichi's book *Akuma no Hōshoku* (The devil's gluttony) (Tokyo: Kadokawa Shoten, 1982); the question that concerned the court was whether Ienaga's description, or the ministry's request, was based on scholarly work established by the time of the screening.

42. In fact he won on four of the six points he had changed at the ministry's request. The complete judgment is printed in Kyōkasho Kentei Soshō o Shien-suru Zenkoku Renrakukai (NLSTS), ed., *Kentei ni Ihō Ari: Ienaga Kyōkasho Saiban Saikōsai Hanketsu*

(The screening is found illegal: the Supreme Court decision on Ienaga's textbook lawsuit) (Tokyo: NLSTS, 1997).

43. Immanuel Wallerstein, "The Construction of Peoplehood: Racism, Nationalism, Ethnicity," in Etienne Balibar and Immanuel Wallerstein, *Race, Nation, Class: Ambiguous Identities* (London: Verso, 1991), 78.

44. Patrick Wright, *On Living in an Old Country: The National Past in Contemporary Britain* (London: Verso, 1985), 24–26.

45. Wada Haruki and Ishizaka Kōichi, "Hajime ni" (Introduction), in Wada Haruki, Ishizaka Kōichi, and Sengo Gojū-nen Kokkai Ketsugi o Motomeru Kai (Group for Requesting the Diet Resolution of Japan's War Responsibility), eds., *Nihon wa Shokuminchi-shihai o dō Kangaete Kita ka* (How Japan has thought about its colonial rule) (Tokyo: Nashinokisha, 1996), 1–5.

46. Critical examination is necessary to understand why many Japanese progressives as well as ordinary people "collaborated" with the government in denying war responsibility. One good critical study is Yoshida Yutaka, *Nihonjin no Sensō kan: Sengo-shi no naka no Henyō* (Japanese views on the war: Changes in the postwar history) (Tokyo: Iwanami Shoten, 1995).

47. Ibid., 160–61.

48. Raymond Williams, *Resources of Hope: Culture, Democracy, Socialism* (London: Verso, 1989), 36–38.

49. Todd Gitlin, *The Twilight of Common Dreams: Why America Is Wracked by Culture Wars* (New York: Metropolitan Books, 1995), 23.

5

Identity and Transnationalization in German School Textbooks

Yasemin Nuhoglu Soysal

In recent decades we have observed a significant change in nation-state identities in response to global and regional political reconfigurations. One such case, the European Union (EU), projects a transnational political entity—a union of nations, regions, and localities. What happens to collective identities and citizenship (historically shaped by the boundaries of the nation-state) in a situation in which centrifugal forces are undermining the premise of national collectivities and the national closure of cultures? Postwar changes in the European state system provide ample opportunity to explore the definition and redefinition of collective identities and nationhood through the institution of education.

In this chapter I aim to capture the shifts in nation-state identities, specifically in Germany, as these are represented in school curricula and textbooks.[1] In comparison with the study of nation-state identities in the textbooks of other countries, Germany provides an interesting puzzle. Unlike its Asian counterparts and more so than other European countries, Germany displays a prudence in representations of national identity in its social science textbooks. Rather than asserting national myths and presenting irredentist narratives as the core components of nationhood, the textbooks focus on the representation of a more globalized and diversified world and the place of a relativized German identity in that world. This departure from the traditional representations of national identity should no doubt be understood vis-à-vis the critical juncture of the Holocaust and World War

II. Given its harrowing nationalist and militarist past, Germany had no choice but to anchor its identity within the prospect of an integrated Europe and a transnational context. I contend, however, that there are other decisive factors that we need to take into account in order to understand the puzzle of postwar shifts in German nation-state identity.

I explicate the postwar identity trends as depicted in German textbooks and offer a set of explanatory factors that explain these trends—the disposition of Germany vis-à-vis the European Union, the institutional structure of the school system and textbook production, and the nature of the actors involved in textbook reformation efforts. My focus is on the official representation of identities in textbooks rather than the extent to which the textbooks themselves affect the attitudes or shape the beliefs of individuals. Furthermore, I do not intend to provide a normative assessment of various representations of identity; instead, I deploy the representations analytically to capture the identity reconfigurations in postwar Europe.

Nation and Identity in Public Debates

The controversies over history and the definition of the nation are not absent from the public sphere in Germany. Since unification in 1989, Germany has had its share of efforts to search for national identity, along with debates on how to interpret its history. The unity and nature of the German nation have been called into question over and over again in struggles over memorials and monuments, the reinterpretation of the Nazi past, and the place of the army in the new Germany.

Indeed, the year 1994 witnessed a heightened public debate over identity and history—not coincidentally, since the year was marked by a series of commemorations of the end of World War II. It was also a presidential election year, with immigration, unification, and the future of Germany among the topics on the electoral agenda. Efforts to redefine the German nation and its history and to discern the role of Germany in a unified Europe were strengthened as events unfolded in 1994.

When the conservative presidential candidate Roman Herzog identified himself as a "patriot" in an interview, stating, "Ich liebe dieses deutsche Volk (I love this German nation)," the routine and rather tranquil parliamentary contest for a ceremonial post turned into a matter for "national soul searching and re-examination."[2] Herzog's comments, interpreted as a drift toward German nationalism, generated reactions across a broad spectrum. Although his words found resonance among many, the ensuing debate was not as much about recovering the German nation as it was about defining a new identity for Germany—involving a break from the past and a striving for normalcy as a nation-state and an assuming of European and global responsibilities.[3] Soon after his election, Herzog committed himself to this vision of a new identity, distancing himself from his earlier *völkisches Denken* (ethnic thinking) and recasting his image as the "president of everyone living in Germany"—German or foreigner.[4]

The controversies surrounding the commemorations of World War II were also signs of a desire to make a sharp break with the past and to reconstitute postwar Germany as an equal among the other European nation-states. Anniversary events in the summer of 1994 highlighted the urge to "move forward." At the same time, the fragility of that same desire in the shadow of the Nazi past came to the fore with the opening of a nationwide exhibition on "German resistance" to the Nazi regime, the quest of the German state to be part of the D-day celebrations, the marching of German troops along with the French on Bastille Day as part of the Eurocorps, and President Herzog's official visit to Poland and his apology on the anniversary of the Warsaw uprising.[5] Each of these events, though they reflected the efforts of Germany to reconcile with its neighbors and allies—and recontextualize its national identity—also revealed the strains of trying to come to terms with a difficult past.

Not so inadvertently, the quest to normalize the German nation and identity has coincided with the flaring up of theories and historical accounts that relativize the Nazi past. Since the mid-1980s, conservative reinterpretations of the Holocaust, which reject the uniqueness of the German experience or deny outright the existence of the Holocaust, have found their way into historians' writings. This perspective, however, has been fiercely opposed by humanist and left-oriented historians.[6] Germany's constitutional court itself ruled that the denial of the Holocaust was unconstitutional.[7] Still, a loosely linked group of writers and historians continues to appeal for a more self-assertive German identity and national pride. And history and national identity remain contested issues as Nazi revivals, Holocaust revisionism, and anti-immigrant violence keep surfacing, despite reactions from wide-ranging segments of German society.

Although the contentions over German history and identity play out in the public arena, the school curricula and textbooks appear to be little affected. Rather, the textbooks reflect a consensus over the condemnation of the Nazi past and the exclusion of references to the past glories and power of the German nation. The significant absence of public struggles over textbooks, which is in sharp contrast to the case of Japan (and also the United States), is part of the puzzle that I try to untangle in this chapter. To do so, I suggest that we need to take into consideration (1) the specificities of institutional (corporatist) arrangements in Germany, (2) the agency and involvement of international actors, and (3) the role of the unification process in Europe. It is these variables that underlie the different trajectory of identity definitions in the European context and explain the immunity of textbooks from controversy in Germany.

Nation and Identity in German Textbooks

National textbooks are representative of officially selected, organized, and transmitted knowledge.[8] They are products of contestation and consensus. Thus, they are indispensable to the explication of public representations of national collectivities and identities. My discussion of the emerging nation-state identity and the changes in the public definitions of citizenship in postwar Germany draws upon an analysis of history and civics textbooks for lower secondary schools, which reflect standardized, mass education.

History textbooks have an amplified significance, for history is not only a definition of the past and present but also an attempt to foster continuity in national memory. This memory in turn is the foundation upon which collective identity is constructed and the future is predicated.[9] Thus, historiography debates do have an important role in shaping the collective meanings of identity. My discussion here, however, is confined to the textbooks themselves rather than the debates ushered in by historians to recast collective memory. In analyzing German textbooks, I focus on three dimensions that delineate the boundaries of the nation-state identity:

1. The extent of the Europeanization and globalization of identities presented and the coverage of topics such as progress, environment, and human rights, which have a transnationalizing content.
2. The existence (or nonexistence) of a renewed emphasis on national identities and the nationalizing content of education; the nature of values, ideals, loyalties, and civic duties celebrated; and the degree of the valorization of the nation.
3. The degree to which cultures and histories of ethnic, religious, and regional minorities are incorporated.

First I turn to some of the "identity" trends as represented in textbooks in the light of these three dimensions along with some comparative remarks.

Transnationalizing Content of Education and the Normalization of the National Canon

As Europe becomes a transnational political entity and sovereignty is increasingly shared between the European Union and the individual nation-

5.1 Symbols of nationalism
The signers of the Tripartite Pact: Benito Mussolini, Adolf Hitler, and Konoe Fumimaro,
Japan's Prime Minister in 1940. The graphic originally appeared in a Japanese 1941 children's
picture book on Hitler. Kuboi, *Nihon no shinryaku sensō,* 81. Used by permission.

states, we observe the penetration of a pronounced European dimension into national education. In practice, this means, for example, the teaching of EU languages in schools; the incorporation of "Europe" as a formal subject of study; and a growing emphasis in school curricula on wider European ideals and civic traditions (broadly defined as democratic principles, social justice, and human rights), replacing the nationalist content and the nationalizing mission of education. School curricula in several German states specifically include four dimensions to be dealt with across all (curricular) subjects: environment, gender equality, intercultural education, and the European dimension. Even in Bavaria, among the more conservative states, the topics that deal with Europe, democracy, and human rights have been assigned a high priority along with more regional themes that stress the *heimat* (homeland, as in "my homeland, Bavaria").[10]

Many of the government officials, educators, and the heads of teachers' associations I interviewed shared their perspectives on the increased prominence given to the European dimension in school curricula. One Ministry of Education official stated that the changes in curriculum were made "in response to the technical, economic, and political developments in Germany, Europe, and the whole world." For him, the direction was clear: "You cannot preach a European Union and at the same time continue to produce textbooks with all the national prejudices of the nineteenth century. . . . We must lose our national prejudices; we must change our point of view."[11] Accordingly, the ministry produces supplementary teaching material specifically designed to strengthen the teaching of the European perspective in history and civics lessons.

Similarly, the head of the German History Teachers' Association stressed the need for a shift in approaches to teaching history:

> The aim is more and more to cover what is important for Europe. For example, in teaching about the towns and cities in the Middle Ages, the older textbooks spoke about the German old towns. And we saw expressed in these towns the typical German character. And now we do not study the German character of these towns, but their European character. For example, we have buildings in Poland like buildings in Germany. In former times, the teacher would say, "Ah! You see in Poland there are the same buildings as in Germany, therefore these buildings were built by Germans." Now we say, "In both countries in this period, people built similar buildings." This is a question of perspective. You can teach the same material from a national perspective or from a European perspective. And now, we have, we want to have a European perspective.[12]

The European dimension is being given more prominent space in the textbooks, and it is becoming visually salient.[13] Figures 5.2 and 5.3 sample

5.2 Fourteenth-century map as symbol of "European unity"
This map from Sebastian Muenster's *Cosmographia* of the fourteenth century, reproduced in one German textbook, projects a rather inclusive political embodiment of Europe — from Italy to Denmark and from Spain to Constantinople. Newberry Library. Used by permission.

the depictions of Europeanness and European identity from two different German history textbooks. Figure 5.2 reaches back in history in the form of a fourteenth-century map that projects a rather inclusive Europe—from Italy and Germany to Denmark and from Spain, Gaul and Hungary to Constantinople. The poster that appears in Figure 5.3 orients Europe to the future and to development. Posters that celebrate Europe show member nations as unmistakably embodied in the European Union—and its youth and future.

In these depictions the nation exists in the history and future of Europe, and national identity is subsumed under a unified, supranational Europeanness (but not necessarily Euronationalism). This is not a static, unchangeable definition of the nation, since it implies growth with others. Neither is it an unequal portrayal of the nations—each contributes to a common future and each is equally "fruitful." And not surprising (for Germany), the use of tree as a symbol of the European body resonates with the strong environmentalist emphasis in German education.

As a corollary to the trend toward Europeanization, we also observe a normalization of national canons that glorify discriminatory uniqueness and naturalistic myths. An example of this is the remaking of the Vikings from warrior forefathers to spirited long-distance traders. This is evident in the increasing celebration of the European heritage of the Vikings in history textbooks. Similarly, Germanic tribes in civics textbooks are often depicted in cultural terms through references to village life, hospitality, foodways, and artistic achievements.[14]

Yet another manifestation of this trend toward normalization of national canons is the deliberate attempt to remedy the conflicting national histories of European countries. Several joint commissions are currently working to harmonize the teaching of historical relations between Germany and its various neighbors, including Poland, the Czech Republic, and France. These commissions produce guidelines and proposals for writing textbooks and for generating a common understanding and vocabulary for the teaching of national histories consistent with European ideals. (I return to this point below.)

Emphasis on National Identities

Responses to Europeanization differ from country to country depending on the country's position within the European Union. Germany, with a secure place in the new Europe and a stronger identification with it, is more open to the transnationalization of its educational curricula and the diversification of collective identities. The countries in the old core of Europe—such as Britain and France—have a higher propensity to react to the intrusions of Europe by accentuating their national identities.

For example, the 1988 Education Reform Act in Britain was intended to institutionalize a "national curriculum" with greater emphasis on national history and English literature. The growing presence of the European Union—and a possible loss of British identity and sovereignty—underscored the debates surrounding the act. The installation of a national curriculum is a major step in the case of Britain, given that education has always been locally organized and the country has never had a nationally designed curriculum. Not surprising, in the new curriculum British history is front and center—accounting for 75 percent of the time allocated

5.3 Organic unified Europe
In this poster, the history textbook celebrates the European Union as the embodiment of member nations and their future. *Geschichte* (History), vol. 4 (Bayerischer Schulbuchverlag, 1986), 202–03. Used by permission.

to history teaching. This percentage is extremely high compared to Germany, where the European dimension and world history share relatively equal curricular time with national history. In Lower Saxony, for instance, the history curriculum for the first year of secondary school allocates 39.9 percent of teaching time to national history as compared to 49.8 percent reserved for European themes and 10.5 percent for non-European civilizations.[15]

No doubt German history books have the customary narratives of the origins, historical progress, and consolidation of the nation, from the Romans and Greeks and Christian Middle Ages to the coming of age of the nation-state. In comparison with textbooks in other European countries, however, contemporary history in German textbooks is given a more prominent place. Ancient and medieval history is relatively marginalized in comparison with coverage of the Weimar Republic, the Nazi period, and the Cold War. For example, one popular secondary school history textbook, *Die Reise in die Vergangenheit* (Travels in the past), reserves three volumes out of six for the history of the nineteenth and twentieth centuries, with separate volumes devoted to the Weimar and Nazi periods and to postwar world history. In *Zeiten und Menschen* (Times and people), another popular textbook, half of the total 237 pages covering twentieth-century history, are devoted to the study of World War II, beginning with the "crisis of the Weimar Republic." This is not coincidental. In all German states, curricula guidelines require extensive teaching of contemporary German history from Weimar on. This disproportionate attention to contemporary history, given its contentious nature, makes it difficult to extol the German nation and people [Volk] through celebratory narratives.

The Incorporation of Minority/Regional Cultures and Languages into National Curricula and Textbooks

By breaching the link between the status attached to citizenship and national territory, the European Union creates a legitimate ground for various subnational groups to make claims for their cultural and linguistic identities within national education systems. More and more societal groups (immigrant organizations, regional movements, religious groups) are mobilizing around demands for inclusion into the definitions and institutions of national education. Since 1983, for example, organizations advocating the use of languages such as Cornish, Sardinian, and Occitan have been working through the European Bureau for the Lesser-used Languages.[16] In the 1990s, various European states, even those which had long resisted linguistic and cultural diversity, as in the cases of France, Italy, and Spain, have passed legislation accommodating and supporting the use of regional languages in schools.

In Germany many local states require "intercultural education" as a part of their curricula. In history textbooks interculturalism has found its way into the teaching about Islamic civilizations. More and more, for instance, chronological accounts are giving way to narratives that depict Islam as a "culture" and a "way of life." Unlike the coverage of Christianity in German textbooks, the chapters on Islam invariably include everyday-life pictures of mosques, prayers, and marketplaces. In civics textbooks interculturalism commonly finds expression in the introduction of the *ausländer* (foreigner) under the thematic title of *Miteinander Leben* (living with each other).

Figure 5.4 is a typical depiction of "us and "others," a class photo from a middle school in Hannover, showing pupils from different countries.

5.4 German interculturalism
This class photo from a middle school in Hannover, Germany, makes a special point of
identifying pupils who came from different countries, simultaneously celebrating "intercultural education" and relativizing German ethnic and national identities. Another textbook version of the photo identifies immigrants by first name and country. *Welt und
Umweltkunde (World and environmental science)* (Braunschweig, Germany: Westerman,
1993), 156. Photo by Barbara Schmidt-Vogt. Used by permission.

The explanation that accompanies the photo introduces the "virtual German student body" to Zerrin, daughter of a Turkish guestworker. Through
Zerrin's visit to the village of her parents in Turkey during the summer
holiday, students learn about Turkish culture, traditions, and village life. Back
in school after the holidays, Zerrin meets another *ausländische Mitschuler*
(foreign classmate), Esra, daughter of a Kurdish refugee from Turkey.
Zerrin learns about the Kurds, their history, traditions, and oppression in
Turkey. (The text implies that Zerrin is learning about the Kurds for the
first time, because discussion of this subject is forbidden back in Turkey.)
So Zerrin meets her "Other" as well. But the chapter does not end there.
After the spring break, a new student arrives in class from yet another
land, Poland. Stefan is introduced to the class as the new German student. To
Zerrin's surprise, however, he speaks very little German. With the introduc-

tion of Stefan, son of an *Aussiedler* (ethnic German repatriate), the picture of Hannover as a multicultural society becomes complete.

The identities presented in this textbook narrative are particular and differentiated along ethnic lines. Pupils of German, Turkish, Kurdish, and *Aussiedler* origin fill the classrooms (the microgeographies of Germany); recognize their differences; and learn about and from each other. The German nation, "us," becomes meaningful together with its others (Turks), and even with their others (Kurds and *Aussiedler*). Hence, the German identity is relativized as one among many ethnic and cultural identities.

The representation of the "Other" in this identity trajectory is rather a positive one, underlining the principles of plurality and harmony and marking a break from an unbefitting past. In this new trajectory, the threat to us (the German nation) no longer emanates from an exogenous Other (the barbaric Turk or some other foreign culture) but from an indigenous one that violates the democratic order and jeopardizes the standing of Germany in international arenas. This indigenous Other materializes in textbooks as the Neo-Nazi youth, who invariably appears as the natural, present-day extension of the Nazi past.

The dangers posed by the Neo-Nazis are taught through extensive and negative coverage of the Nazi history as a time of violence, persecution, death, and destruction. And not coincidentally, in civics textbooks the sections on *Neonazis heute* (Neo-Nazis today) follow the visual and narrative denunciations of Nazi times and explicitly connect Neo-Nazis to National Socialism through comparisons of ideology, activities, and propaganda.[17]

In one of the civics textbooks, the students are asked to describe and search for similarities between the picture of a Neo-Nazi gathering from 1990 (uniformed youth in a forest area with flags, drums, and a campfire) and one of Hitler Youth from 1934 (assembled in a campsite in military style).[18] In another textbook the section on current Neo-Nazi propaganda against foreigners warns students that similar propaganda existed before 1933 and that is "how it all started, leading from hateful speech and race talk to war and extermination camps."[19]

Narratives of suffering and tragedy also connect the Neo-Nazi youth to the Nazi past. The verbal and physical attacks suffered in school by Nina and Sergül (a black and a Turkish student) in the 1990s are juxtaposed against the experiences of Hanna and Peter (two Jewish students) in 1933. The students are asked to think about Hanna and Peter when recounting how Nina and Sergül may have felt.[20] Similarly, a wall painted with swastikas and Neo-Nazi graffiti—"Deutschland den Deutschen" (Germany for Germans) and "Türken Rauss"—(Turks Out)—recalls a

Nazi sign from 1938 that prohibited Jews from entering a neighborhood.[21] Through references to these lessons of the past, civics textbooks emphasize how necessary it is today to understand the "other" and have solidarity with them as fellow human beings.

Explaining the Postwar Trends in German Textbooks

The identity trends to which I referred in the previous section point to the three distinct ways of conceptualizing identities: European/transnational, national, and ethnic/community-based. These identity positions are generally set against one another and generate much heated debate in popular and scholarly circles. When conceptualizing identities and engaging in political action, people discuss globalization in opposition to localisms and set nationalisms against regionalisms. I argue, however, that such strict dichotomizing is not productive, either theoretically or empirically. My research on textbooks reveals that different identity positions coexist in postwar Europe, not necessarily opposing or replacing one another. More often than not, they are interpreted by each other, and redefined in the process.

German textbooks situate the nation and identity within a transnational context. As such, the German case does not fit a conventional perspective that poses a conflict between the national and transnational. In the case of Germany, national identity is explicated and recast by the transnational. This sets Germany apart from the cases of Japan, South Korea, and China, in which the national dimension still plays a visibly larger role in matters of defining identities through education.

I offer three explanatory factors to account for the dominance of the transnational dimension in German textbooks. The first of these factors has to do with the distinct identity position of Germany vis-à-vis the international community in the postwar period. The other two concern the institutional structure of education and the nature of actors involved in the production of textbooks and curricula.

The international arena provides "collective expectations and norms" for the proper behavior of states as actors, as studies by John Meyer and Peter Katzenstein have shown.[22] Hence, the nature of the international community in which the countries are immersed has an important role to play in shaping nation-state identities. After World War II, while Germany has followed the course of European integration (economic and political) as a possible way to deal with its defeat and regain national sovereignty, Japan's approach has been to focus on economic security and competition with the United States.[23] As Japan's nation-state identity has taken shape vis-à-vis the United States, both on economic and sym-

**5.5 German soldiers and prisoners during the destruction
of the Warsaw ghetto**
German texts dedicate substantial sections to self-critical discussion of World War II,
presenting the war as the cause of European mistrust of Germany, created by actions
like this arrest of Poles during the destruction of the Warsaw ghetto. NARA, NWDNS-
238–NT-288, War and Conflict no. 1124.

bolic grounds—and mainly in an oppositional configuration—German
nation-state identity has evolved within the unifying project of Europe.

As Katzenstein notes, in the process of integrating with Europe and
East Germany, "Germans have eliminated the concept of 'power' from
their political vocabulary. They speak the language of 'political responsibility' instead."[24] Symbolic and vociferous manifestations of identity
struggles in Europe are still apparent; for example, during the European
Cup matches or in the case of Britain's insistence on serving beef during
a European Summit at the height of the mad cow disease crisis. However,
the integration process itself and the institutional framework for the process facilitate denationalization by creating normative expectations of
equal and tamed nation-states. The dichotomy between transnational and
national does not appear natural in the context of European unification,
for the member states have to prove themselves as proper players within
tightly interlinked transnational security arrangements. In Asia, in con-

trast, internal and external security are the domain of national governments, and so national boundaries and identities are more salient.[25]

This difference in international dispositions is clearly reflected in the identity definitions and markings of boundary in textbooks. Embedded as it is in a larger unifying project, Germany has felt considerable outside pressure to adopt a collaborative attitude in the negotiation of its identity and relationship with its neighbors. Japan has managed to shield itself from such pressures and has resisted the demands of its neighbors to collaborate in rewriting the history of World War II in Asia. As recently as August 1997, the Japanese government rejected proposals by South Korea for a joint history textbook commission with Japan, Germany, Poland, and South Korea.[26]

Another explanatory factor I would like to highlight is the peculiarity of the institutional structure of the German educational system. In Germany a tight network exists among the state, the academy, school systems, and the publishing industry, mediated by a set of corporatist institutional arrangements.[27] The close connection between educational authorities and other interest associations—business associations; teachers' unions; teachers' associations of geography, history, and social studies; parents' associations; churches; and universities—creates a basis and a strong incentive for consensus in developing curricula and producing textbooks.

Germany's federalist system delegates control over educational matters to the local states, where curriculum matters are the responsibility of the Ministry of Education. Curricula are reviewed and revised every ten years by a committee that consists of representatives from the ministry, teachers' unions, teachers, and academics. Together they set up the themes, the content of the subjects to be taught, pedagogical guidelines, and the goals and extent of the curriculum. The curriculum is widely circulated among a variety of interested parties for commentary and suggestions. In Lower Saxony, for example, the draft curricula are sent to 400 associations, institutions, and universities throughout Germany for comments and feedback.[28]

Teachers and academics who serve on the curriculum committees are usually commissioned by publishing companies to write and revise textbooks. Approval of the textbooks for use in state schools is the responsibility of the state's ministry of education.[29] Germany's tight corporatist and consensus-oriented arrangement contrasts starkly with the state-centric textbook production and curriculum development in Japan and South Korea.[30]

The existence of corporatist arrangements in the production of curricula and textbooks does not necessarily imply the absence of conflict in Germany. In the aftermath of unification, sex and religious education in particular have been major areas of contention. This is due in part to the merger of two ideologically very different education and institutional systems and also to the increasing visibility of religious diversity in Germany. The German constitution allows denominational religious instruction in schools, the content of which has to be approved by the churches (Protestant and Catholic). Although not to the same extent, both Jewish and Muslim communities are also consulted in matters related to religious education. Religious minority students (Jewish and Muslim) are usually exempted from these classes. The extension of religious education to the new states in the east has created considerable strains over the nature and content of religious education and the place of religion in schools. Many new states, as well as some from the west, offer "values and ethics" instruction, where the emphasis is on teaching world religions (including Judaism, Islam, Hinduism, and Confucianism) in lieu of religious teaching.[31]

The major conflict over national curriculum, however, arose in the late 1960s in West Germany, when the state of Hessen altered its educational system in a rather revolutionary manner—in terms of both organization (introduction of comprehensive schools as an alternative to the stratified system) and content. One of the major actors behind the Hessen reforms was the Young Socialist Student Union, which pushed for open discussion of the Nazi period, a greater emphasis on contemporary German history, and equal access to higher education. The inspiration for these revisions came from the postwar reeducation program initiated by the U.S. occupation forces in Germany, who founded the first comprehensive school and introduced the study of Nazi Germany as a compulsory subject.[32]

The Hessen reforms were eventually taken up by other German states, and by the end of the 1960s there emerged a consensus among political parties for a need to reform the whole education system. One consequence of these reforms was democratization and inclusion of a wider spectrum of interest groups in the decisionmaking process. This led to the current institutional basis for consensus. Another consequence of these reforms was the incorporation of Germany's Nazi past into the curricula and the devalorization of the "national" in education about German identity. The current curricula and textbooks still carry the imprint of the normative principles and institutional framework established at the time of the educational reforms of the late 1960s.

One has to take into consideration the difference in the nature of actors involved in the postwar efforts to normalize history teaching in Germany and Japan. Whereas in Japan the government has had much more direct control over these efforts, in Germany the bodies and organizations that have been particularly active are mostly nongovernmental, both inter- and transnational.

In Europe international attempts to reexamine and revise textbooks go back to the interwar period. The national and international committees set up by the League of Nations, in cooperation with teachers' associations in different countries, sought to eliminate national prejudices and stereotypes from textbooks. In the 1930s, bilateral consultations were already in place between German and French and German and Polish historians. With the foundation of UNESCO and the Council of Europe after World War II, however, these efforts gained a more institutional basis. Especially effective was the German Commission for UNESCO, whose activities culminated in the foundation of the Georg Eckert Institute for International Textbook Research in 1951. Assisted by UNESCO and the Council of Europe, the institute has facilitated several international collaborative projects and promoted the exchange of history and geography textbooks between countries.[33] Joint commissions between Germany and France, Poland, and Israel have produced recommendations for normalizing contentious histories and bringing about a rapprochement among "former enemies."[34] With the goal of "integrating national units [in]to international ones," the institute has been focusing on the teaching of Europe, environmental education, human rights, and multicultural society—themes that are supported by UNESCO and the Council of Europe and integrated into the curricula in many German states.

Education is a priority of member states in the European Union. An advisory committee of national administrators exists at the European level, but education is still a battleground for sovereignty. There are no formal European Community directives, and education as a policy area is only marginally incorporated into the Maastricht treaty.[35] Nevertheless, over the years, the European Union has established several educational programs, most of which deal with issues of vocational education, harmonization of credentials, student exchange, and the incorporation of the European dimension and heritage into national curricula. More important, numerous groups, committees, professional associations, and advocacy organizations for regional languages—loosely associated and funded by the EU—have been extremely active in the forging of European education and standards. Experts and academic specialists conduct studies on behalf of the European Union and give advice on technical as well as substantive aspects. They supply and translate curricula, form teams to evaluate national education systems, and compare and rank member-state education systems by performance and achievement.

5.6 Liberated orphan
This six-year-old war orphan waits for his name to be called at Buchenwald camp, for departure to Switzerland. In 1945 the only future imaginable for the few children who survived the camps was to leave Germany. This is the legacy that "intercultural" educators hope to overcome. NARA, NWDNS-111–SC-208199, War and Conflict no. 1109.

Thus, the rather less-structured and less-formalized nature of education as European Union policy field (unlike the situation for monetary,
economic, and security issues) provides an opportunity for various groups
to seize initiative and create networks outside the strict intergovernmen-
tal negotiation structures.

The European Standing Conference of History Teachers Associations
(EUROCLIO) and the European Academy are two among many organizations that have done just that. EUROCLIO, in existence since 1993, aims to
"[eliminate] prejudice in the teaching of history by emphasizing positive
mutual influences between countries, religions, and ideas in the historical
development of Europe . . . and [ensuring] that national history does not
become nationalist history . . . and include a genuine pan-European dimension."[36] The European Academy was founded in Berlin by "concerned
Europeanists" (party members, heads of trade unions, business representatives, academics) in the early days of the Europeanization movement in the
1960s and 1970s. The activities of the academy are funded by German
federal institutions, the Berlin government, and the European Union. Both
of these organizations run periodic, practice-oriented conferences that bring
together teachers, textbook authors, and curriculum experts from various
countries.[37] They also produce what is referred to as "gray literature," covering topics not necessarily included in textbooks but required as part of the
curriculum. These complementary materials find wide distribution among
teachers.[38] All these activities extend European networks, both organiza-
tionally and symbolically, and facilitate a climate of Europeanness and the
reconsideration of national canons in education.

National approaches come to the fore quite regularly in international
collaborative efforts. Historically embedded pedagogical and institutional
differences prove to be the main barriers to the realization of a unified
European education. Nevertheless, ideas diffuse and educational norms
evolve, and these expedite standardization at the national level in terms
of both teaching technologies and subjects covered.

Conclusion

We think of textbooks singularly as tools for teaching national priorities and building unified national communities. We have seen in the
case of Germany, however, that textbooks promote not only national
but increasingly local and transnational identities and responsibilities. In contrast to dominant conceptualizations, national, local, and
transnational identities do not appear to be exclusionary.

The increasing pronouncement of local/ethnic and transnational identities does not necessarily result in the displacement of national identity. On the contrary, in the process of teaching and expressing identities, the nation is being reinterpreted and recast anew. What we are accustomed to thinking and teaching as national culture—the typical civic values: democracy, progress, human rights, equality—become part of the transnational and define Europeanness. Concurrently, transnational institutions (UNESCO, the Council of Europe, and the European Union) legitimate the proliferation of ethnic, religious, and regional identities by upholding the principle of the right of each people to its own culture and sovereignty. Hence, we all have our particularistic identities and cultures to be proud of and to secure and celebrate. The nation loses its singularity as the principle of identity. In the process, national identities become more and more rationalized across nation-states as equally valid identity positions and comparable cultural heritages, undermining mythical geneses and naturalistic canonizations.

In Germany and Europe, as in other parts of the world, the questions of history and identity in education are periodically revisited and contested. However, the corporatist institutional structure of the German textbook production system and, more important, Germany's disposition within the European Union and vis-à-vis European integration have led to the relative insulation of textbooks from ongoing public struggles over national history and identity. German textbooks are the product of complex and wide-ranging consultations and negotiations within Germany and between Germany and its neighbors. As Europe expands, national and European actors and networks involved in this process multiply and textbooks become a matter of growing transnational action.

The postwar evolution of German textbooks and curricula illustrates the changing context and meaning of identity in a world where the national is increasingly subjected to reinterpretation by the transnational. In that respect, European integration provides a unique opportunity to sharpen our analytical and conceptual tools as we scrutinize the relationship between textbooks and emerging nation-state identities.

Notes

1. This chapter draws upon my current project, which explores the emerging forms of claims-making and mobilization by minority and regional groups on national education and investigates the changes in nation-state identities through a comparative analysis of history and civic textbooks in postwar Europe. The data for the project come from national textbooks and public school curricula for lower secondary schools in four Euro-

pean countries (Germany, France, Britain, and The Netherlands). I sample the history and civics textbooks and curricula in these countries from three time points, the 1950s, 1970s, and 1990s, when major educational reforms took place. I also examine public debates, conflicting claims, and court cases that surround national education systems and national curricula, as well as the incorporation of minority cultural/religious provisions into public education systems. I make use of interviews I conducted with officials from state educational boards and ministries, school authorities, teachers' and parents' associations, the representatives of European and national-level associations and networks on textbook and curricular study, and with the leaders of immigrant organizations and regional movements.

2. Interview with Roman Herzog, *Focus*, May 9, 1994, 20–25.

3. See the interviews with Johannes Rau, the presidential candidate for the Social Democrats (*Die Zeit*, May 6, 1994); Hildegard Hamm-Brücher, the candidate for the Liberal Democratic Party (*Die Zeit*, May 13, 1994); and Hans Otto Bräutigam, the justice minister of the state of Brandenburg (*Frankfurter Rundschau*, May 10, 1994). Also see the statements by Rita Süssmuth, the president of the parliament from the Christian Democratic Party, and Richard von Weizsäcker, the outgoing president (*Der Tagesspiegel*, July 2, 1994).

4. After being elected, Herzog paid a symbolic visit to the Turkish community, and presented a "medal of honor" to the mother of Turkish children who were burned to death when Neo-Nazis set fire to their house in Sollingen.

5. For the portrayal of these controversies in the German press, see "Keine Ruhe vor der Geschichte" (No rest from history), *Der Tagesspiegel*, July 20, 1994; "Das Band der Sippenhaft: 50 Jahre nach dem Hitler-Attentat vom 20. Juli 1944, der Streit um den richtigen Widerstand" (The bond of kinship: 50 years after the attempt on Hitler's life, July 20, 1944, the conflict over proper resistance), *Süddeutsche Zeitung*, August 2, 1994; "Es lebe das freie Polen! Gedenken an den Aufstand" (Let free Poland live! Thoughts on the uprising), *Frankfurter Allgemeine Zeitung*, August 2, 1994; and "Herzog bittet um Vergebung für Deutsche Verbrechen und bietet den Polen Deutschlands Freundschaft an" (Herzog asks forgiveness for German crimes and offers the Poles Germany's friendship), *Süddeutsche Zeitung*, August 2, 1994.

6. Daniel Levy, "The Future of the Past: Comparing Historians' Disputes in Germany and Israel," paper presented at the annual meeting of the Social Science History Association, New Orleans, November 1996.

7. The Constitutional Court, deciding on a freedom of speech case brought by the extreme right National Democratic Party (NDP), argued that "to deny that Jews died in Nazi camps was to deny a fact, and that the severity of the insult to the Jewish Community meant the right of free speech did not apply." The case concerned the banning of a talk by David Irving (a British revisionist historian) at an NDP congress (*International Herald Tribune*, April 27, 1994).

8. See M. Young, ed., *Knowledge and Control* (London: Collier Macmillan, 1971); Ivor Goodson, *The Making of Curriculum: Essays in the Social History of Schooling* (London: Falmer Press, 1987); Ivor Goodson, ed., *International Perspectives in Curriculum History* (London: Falmer Press, 1987); John W. Meyer et al., *School Knowledge for the Masses: World Models and National Primary Curricular Categories in the Twentieth Century* (Washington, DC: Falmer Press, 1992).

9. Charles Maier, *The Unmasterable Past: History, Holocaust, and German National Identity* (Cambridge: Harvard University Press, 1988); Levy, "The Future of the Past."

10. A 1991 circular from the ministry of education in Bavaria states that "the European dimension should be introduced into all subjects" and "pupils should become aware of Europe's intellectual and cultural heritage and of common European values such as democracy and human rights" (Council of Europe, Education Newsletter, 4, Strasbourg, 1991).

11. Interview with the official responsible for curriculum in the ministry of education in Lower Saxony, November 23, 1995.

12. Interview with the head of the German History Teachers' Association, Jacobson-Gymnasium, Seelen, November 30, 1995.

13. Falk Pingel, ed., *Macht Europa Schule? Die Darstellung Europas in Schulbüchern der Europäischen Gemeinschaft* (Power of European schools? Representation of Europe in textbooks in the European Union countries), Schriftenreiche des Georg-Eckert-Instituts, vol. 84 (Frankfurt: Verlag Moritz Diesterweg, 1995).

14. See, for example, *Welt- und Umweltkunde 5/6, Niedersachsen* (World and environment science 5/6) (Braunschweig, Germany: Westermann, 1993), 138–53, and *Menschen, Zeiten, Räume 5/6 Arbeitsbuch für Welt- und Umweltkunde in der Orientierungsstufe* (People, times, places: Workbook for world and environment science for junior high 5/6) (Berlin: Cornelsen Verlag, 1993), 188–231. Following the chapter on Romans and Germans, both books present the "culture" and the "village life" of Turkish migrants and Native Americans, expressively equating all three peoples across time and space.

15. Karl-Ernst Jeismann and Bernd Schönemann, *Geschichte amtlich: Lehrpläne und Richtlinien der Bundesländer* (Institutional history: curricula and instruction guides in federal states), Schriftenreiche des Georg-Eckert-Instituts, vol. 65 (Frankfurt: Verlag Moritz Diesterweg, 1989),75.

16. The European Bureau for the Lesser-used Languages is directly financed by the European Union and has the goal of protecting fifty minority languages in the member states of the EU.

17. *Welt- und Umweltkunde 5/6*, 226–29; *Menschen, Zeiten, Räume 5/6*, 272–75.

18. *Menschen, Zeiten, Räume*, 160, 272.

19. *Welt- und Umweltkunde*, 226.

20. *Menschen, Zeiten, Räume*, 266, 274.

21. Ibid.

22. John W. Meyer, "The World Polity and the Authority of the Nation-State," in A. Bergesen, ed., *Studies of the Modern World-System* (New York: Academic Press, 1980); Peter J. Katzenstein, ed., *The Culture of National Security: Norms and Identity in World Politics* (New York: Columbia University Press, 1996).

23. Peter J. Katzenstein and Nobuo Okawara, "Japan's National Security: Structures, Norms, and Policies," *International Security* 17 (1993): 84–118.

24. Peter J. Katzenstein, ed., *Tamed Power: Germany in Europe* (Ithaca, NY: Cornell University Press, 1997), 116.

25. Peter J. Katzenstein, *Cultural Norms and National Security: Police and Military in Postwar Japan* (Ithaca, NY: Cornell University Press, 1996).

26. Reiner Drifte, "Is the Mombusho Running One of Japan's Most Sensitive Bilateral Relationships?" Article distributed through SSJ-Forum, Institute of Social Science, University of Tokyo (ssjmod@shaken.iss.u-tokyo.ac.jp), August 15, 1997.

27. Peter J. Katzenstein, *Policy and Politics in West Germany: The Growth of a Semisovereign State* (Philadelphia: Temple University Press, 1987); Yasemin Nuhoglu Soysal, *Limits of Citizenship: Migrants and Postnational Membership in Europe* (Chicago: University of Chicago Press, 1994).

28. Interview with the official responsible for curriculum in the ministry of education in Lower Saxony (November 23, 1995).

29. Each ministry publishes a list of generally four or five textbooks that conform with the established curricular norms and requirements. The schools have the option of selecting books from this list.

30. In Japan the government authorizes textbooks to be used and has a right to censor "undesirable" content, as exemplified in the recent controversy over the treatment of Japa-

nese war crimes in history textbooks. In South Korea, the textbooks are issued by the state itself.

31. For the controversy over "values and ethics" instruction in the state of Brandenburg, see Achim Leschinsky, *Vorleben oder Nachdenken? Bericht der wissenschaftlichen Begleitung über den Modellversuch zum Lernbereich "Lebensgestaltung-Ethik-Religion"* [Anticipation or retrospect? Report on the scholarly debates accompanying the search for models in teaching the "lifestyle, ethic, and religion" course] (Frankfurt: Verlag Moritz Diesterweg, 1996).

32. Interview with Professor Ingrid Haller, University of Kassel. Haller was a key figure in the conceptualization and implementation of Hessen reforms.

33. Like many German institutions, the Georg Eckert Institute has a public standing and is sponsored by the local states. The governing board includes representatives from the states, the Foreign Office, the Federal Ministry of Education and Science, the German Commission for UNESCO, as well as independent scholars. The foundation act of the Institute aims to submit recommendations for making "more objective" the historical, political, and geographic representations of Germany and other countries in textbooks; to organize international meetings of experts for examining and revising textbooks; and to advise authors and publishers of textbooks.

34. The recommendations include the "German-French Agreement on Controversial Problems of European History" (1951), the "Recommendations for Textbooks of History and Geography of the Federal Republic of Germany and People's Republic of Poland" (a product of the German-Polish Commission on textbooks, which has been in place since 1972), and the "German-Israeli Textbook Recommendations" (1985). Also, since 1981 the French-German Commission has been working on recommendations for the treatment of the Weimar Republic, National Socialism, and the Vichy regime. The recommendations of the joint commissions have been substantially incorporated into the curricula and textbooks in the respective countries (interviews with experts and researchers at the Georg Eckert Institute, Braunschweig, November 1995).

35. The Maastricht treaty was signed in 1991, creating the European Union out of the European Community. The treaty was a comprehensive agreement designed to regulate the transition of Europe into a union with a common currency and without internal borders. The treaty dealt primarily with economic issues, but it also emphasized the commitments of EU member states to "humanitarian traditions" of Europe and created the status of the citizen of the Union, leading the way beyond nation-state citizenship to European citizenship.

36. *EUROCLIO Bulletin*, 5 (1996): 15.

37. Many of the participants of EUROCLIO conferences are practicing teachers, active in their national associations. In 1994 about ninety history teachers were involved in a year-long project to discuss the "theoretical and practical aspects of encouraging democratic values through history education." In 1995, working with the Council of Europe, EUROCLIO organized the conference, "Philip II and His Times," a prominent and controversial personality in European history, with the goal of comparing varied interpretations and methods of teaching. Similar conferences have been held with the former Soviet republics (Latvia, Lithuania, and Russia) to reform history teaching and others to deal with the question of representing women, ethnic minorities, and human rights in textbooks.

38. The European Academy, for instance, is the publisher of two of the most widely used single examples of gray literature on Europe: Günter Renner and Peter Czada, *Vom Binnenmarkt zur Europäischen Union* (From market to European Union) and *Euro and Cent: Europäische Integration und Währungsunion* (Euro and cent: European integration and monetary union).

6

The Vietnam War in High School American History

James W. Loewen

American history is the least-liked subject in high school. Research shows that it is also the most dependent on textbooks. The latter is an astounding fact. Surely plane geometry, say, offers less opportunity to use books from the library, interview members of the community, or explore on the Internet. Many high school history teachers don't know much history: a national survey of 257 teachers in 1990 revealed that 13 percent had never had a single college history course, and only 40 percent had a B.A. or M.A. in history or had a major with "some history" in it. Unprepared teachers are not likely to encourage students to go beyond the textbook, because the textbook is all the history they know. According to educational researcher Seymour B. Sarason, teachers rarely say "I don't know" in class and rarely discuss how one would then find out. "I don't know" violates a norm. The teacher, like the textbook, is *supposed* to know. Teachers can end up afraid not to be in control of the answer, afraid of losing their authority over the class. To avoid exposing gaps in their knowledge, too many teachers hide behind the textbooks, allowing their students to make "very little use of the school's extensive resources," according to Linda McNeil, who completed three studies of high school social studies classes between 1975 and 1981.[1]

Moreover, most teachers do not like controversy: a study some years ago found that 92 percent said they didn't initiate discussions of controversial issues, 89 percent didn't discuss controversial issues when students brought them up, and 79 percent didn't believe they should. Among the topics that teachers felt students were interested in discussing but that most teachers believed should not be discussed in the classroom were politics, race relations, and the Vietnam War.[2]

Accordingly, to learn what high school students are taught about the Vietnam War, it is appropriate to start with their textbooks. Unfortunately, textbooks in American history stand in sharp contrast to the educational materials used in the rest of our schooling. Their contents are muddled by conflicting desires to promote inquiry and indoctrinate nationalism. Publishers stress nationalism in their advertisements for these books; Houghton Mifflin, for example, brags that its book provides "major emphasis on America's heroes, America's citizens, and the nation's achievements," so it "instills pride in America's heritage." "Take a look in your history book, and you'll see why we should be proud," goes an anthem often sung by high school glee clubs. But we need not even take a look inside. The difference begins with some of their titles: *The Great Republic*, *The Great Experiment*, *The American Way*, *Land of the Free*, *Land of Promise*, *Rise of the American Nation*.[3] Such titles differ from those of textbooks in all other fields. Chemistry books are called *Chemistry* or *Principles of Chemistry*, not *Rise of the Molecule*. Even literature collections are likely to be titled *Readings in American Literature*. And you *can* tell these history books from their covers, graced with American flags, eagles, and the Statue of Liberty.

How do these textbooks handle the Vietnam War, given that publishers like to place "major emphasis on the nation's achievements"?

Textbooks Examined

In 1995 I published *Lies My Teacher Told Me: Everything Your American History Textbook Got Wrong* (New York: New Press, 1995), based on close reading of twelve high school American history textbooks. They were:

- Thomas A. Bailey and David M. Kennedy, *The American Pageant* (Lexington, MA: D.C. Heath, 1991)
- Nancy Bauer, *The American Way* (New York: Holt, Rinehart and Winston, 1979)
- Carol Berkin and Leonard Wood, *Land of Promise* (Glenview, IL: Scott, Foresman, 1983)
- James West Davidson and Mark H. Lytle, *The United States—A History of the Republic* (Englewood Cliffs, NJ: Prentice-Hall, 1981)

- John A. Garraty, with Aaron Singer and Michael Gallagher, *American History* (New York: Harcourt Brace Jovanovich, 1982)
- Robert Green, Laura L. Becker, and Robert E. Coviello, *The American Tradition* (Columbus, OH: Merrill, 1984)
- Allan O. Kownslar and Donald B. Frizzle, *Discovering American History* (New York: Holt, Rinehart and Winston, 1974)
- Ira Peck, Steven Jantzen, and Daniel Rosen, *American Adventures* (Austin: Steck-Vaughn, 1987)
- Philip Roden, Robynn Greer, Bruce Kraig, and Betty Bivins, *Life and Liberty* (Glenview, IL: Scott, Foresman, 1984)
- Robert Sobel, Roger LaRaus, Linda Ann De Leon, and Harry P. Morris, *The Challenge of Freedom* (River Forest, IL.: Laidlaw, 1982)
- Social Science Staff of the Educational Research Council of America, *The American Adventure* (Boston: Allyn and Bacon, 1975); and
- Paul Lewis Todd and Merle Curti, *Triumph of the American Nation* (formerly *Rise of the American Nation*) (Orlando: Harcourt Brace Jovanovich, 1986 and numerous earlier editions.)

Ten of these textbooks were the usual narrative kind. *Discovering American History* and *The American Adventure* were "inquiry texts"—books that included primary documents and got students to advance the narrative by asking questions of them. Inquiry texts were part of a reform movement called "the new social studies" that rose in the 1970s and has since sunk, pretty much without a trace. To include inquiry texts I had to use books from 1974 and 1975.

Critics of *Lies My Teacher Told Me* have pointed out that the textbooks reviewed there date from 1991 back to 1974. Although they acknowledge my appraisal (and not just on Vietnam), some critics claim that newer textbooks have improved. To test their optimism, I examined four new high school history textbooks:

- the 1990 edition of *Triumph of the American Nation*, the best-selling textbook between 1965 and 1990
- the 1994 edition of *The American Pageant*
- Daniel J. Boorstin and Brooks Mather Kelley, *A History of the United States* (Needham, MA: Prentice Hall, 1996) (hereafter Boorstin and Kelley to avoid confusion) and
- Gary B. Nash and Julie R. Jeffrey, editors, *The American People*, (New York: Longman, 1998).

I also considered an anomalous product, Joy Hakim's *All the People*, volume 10 of her series *A History of US* (New York: Oxford, 1995). *A History of US* is not a typical textbook, was not written by committee as so many textbooks are, and was not published by a textbook publisher. It has been a surprise best-seller as a sort of trade book for Oxford University Press and is now getting adopted by some school systems as a textbook for middle schools.

Visual Images of the War

To avoid the charge that I am attacking textbooks merely for putting forth a different analysis than my own about the war, I focus first on something easily quantifiable: the visual images they supplied. More than any other war in our history, the Vietnam War was distinguished by a series of images that seared themselves into the public consciousness. I asked dozens of adults old enough to have lived during the war to tell me what they remember visually about it; they supplied a list of images showing remarkable overlap. A short list includes these five specific images:

- the little girl running naked down Highway One, fleeing a napalm attack
- a Buddhist monk sitting at a Saigon intersection immolating himself to protest the South Vietnamese government
- the national police chief executing a man suspected of being in the Viet Cong, with a pistol shot to the side of his head
- the bodies in the ditch after the My Lai massacre
- Americans evacuating the U.S. embassy by helicopter, while desperate Vietnamese try to climb aboard

The list would also include at least two generic images: B52s with bombs streaming below them into the pock-marked countryside of Vietnam and a ruined city such as Hué, with nothing but rubble in view, as Americans and South Vietnamese troops move in to retake it after the Tet offensive.[4]

Merely reading these short descriptions prompts most older Americans to remember these images in sharp detail. Several remain "among the most well-known images in the world even now [1991]," according to Patrick Hagopian, who has studied the ways America memorialized the Vietnam War.[5] The emotions that accompanied them come back vividly as well. But younger people have little chance to see or recall them unless their history books provide them. Most don't. Of the twelve American history textbooks in my original sample, one book, *The American Pageant*, included one picture, the police chief shooting the terrified man. No other textbook included any.

6.1 The U.S. military in action

U.S. textbooks typically present the Vietnam War through images like this one of jets refueling en route to bomb Vietnam rather than any of the famous pictures that symbolized the war to Americans at the time. NARA, Lt. Col. Cecil J. Poss, USIA/NARA, (NWDNS–306–MVP-14 (28), War and Conflict Photo # 416.

Leaving these images out of history textbooks shortchanges today's students, for not only did these photos report the war, but they also *made* history, for they affected the way Americans—and Vietnamese—thought about the war. Quang Duc's self-immolation, for example, shocked the South Vietnamese and American public. Before the war ended, several other Vietnamese and at least one American followed his example. According to Michael Delli Carpini, an authority on media coverage of Vietnam, the "devastating" image of Nguyen Ngoc Loan casually shooting the terrified young man on a Saigon street helped persuade Americans that their side was not morally superior to the Communists.[6] The image is so haunting that decades later, I have only to cock my fingers like a gun and people who were old enough to read newspapers or watch television in 1968 immediately recall it and tell about it in some detail. After the Tet offensive, television images and photographs of what U.S. bombs and shells had done to Ben Tre, Hué, and other cities and towns in South Vietnam as U.S. forces retook them persuaded many Americans to oppose the war. But images of the war in the original textbooks I examined were much prettier. Not one showed any damage done by the U.S. side.

What about the newer textbooks in American history? One did mark an improvement: *The American People* includes the little girl running naked down Highway One, the national police chief executing the man, and a photograph of an immolation. The new edition of *Triumph of the American Nation* has not improved. It still offers just two images of the war, giving each nearly half a page: American troops happily surrounding President Lyndon Johnson when he visited the huge U.S. base at Cam Ranh Bay and cars, trucks, and pedestrians streaming down a highway toward Saigon at the end of the war. The new version of *The American Pageant*, in contrast, with David M. Kennedy added to replace the deceased Thomas A. Bailey as author, dropped its photo of the police chief shooting the terrified man. It now contains none of the important images, although it does include a confusing photograph of an American punching a Vietnamese, probably to keep him off a helicopter evacuating Vietnam. Boorstin is quoted from another published work saying, "The Vietnam War was the first American war which was a television experience," but Boorstin and Kelley contains none of the seven images.

The book that supplies the widest range of images of the war is not a high school textbook at all but Joy Hakim's *All the People*. She includes photographs of the police chief shooting the man, a guard threatening a Vietnamese POW with a knife, and a town destroyed by "our side" and the most famous image of the My Lai massacre. Surprisingly, Hakim also gives her readers an image of the little girl running naked down Highway

One. This is surprising because textbook publishers follow the rule of no nudity—as one editor told me, "In elementary books *cows* don't have udders." It is a disturbing image; a college student of mine wrote, "To show a photograph of one naked girl crying after she has been napalmed changes the entire meaning of that war to a high school student."

If most textbooks omit all the important photographs of the Vietnam War, what images *do* they include? Uncontroversial shots, for the most part—servicemen on patrol, walking through swamps, or jumping from helicopters. Boorstin and Kelley includes a refugee "carrying household goods"; most older books similarly show refugees or damage caused by the *other* side, but since such damage was usually less extensive than that caused by U.S. bombardment, the pictures, like this one, are not very dramatic. No wonder college students don't remember anything they learned about Vietnam in high school! Most textbooks have edited out every image older adults found memorable about the war.

The Antiwar Movement

Most authors also leave out most of the acts, words, and images of the growing movement that opposed the Vietnam War. Martin Luther King Jr., the first major leader to come out against the war, opposed it in his trademark cadences: "We have destroyed their two most cherished institutions: the family and the village. We have destroyed their land and their crops. . . . We have corrupted their women and children and killed their men." No textbook of my original twelve quotes him; neither do the four new high school texts. Even more famous was the dissent of Muhammad Ali, then the heavyweight boxing champion of the world, who refused induction into the military, for which his title was stripped from him. Ali said, "No Viet Cong ever called me 'nigger,'" but every textbook in my original sample left out that line too. Not one included the famous question of John Kerry, then a leader of Vietnam Veterans Against the War, now a U.S. senator: "How do you ask a man to be the last man to die for a mistake?" After the Tet offensive, a U.S. major involved in retaking Ben Tre said, "It became necessary to destroy the town to save it." One textbook, *Challenge of Freedom*, offered this pallid paraphrase: "Other doves believed that the war was harming South Vietnam. These people said that there was not much sense in destroying the country to save it from communism." Otherwise, none quoted the notorious line. Textbooks likewise excluded the antiwar songs, the chants, and, above all, the emotions.

On this point some recent texts do better. *Lies My Teacher Told Me* pointed out that virtually the only people quoted by older books were Presidents Johnson and Richard Nixon. In a typical passage quoted in *The American*

6.2 Muhammad Ali refused to fight in Vietnam
None of the conventional textbooks discuss the ways in which the Vietnam War became a new site for domestic debate over racism and the treatment of African Americans at home, even though that connection was made very clearly at the time by heavyweight boxing champion Muhammad Ali and others. Here, Ali is escorted from the Armed Forces building in Houston on April 28, 1967, after he refused Army induction. AP/WIDE WORLD PHOTOS. Used by permission.

Pageant, Nixon says, "America cannot—and will not—conceive all the plans, design all the programs, execute all the decisions, and undertake all the defense of the free nations of the world." The passage does not help to clarify the war or the opposition to it. The 1994 version of *Pageant*, which came out at the same time as *Lies*, has improved dramatically on this score:

it drops the deceptive Nixon quote and tells how "hundreds of thousands of marchers filled the streets of New York, San Francisco, and other cities, chanting 'Hell, no; we won't go!' and 'Hey, hey, LBJ, how many kids did you kill today?'" *The American People* and Boorstin and Kelley also include the latter slogan. *People* also quotes Muhammad Ali, "I ain't got no quarrel with them Viet Cong," Women Strike for Peace, and the general slogan, "Make love, not war." Boorstin and Kelley includes a photo of a street demonstration near the nation's capitol; *People* contains a photograph of Mario Savio of the Free Speech Movement at Berkeley, the famous image of the grief-stricken woman over the dead body at Kent State, and photographs and captions of antiwar demonstrators in California and at the 1968 Democratic National Convention.

Again, Hakim's *All the People* provides the fullest coverage. Her series is broken up by sidebars and marginal notes, which sometimes distract but here seem appropriate. The resulting montage of such disparate items as images of protesters at the Pentagon, Coretta Scott King in a crowd protesting the war outside an unnamed gate, a big antiwar demonstration in Des Moines, a body on the sidewalk at Kent State, a tiny photograph of hands giving the peace sign, a minibiography of Dorothy Day protesting the war in her last years, and other written material about opposition to the Vietnam War, commingled with prose and photos about the counterculture, race relations, and the women's movement, give readers something of the feel of the confused late 1960s.

The Origin of the War

Having excluded the sights, the sounds, and the feelings of the Vietnam era, the authors of the twelve textbooks in my original sample proceeded to muddy or exclude the issues. Frances FitzGerald, author of *Fire in the Lake*, a fine book about Vietnam, called the textbooks she reviewed in 1979 "neither hawkish nor dovish on the war—they are simply evasive." She went on to say, "Since it is really quite hard to discuss the war and evade all the major issues, their Vietnam sections make remarkable reading."[7]

Any reasonable treatment of the Vietnam War in American history textbooks would discuss at least these six questions:

- Why did the United States fight in Vietnam?
- What was the war like before the United States entered it? How did we change it?
- How did the war change the United States?
- Why did an antiwar movement become so strong in the United States? What were its criticisms of the war in Vietnam? Were they right?
- Why did the bulk of the Vietnamese people oppose us? Hence, why

6.3 The antiwar movement

Textbooks mention the antiwar movement but fail to explain why Americans disagreed so profoundly about the war. Even the military was deeply divided, as evident in this demonstration on July 4, 1994, by active-duty GIs who demanded both better veterans' benefits and cessation of aid to the South Vietnamese government. VVAW, Inc. Used by permission.

did the United States lose the war?
- What lesson(s) should we take from the experience?[8]

Simply to list these issues is to recognize that each of them is still controversial. Take the first. Some people still argue that the United States fought in Vietnam to secure access to its valuable natural resources. Others still claim that we fought to bring democracy to its people. More common are analyses of our internal politics: Democratic Presidents Kennedy and Johnson, having seen how Republicans castigated Harry Truman for "losing" China, did not want to be seen as "losing" Vietnam. Another interpretation offers the domino theory: although we know now that Vietnam's Communists are antagonists of China, we didn't then, and some leaders believed that if Vietnam "fell" to the Communists, so would Thailand, Malaysia, Indonesia, and the Philippines. Yet another view is that America felt its prestige was on the line, so it did not want a defeat in Vietnam, lest Pax Americana be threatened in Africa, South America, or elsewhere in the world. Some economic determinists go even further and claim that big business fomented the war to help the economy. Other historians take a longer view, arguing that our intervention in Vietnam derives from a cultural pattern of racism and imperialism that began with the first Indian war in Virginia in 1622, continued in the nineteenth century with Manifest Destiny, and is winding down in the "American century" of the present. A final view might be that there was no clear cause and certainly no clear purpose, that we blundered into the war because no later administration had the courage to undo our 1946 mistake of opposing a popular independence movement. "The fundamental blunder with respect to Indochina was made after 1945," wrote Secretary of State John Foster Dulles at the time of the Geneva Convention, when "our Government allowed itself to be persuaded" by the French and British "to restore France's colonial position in Indochina."[9]

Perhaps the seeds of America's tragic involvement with Vietnam were sown at Versailles in 1919, when Woodrow Wilson failed to heed Ho Chi Minh's plea for his country's independence. Perhaps they germinated when Franklin Roosevelt's tentative policy of not helping the French recolonize Southeast Asia after World War II terminated with or perhaps just before his death. None of the twelve books in my original sample looked before the 1950s to explain the Vietnam War. Most of them simply dodged the question of why we fought. Here is a representative analysis, from *American Adventures*: "Later in the 1950's, war broke out in South Vietnam. This time the United States gave aid to the South Vietnamese government." "War broke out"—what could be simpler!

Three of the four new high school textbooks do somewhat better, al-

6.4 Why did the United States fight in Vietnam?
Americans poured vast resources into the Vietnam War, as is illustrated in this 1968 photo of M-113 armored personnel carriers overseeing the evacuation of the village of My Tho. Yet U.S. textbooks do not explain why. NARA, NWDNS–111–SC–646675.

though not the 1990 edition of *Triumph of the American Nation.* The 1994 version of *The American Pageant* provides three sentences: "Nationalist movements had sought for years to throw off the French colonial yoke in Indochina. The Vietnamese revolutionary, Ho Chi Minh, had tried to appeal personally to Woodrow Wilson as early as 1919 to support self-determination for the peoples of Southeast Asia. Franklin Roosevelt had likewise inspired hope among Asian nations." *Pageant* goes on to tell that Asian leaders became increasingly Communist while the United States became increasingly anti-communist after World War II. *The American People* describes how Ho Chi Minh "sought to expel the Japanese conquerors" during World War II. It mentions that FDR opposed colonialism and goes on to tell how he had backed down to France's desire to regain its colony by the time of his death. "Meanwhile, Ho Chi Minh had established the Democratic Republic of Vietnam in 1945," *People* explains, as does Boorstin and Kelley; only one of the other fourteen high school textbooks says this. "Then the French began to become difficult," according to Boorstin and Kelley. "Like other old imperial powers after World War II, France, even including Communists, wanted to hold onto its former colonies. Now the French moved to bring down Ho and replace him with their own puppet." *People* notes that President Truman recognized the French puppet government instead. Boorstin and Kelley, like several older texts, tells how "the U.S. began helping the French with money and arms."

Hakim devotes an entire four-page chapter to the start of the conflict. She begins with definitions of "colonialism" and "imperialism" and points out, "We had once been an English colony and we hadn't liked it a bit." She tells how Ho not only sought independence from Wilson in 1919 but also "wrote eight letters to President Truman asking for help in making Vietnam free." She provides five paragraphs of information about Ho, not all of it positive, and explains carefully why the French failed to defeat his forces and why the United States supported the French.

To answer what the war was like before the United States entered it raises an element of definition: was it a war of Communist aggression? a civil war? an American invasion? Some textbooks claim that South Vietnam was an independent country created at Geneva; others state that the partition between the two zones of Vietnam was intended to last no more than two years, with nationwide elections reuniting the nation. The historical record leaves no doubt: the latter is fact. Four books of my original twelve treat Vietnam as one nation with two zones; six, including *Triumph of the American Nation*, treat it as two separate nations; two, including *The American Pageant,* take no clear position. The new *Pageant* observes that Vietnam was divided "supposedly temporarily" but then states, "The Vietnamese"—not "Diem" or "the South Vietnamese government"!—"never held the promised elections." *Triumph* still treats South Vietnam and North Vietnam as two "new nations," like Laos and Cambodia. The 1998 edition of *The American People* begins its treatment of the Vietnam War with the perplexing sentence, "The Geneva agreement created two Vietnams." This is puzzling because an earlier edition, published in 1990, was much closer to the mark, telling how the Geneva conference "divided Vietnam along the 17th parallel, with elections promised in 1956 to unify the country and determine its political fate."

Equally puzzling is Boorstin and Kelley. They preface their treatment of the war with the feel-good distortion, "Wherever they looked around the world, JFK and his advisers saw tests of America's determination to stand for peace and freedom." How America stood for "peace and freedom" in Vietnam is hard to fathom. Boorstin and Kelley then give a lengthy analysis of "Why we were in Vietnam," but as everywhere in this textbook, phrases contradict each other. Most authors assert that the Vietcong were largely the creation of North Vietnam so they can claim that the war was one of Communist aggression. But Boorstin and Kelley do call the conflict a "civil war in

South Vietnam" and say it began "after South Vietnam refused to take part in elections." Then, however, they give as one of three reasons why the United States got into the war: "to stop aggression. Early in 1965 there were still only a small number of North Vietnamese soldiers in South Vietnam. But American military leaders remembered how Europe had fallen to the Nazis. . ." If "only a small number of North Vietnamese soldiers" were in South Vietnam, compared to many more U.S. soldiers, critical readers might legitimately ask who was the aggressor. But Boorstin and Kelley immediately state a more believable cause: to "protect our reputation" and "credibility" around the world. Hakim again is clearer: "The division was meant to be temporary," and she points out that the two halves of Vietnam were economically interdependent, with most agriculture in the south, most industry in the north.

Moral Issues in the Vietnam War

I cannot address all the questions about the Vietnam War enumerated above. However, we cannot overlook the moral element in several of these issues. Answers to why the United States fought in Vietnam shade into *"Should* it have?" Discussions of how the entry of the United States changed the war lead directly to how the United States fought it, including such matters as the My Lai massacre. In turn, answers to these questions help explain why the antiwar movement became so strong. To ask whether its criticisms of the war in Vietnam were right is partly a moral question, of course. And among the lessons Americans should take from the experience might be moral ones. In *The Debate over Vietnam*, David Levy points out that throughout the war debate was couched mostly in moral terms: "Was intervention right or wrong?" Yet most textbooks avoid this question. William Griffen and John Marciano wrote an entire book called *Teaching the Vietnam War*. After examining how twenty-eight textbooks present the Vietnam War, they conclude that authors may concede American errors and brutality but never question the legitimacy of the entire enterprise.[10] Their description fits eleven of the twelve books I originally surveyed. Only *Discovering American History*, the oldest book in my sample, written in 1974, directly asks, "Do you think the United States was right to intervene in the affairs of Vietnam? Explain." *Discovering* also asks if the war was unconstitutional and if the United States should intervene in a similar situation in another part of the world.

Some textbooks appear to raise moral issues but veer away. For example, *Challenge of Freedom* asks, "Why did the United States use so much military power in South Vietnam?" Attempting to answer this question could get quite interesting: Because its antagonists weren't white?

Because they couldn't strike at the United States? Because the United States has a history of imperialism vis-à-vis "primitive" peoples, from the early Indian wars through the Philippine-American War of 1899–1913 to Vietnam? Because like most other nations, the United States behaves not by standards of morality but of realpolitik? The answer that *Challenge* suggests to teachers, however, shows that the authors don't really want students to think about why the United States intervened and certainly not about whether it should have done so. It is content to regurgitate President Johnson's stated rationale for so much bombing [which the book has previously supplied]: "To show the Vietcong and their ally, North Vietnam, that they could not win the war." This answer is mystifying, since the Vietcong and North Vietnam *did* win the war; moreover, the authors' claim to know Johnson's motivation arrives without evidence. In the rhetorical climate created by this textbook, for a teacher to raise a moral question would come across as a violation of educational norms.

Two textbook authors, James Davidson and Mark Lytle, are on record elsewhere as knowing of the importance of My Lai and other examples of American wrongdoing. "The American strategy had atrocity built into it," Lytle said to me. They devote most of a chapter to the My Lai massacre in their interesting book *After the Fact*, often read by college history majors. There they tell how news of the massacre stunned the United States. "One thing was certain," they write, "the encounter became a defining moment in the public's perception of the war."[11] Yet their high school history book, *The United States: A History of the Republic*, like seven others in my sample, never mentions My Lai. Lytle characterized his textbook as "a McDonald version of history—if it has any flavor, people won't buy it." Like several other authors, Lytle claimed that he and Davidson suffered no editorial interference. The publishers were in charge, however: "They didn't want famous people, because we'd be more tractable," Lytle told me, explaining why a major publisher had sought out him and Davidson, relative unknowns. "Were you?" I asked. "We were reasonably tractable," he admitted. In short, editors could use a light touch because authors omitted most unpleasantries and moral controversies on their own. Many textbooks are not written by their "authors." Lewis Todd and Merle Curti may have written the first draft of *Rise of the American Nation*, back in 1949, but by the 1990 edition, Curti was in his nineties and Todd was dead. When Harcourt came out with a new edition of *Triumph* in 1994, editors found it hard to pretend that either author had anything to do with it, since Curti had also died, so they moved Todd and Curti's names into the title and put a new author's name below theirs.

Newer textbooks continue to duck moral issues. The 1990 version of *Triumph of the American Nation* avoids "why" questions by sticking with "how" questions, like, "Trace the steps of American involvement in South Vietnam starting in 1962," and "How was the conflict between North and South Vietnam finally resolved?" Boorstin and Kelley tend to ask regurgitation items such as "Identify Dean Rusk," occasionally interspersed with "critical thinking" questions such as "How did the Tonkin Gulf incident lead to our increased involvement in Vietnam?"[12] Real "critical thinking" might lead students to conclude that the question has it backward: our increased involvement in Vietnam led to the Tonkin Gulf incident, especially since the Tonkin Gulf incident probably never happened. Except *Discovering American History*, all high school history textbooks I surveyed shy away from prompting students to think critically.

American Pageant at no point suggests that U.S. intervention might have been morally flawed from its outset. Language in the 1998 edition of *The American People* likewise implies that the United States was basically acting morally: "Kennedy understood the importance of popular support for the South Vietnamese government if that country was to maintain its independence [*sic*]." Of course, the *independent* government in Vietnam was always Ho Chi Minh's, and the South Vietnamese regime was always held up only by outside American intervention and collapsed promptly when that intervention came to an end. Boorstin and Kelley's language similarly implies that the war was moral: U.S. troops are a "commitment," not an invading force, and American leaders repeatedly seek diplomatic solutions only to be frustrated by North Vietnamese intransigence.

By way of contrast, Hakim's *All the People*, which like *Pageant* asks no questions, ends its main chapter on the war with this passage:

> We thought we were doing the right thing when we began. We really were unselfish. We weren't imperialists. We didn't want to make Vietnam a colony. And we left much of our national wealth in that nation halfway around the world. So why did we make such a terrible mistake?
> We didn't understand what the war was all about.
> It was about freedom. The Vietnamese wanted to be free of foreign rule. They wanted to choose their own leaders. They wanted freedom even to make the wrong decisions. . .
> . . . Didn't we remember that people fighting for their own freedom are apt to be unbeatable? What had happened to us?"

Whether one accepts the view that the Vietnam war was a "mistake," compared to other textbooks it is a breath of fresh air. And its final question is a potential depth charge whose detonation has the power to maim

6.5 Losing the war for hearts and minds

American texts neither clearly explain important facts about the war nor address moral issues raised by those facts. For example, this photo shows one of the few occasions when a B-52 bomber was shot down over Hanoi during the Christmas bombings of December 1972, which killed over 1,600 civilians. American texts are far more likely to show destruction by the other side, despite vastly superior U.S. firepower. Lou Dematteis, *A Portrait of Vietnam* (New York: W.W. Norton, 1996), 72. Used by permission.

various weary denizens of the cultural deep that other textbooks are still peddling, including automatic progress and ethnocentrism.

Are Textbooks Getting Better?

Hakim to the contrary, by excluding the primary texts and emotions of the war, by telling their narrative in a monotone, and by selecting unimportant photographs, authors have reduced the Vietnam War to a boring monologue. Are the newer textbooks improving? Some early textbook treatments were so bad that one could not imagine their getting worse. In 1966 *Rise of the American Nation*, for example, gave this "explanation" for the beginning of the conflict: "Ever since the end of WWII, Indo-China, a French colony, had been torn by armed conflict. The Vietminh, a Communist group, had been fighting to win control of the entire country from the French and their loyal, anti-Communist allies, the Vietnamese. When it became clear that Communist China was actively aiding the Vietminh, the United States began to send military equipment to the Vietnamese and French armies." This paragraph blandly says that Indochina was a French colony, ignoring the Japanese takeover during World War II and Ho Chi Minh's declaration of nationhood in 1945. The memorable implication is that "the Vietnamese"—the whole people—were the "loyal, anti-Communist allies" of the French. It is astounding that Merle Curti, a respected diplomatic historian listed as one of the book's two authors, would allow his name to be associated with such a paragraph.

By 1982 someone—probably functionaries deep within the bowels of Harcourt Brace Jovanovich, the publisher—had revised that passage to read: "A group of revolutionary nationalists, the Vietminh, who were mainly Communists, had been fighting to win control of the entire country from the French and their Vietnamese allies." The other sentences in the paragraph went unchanged, however, implying that the United States was merely responding to outside intervention by China. The paragraph remains the same in the most recent edition of the textbook, published in 1990 under the new title *Triumph of the American Nation*.

Although *Rise/Triumph* thus improved slightly, comparing all the textbooks by publication date offers no ground for optimism. Within my original sample of twelve, treatments of the war grew *less* competent, not more, with the passage of time. The only textbook among them to provide a serious treatment of My Lai, for example, was *Discovering American History*, published in 1974. Three others mentioned My Lai; published in 1975, 1983, and 1984, they were among the next oldest books in my sample. Eight books never mentioned My Lai or any similar incident or problem;

their publication dates ranged from 1979 to 1990 and averaged 1985. The 1998 *American People* now joins the oldest with a competent treatment of My Lai. In contrast, Boorstin and Kelley grant just two sentences to My Lai, and their real purpose is to raise readers' ire against the Vietcong: "Shortly after Tet, the American public was shocked to hear that United States troops had killed some 300 civilians, mostly women and children, in the little village of My Lai. The fact that the Viet Cong had murdered many hundreds of civilians during their month-long occupation of Hué was lost in the American distress over the atrocity committed by U.S. troops in My Lai." Again, Hakim's middle school textbook does better—she devotes a page to the massacre and includes an analysis by Neil Sheehan tying that incident to the more general policies of the U.S. military command. She alone also tells what happened to Lieutenant William Calley, who led the massacre. In its 1990 edition *The American People* had told of his reduction in sentence, but nothing about Calley survives the 1998 revision.

Hakim also does something unusual in her discussion of Calley—she displays a point of view: "Lt. William Calley, Jr., who had directed much of the massacre (and who personally killed 109 Vietnamese, including babies), was the only soldier convicted of a crime. He was court-martialed and sentenced to life in prison at hard labor. But President Nixon intervened (to his and America's shame), and Calley was released after three years of house arrest in his own apartment." Her parenthetical statement, only five words, is refreshing after reading sixteen standard textbooks whose authors would never risk such a departure from the usual omniscient authorial monotone. In *America Revised*, a 1979 study of changing fashions in American history textbooks, Frances FitzGerald pointed out that textbooks before World War II displayed some personality. Only *Pageant* among my sixteen high school textbooks ventures any personality today, and then only in Bailey's quips. None manifests a point of view, let alone one critical of the government, as Hakim is here. All of the traditional textbooks *have* points of view, of course, but this fact is masked by their godlike rhetoric.

Hakim is new, the prose in *The American Pageant*'s is somewhat more truthful (although its photo selection deteriorated), and *The American People* is the second most forthcoming among all standard textbooks, so one might justifiably conclude that textbooks are getting better in their treatment of the Vietnam War. But because the best standard textbook, *Discovering American History*, was the oldest book in my sample, dating from 1974, and because Hakim is not a standard textbook product, such a conclusion must be advanced with caution. Moreover, between 1990 and 1998 *The American People* chopped its discussion of the Geneva conference and its aftermath; its analysis suffers accordingly.

If textbooks are a bit better, the improvement may reflect that the Vietnam War is no longer very controversial. Since the late 1970s, opinion polls have told us that more than two of three adult Americans consider it to have been morally wrong as well as tactically inept.[13] Authors may be coming to treat the Vietnam War more forthrightly, as they now treat slavery, now that the Cold War, like formal segregation of African Americans, has ended. Like slavery, the Vietnam War is treated as a minor detour on America's basically ethical path as a nation. Then authors can depict the war, like slavery, as having no real relevance to the present. These last sentences are debatable, of course—but not within most high school history textbooks. Wedded as most of them are to portraying America-the-good and history as automatic progress, they do not risk a portrayal of the Vietnam War that might challenge either of those central archetypes.

Most Teachers Never Get to the War at All

We have seen that many teachers are loathe to teach "against" their textbooks, especially on a topic they deem controversial. Some teachers do challenge the lifeless and distorted accounts of the Vietnam War that most high school history textbooks offer. Not only do they "get away" with doing so, their students often respect them for it and end up choosing history as a favorite subject. The January 1988 issue of *Social Education* tells how some teachers have approached the subject and directs readers to useful primary sources, many of which are now on the Web. It turns out that most students never encounter their textbook treatments of the war *or* any supplements from their teachers, however, because teachers rarely reach even the Korean War in high school American history courses. Sociologist Jim De Fronzo found that only 2 to 4 percent of college students said that they had any substantial treatment of the Vietnam War in high school. Linda McNeil reports that most teachers don't want to teach about Vietnam: "Their memories of the Vietnam war era made them wish to avoid topics on which the students were likely to disagree with their views or that would make the students 'cynical' about American institutions." Many teachers (and most textbook writers) somehow imagine they are holding their fingers in the dike that protects American civilization. Although *they* criticize our government and society, they do not trust students to do so. Hence, the less said about Vietnam the better—so the average teacher grants the Vietnam War 0 to 4.5 *minutes* in the entire school year![14]

My undergraduates confirmed that the Vietnam War is simply not taught in most high school American history courses. I taught large courses in introductory sociology at the University of Vermont between 1975 and

1996. These classes, composed mainly of first-year students, provided an interesting window on what goes on in high school. More than half of all University of Vermont students come from out of state, so they can tell us something about high school across the United States, not just in the Green Mountain State. Discussions of the Vietnam War increasingly drew blank looks.[15] By the early 1980s, only two-thirds of my students knew the meaning of "hawk" and "dove," and by the end of that decade just one-third did. In 1989 I taught a group of advanced undergraduates in a course conveniently titled "Lies My Teacher Told Me" after the book I was writing at the time. On the first day of class, responding to a question on a quiz I gave them that asked, "The War in Vietnam was fought between _____ and _____, 22 percent of them replied "North and South *Korea*." These responses were so outlandish that some readers have concluded that my students were pulling my leg, but they took the quiz quite seriously—indeed, they wanted to know how much of their semester grade would depend on it. One student even wanted partial credit for getting "North" and "South" correct.[16] To my scolding, they replied that they were only small children when the war ended, and their high school American history teachers never got much past World War II.

Citizenship and Thinking About the Vietnam War

When Americans encounter no treatment or mystifying coverage of the Vietnam War in high school and are not encouraged to think critically about it, we must be alarmed. Only one American in six goes on to take any history in college—partly because high school history was so boring. If they don't learn about Vietnam in high school, therefore, many won't learn about it at all. Should they?

I suppose that depends on why we teach history. Too often we simply assert history is "good for us," without thinking about why. Surely one reason to ask young Americans to learn something about their nation's history is so they can understand what has caused what in the past, so as to apply such lessons to the present. When political leaders or newspaper commentators invoke history, usually it is the history of the previous thirty years or so. Thus, politicians across the spectrum cited "the lessons of Vietnam" as they debated intervening in Angola, Lebanon, and Kuwait. Bumper stickers reading "El Salvador is Spanish for Vietnam" helped forestall sending U.S. troops to Central America. "The lessons of Vietnam" have also been used to inform or mislead discussions about secrecy, the press, how the federal government operates, and even whether the military should admit gays. It is clear that adults feel the history of the Vietnam War is more important today than the history of, say, the War of 1812. High school graduates have a right to enough knowledge about the Vietnam War to respond intelligently when it is mentioned in ongoing political debates.

Yet high school students learn more about the War of 1812, which lasted only half as long, than about the Vietnam War. This theft of the recent past by textbooks and teachers is a crime that schools perpetrate on high school students, depriving them of perspective about the issues that most affect them. Leaving out the recent past ensures that students will take away little from their history courses that they can apply to the world into which they graduate.

Even a worse offense is the way that textbooks and teachers fail to help students think critically about the Vietnam War and marshal historical evidence to support their conclusions. This crime robs students of the tools to understand their own society today and also fails to give them any grasp of how American citizens have affected and sometimes have failed to affect the policies of their government. Such schooling perverts citizenship—unless by "citizenship" we mean the unthinking nationalism that helped get us into Vietnam in the first place. Judged by the flag-waving ads publishers use to sell their textbooks, such limited citizenship may be just what they have in mind.

Notes

1. Charlotte Crabtree and David O'Shea, "Teachers' Academic Preparation in History," *Newsletter* (National Center for History in the Schools) 1, 3 (November 1991): 4, 10; Linda McNeil, "Defensive Teaching and Classroom Control," in Michael W. Apple and Lois Weis, eds., *Ideology and Practice in Schooling* (Philadelphia: Temple University Press, 1983), 116.

2. Hillel Black, *The American Schoolbook* (New York: Morrow, 1967), 91–95; Jack L. Nelson and William B. Stanley, "Academic Freedom: Fifty Years Standing Still," *Social Education* 49 (1985): 663; John Goodlad, "A Study of Schooling," *Phi Delta Kappan*, March 1983, reprinted in James W. Noll, ed., *Taking Sides: Clashing Views on Controversial Educational Issues* (Guilford, CT: Dushkin, 1989), 145.

3. In the aftermath of the Vietnam War, Harcourt Brace renamed this last one *Triumph of the American Nation*, exemplifying a Rambo approach to history: we may have lost in Southeast Asia, but we'll win on the book covers.

4. Lewis Lapham, editor of *Harper's*, agrees that what he terms "a sequence of brutal images" played an important role during the war. He describes three images, including the first, third, and seventh of those I list. See *America's Century Series Transcript* (San Francisco: KQED, 1989), 57–58. Note that the most famous evacuation photo was not actually shot at the embassy but at the roof of a nearby building.

5. Hagopian specifically refers to the naked napalmed girl and the My Lai massacre victims and cites another student of photojournalism who adds the monk's immolation and the police chief's shooting the Vietcong suspect. See Patrick Hagopian, "Vietnam

Veterans and the Right to the Past" (Baltimore: American Studies Association, 1991), 14.

6. Delli Carpini, "Vietnam and the Press," in D. Michael Shafer, ed., *The Legacy* (Boston: Beacon, 1990), 142.

7. Frances FitzGerald, *America Revised: History Schoolbooks in the Twentieth Century* (New York: Vintage Books, 1979), 126.

8. These questions hardly amount to a full treatment of the war; for one, they do not include what the war did to the nation of Vietnam.

9. Quoted in William Appleman Williams, ed., *America in Vietnam* (New York: W.W. Norton, 1989), 167.

10. William Griffen and John Marciano, *Teaching the Vietnam War* (Montclair, NJ: Allanheld, Osmun, 1979), 167, 171.

11. James Davidson and Mark Lytle, *After the Fact: The Art of Historical Detection*, vol. 2 (New York: McGraw-Hill, 1992), 371.

12. The teacher's edition of Boorstin and Kelley does offer a "writing process activity" that might prompt students to raise moral questions about the war: "Recognizing Bias: Ask students to imagine they are college males of draft age in 1965." They then suggest asking students to write letters "to their parents explaining why they are or are not going to Washington, D.C., to protest the war in Vietnam."

13. For example, Gallup Poll, November 1986; Roper Poll, August 1984.

14. Jim De Fronzo, "How Sociologists Can Help Prevent War," typescript, Storrs, CT, n.d.; McNeil, "Defensive Teaching," 116, 126–27.

15. My questions and student responses are discussed in chapter 12 of *Lies My Teachers Told Me*.

16. I replied, "What if you'd written North and South *Dakota*?"

7

War Crimes and the Vietnamese People:
American Representations and Silences

David Hunt

"War crimes" were in the logic of the Vietnam War. As the U.S. military sought to extirpate guerrillas living in the midst of the rural population, Vietnamese peasants paid a high price. With memories of World War II still fresh, the Tokyo and Nuremberg Trials provided the antiwar movement a framework for making sense of the carnage. Veterans led the way in documenting the case, most notably at the Citizens Commission of Inquiry (December 1970, Washington D.C.) and the "winter soldier" investigation (January 1971, Detroit), during which returning soldiers described atrocities they had witnessed and perpetrated in Southeast Asia.

The "winter soldiers" were heroes of the Vietnam War. Public testimony was part of an effort to recover from combat trauma, and perhaps there was a hope for atonement as well. But the hearings were primarily an act of citizenship, an attempt to force on the American public a recognition of what was going on in Vietnam. As one veteran put it, the willed incomprehension of friends and family and of participants in public discussion of the war impelled him to speak. "The fact that they didn't want to know," he declared, "told me they had to know."[1]

The winter soldiers were not satisfied with fixing blame for crimes committed. Refusing a solipsism that portrayed the war as a dispute among Americans, they insisted on the reality of Vietnam. According to their logic, a society guilty of atrocities could recover its humanity only in connecting to the humanity of the victims. As part of a collective effort to recover, veterans demanded reconstruction assistance for Vietnam and anticipated peaceful exchanges between the two countries and a wider understanding of Vietnamese history and culture in the United States.[2]

Survey texts assigned in college courses on the Vietnam War convey a sense of how such issues are remembered in the United States (see appendix at the end of this chapter for a list and description of the books considered here). Redressers of wrongs, the winter soldiers also called for a recognition of the Vietnamese as participants in their own history, with the implication that they, too, were party to questions of power and responsibility raised during the war. In order to meet the winter soldier challenge, survey authors must enter into the war crimes debate, and they must engage with the Vietnamese side of the Vietnam War. Having dealt elsewhere with images of the Viet Cong, I focus here on how representative texts present the leaders and citizens of the Saigon-based Government of Vietnam (GVN) and the North Vietnamese Democratic Republic of Vietnam (DRV).[3]

Triumph and Eclipse of the Winter Soldiers

A few weeks after the winter soldier hearings (March 28, 1971), the *New York Times Magazine* published an article by Neil Sheehan entitled, "Should We Have War Crime Trials?" When he was first stationed in Vietnam, Sheehan regarded the "Hun-like" behavior of U.S. personnel as "unnecessarily brutal and politically counter-productive," but it had not occurred to him that such conduct might be classified as criminal. By the time of the article, he was both advocating and expecting "a long and painful inquest into what we are doing in Southeast Asia." Alarm and indignation at the suffering of the Vietnamese had spread widely within the United States.

Postwar revisionism was launched in this atmosphere, shaped by the antiwar movement. Guenter Lewy's *America in Vietnam*, which sets out to establish the legality and morality of U.S. war making, portrays the winter soldiers and other activist veterans as "emotionally disturbed individuals" who spoke of atrocities to gain "approval and acceptance" from the public, or simply as impostors and liars. At the same time, Lewy is obsessed with war crimes testimony. Although he exculpates U.S. policymakers and characterizes the Vietnamese as victims of Communism who needed American help, he recognizes that the countryside was full of persons the GIs "had good reason to consider unfriendly." Troubled by the implication that a general assault on the rural population was required to win the war, he both defends forced population relocations, seen as admissible according to the Geneva Convention, and recognizes that this tactic demoralized the peasantry. Napalm, defoliants, and tear gas were also not illegal, but Lewy gives a hearing to humanitarian arguments against their use. My Lai-type massacres did not happen "all the time," as critics maintained, but "the lives of Vietnamese were cheap and not protected by the law of war." In a remarkable passage, Lewy suggests that if Japanese general Yamashita Tomoyuki, who led Japan's 1932 advance through Southeast Asia, had been properly condemned at the end of World War II for failing "to take all possible measures to prevent such crimes," then General William Westmoreland, who turned a blind eye to the travails of the indigenous population, should be found culpable as well.[4]

Roused to fury by the defamatory character of attacks on U.S. policy (the "war crimes" argument equated the United States with the Axis Powers of World War II), Lewy confronts polemical adversaries on their own ground. Working his way through the dossier, he repeatedly stumbles over evidence of massive firepower trained on an enemy who lived and fought in the midst of the Vietnamese people. Determined to establish that the Americans waged a just war, he makes clear that it was a dirty war.

Moral questions imposed on the American conscience by counter-insurgency also haunt Marilyn Young in *The Vietnam Wars*, but in other survey texts published after *America in Vietnam*, the war crimes debate recedes from view. The authors of these books are critical of Pentagon strategy and tactics. But to employ the distinction drawn by Sheehan, they tend to characterize U.S. intervention as "unnecessarily brutal and politically counter-productive" rather than as a criminal enterprise. Treatments of the My Lai massacre in these books are less extensive than the analysis offered by Lewy and Young and do not emphasize, as they do, that some Americans at the time thought Washington leaders were war criminals. The issue is further obscured when terrorist acts by the enemy, such as the Hué "massacre," are made to seem more wanton than U.S. atrocities.[5]

Even so, the winter soldier message has not been entirely effaced. When I began to think about Lewy's work and other surveys texts, I assumed that most would dwell on the U.S. role and marginalize the people of Vietnam. But if one adds up pages devoted to Vietnam's pre-1945 history, the Viet Minh, the GVN, the DRV, and the Southern guerrillas of the National Liberation Front (NLF), it emerges that the Vietnamese occupy center stage in over 40 percent of our collective text.

This near parity with the U.S. side is unique in the annals of U.S. scholarship on foreign wars. College textbook treatments of Vietnam are unfinished, but their qualities are obvious when compared to surveys of other U.S. military interventions in Asia. No Vietnam War study comes

7.1 War crimes and prisoners of war
Did the United States commit war crimes in Vietnam? This 1968 photo of a bleeding and bound prisoner is captioned, "A youthful hard-core Viet Cong, heavily guarded, awaits interrogation." Images like this one troubled Americans during the war but rarely appear in college texts. NARA, NWDNS-306–MVP-21(1). War and Conflict no. 414.

close to the racism of Max Hastings, *The Korean War*, which declares that Korea "stank" and in which the political tendencies and even dietary preferences of Koreans are treated with contempt. Their discussions of the DRV are not satisfactory, but the Vietnam War authors do not write off Hanoi statements, as does Hastings when explaining why he paid no heed to North Korean perspectives. They fail to resolve every question, but the surveys do open the way toward a discussion that is attentive to the place of the war in Vietnam's recent history. The winter soldiers helped to fashion a scholarly literature.[6]

Story of a Betrayal

Guenter Lewy, Timothy Lomperis, and Anthony James Joes stand out among the survey authors in their relative sympathy for the GVN and their unwillingness to write it off as a lost cause. These scholars agree on a number of propositions: that the introduction of U.S. ground forces, necessary to stave off defeat in 1965, quickly became an obstacle to progress; that Vietnamization was a welcome, if belated, step; that the GVN was headed in the right direction in the years leading up to 1975; and that the withdrawal of U.S. assistance after the Paris Peace Agreement constituted a fatal blow to Saigon.

Joes's treatment of these themes is squarely within the "betrayal-of-an-ally" paradigm characteristic of right-wing retrospectives on the war. "The United States could have sustained the south indefinitely," he writes, "but chose not to. The United States could have stopped the final offensive against Saigon dead in its tracks, but chose not to. And so, in a real sense, the Americans defeated the South Vietnamese, and themselves." A similar interpretation is suggested by Lomperis, who writes that "at the time of the signing of the Paris Peace Agreement in January 1973, the South Vietnamese government had attained passive legitimacy." But before "passive" could become "active" support, the Americans "let [the GVN] down." Lewy portrays the peace agreement as an abandonment of South Vietnam by its U.S. ally and even (quoting an Australian observer) a "shameless bug-out." He condemns the "folly" of the antiwar movement and declares that the "very improvement of the GVN and the greatly weakened posture" of the Vietcong prompted Hanoi to launch its 1975 offensive.[7]

The GVN Polity

This line of argument leads toward a portrayal of Saigon's leaders as victims of the Americans as well as of the Communists. But the history of the regime, as narrated in the surveys, does not support such a view. With respect to the electoral sphere, Joes is enthusiastic about the 1955 referendum asking voters to choose between Premier Ngo Dinh Diem and Emperor Bao Dai (it provoked a "massive turnout of voters" in support of a republic led by Diem), but everyone else thinks the contest was rigged. Joes and Lewy offer justification for cancellation of the Geneva vote scheduled for 1956, whereas the other authors are critical, with George Herring, Michael Maclear, George Moss, James Olson and Randy Roberts, and Marilyn Young specifying that Ho Chi Minh would have won if the Vietnamese had been allowed a choice. On the suspension of village elections by Diem in 1956, the verdict is unanimously negative, with even Joes, after some hesitation ("there was justification for this move"), expressing disapproval ("an unpopular mistake").[8]

Electoral contests in the era of President Nguyen Van Thieu prompt a somewhat more spirited exchange. Joes regards constituent assembly and presidential campaigns of 1966–1967 as a breakthrough and adds that they were "the fairest ever conducted in Viet Nam." Lomperis offers a more guarded endorsement, saying that the elections appealed to "modernists" by "at least going further than Hanoi in establishing legitimate constitutional government." He adds that many legislators in the national assembly, chosen soon after Thieu's victory at the polls, "did see themselves as modern ombudsmen and developed links with the constituents."[9]

These judgments are not seconded in the other texts. Gary Hess declares that the 1967 vote revealed "the shallowness of the Saigon government's support," and Herring arrives at a similar conclusion. Stanley Karnow avers that, "Thieu performed miserably" and dwells on his "astonishingly poor" score. Moss remarks that the election revealed Thieu's dependence on "the backing of the Americans," and William Turley concludes that it pinpointed and sharpened divisions within the Saigon elite.[10]

Perhaps most prominent among the skeptics when it comes to these elections is Lewy. While citizens trooped to the polls, Lewy notes, "the government continued to protect a power structure based on the wealthy urban elements of society." At the grassroots, "GVN officials, usually drawn from the urban elite of the country, displayed a contemptuous attitude toward the people they governed." Lewy's interest is stimulated more by Thieu's decision to restore village elections in 1970, especially since this democratic local leadership was given control over budget funds, paramilitary forces, and implementation of the "land-to-the-tiller" redistribution program: "A shift of political allegiance toward the GVN on the part of the rural population seemed to be in the making." But then, a few pages later, Lewy notes that, "The South Vietnamese government, despite belated reforms like the land-to-the-tiller program, had been unable to mobilize mass support in the countryside. In a series of moves in 1972 and 1973, Thieu once again seriously weakened local self-government by abolishing authority for the election of hamlet chiefs."[11]

The survey authors come close to unanimity in their evaluations of the GVN polity, and in addition to noting the limits of its electoral practice, many refer to press censorship, concentration or "reeducation" camps, and thousands of executions. Several texts underscore Diem's authoritarianism, with Herring affirming that his model was the nine-teenth-century emperor Ming Mang, Hess noting his regime's "contempt" for the people, and Moss characterizing the government as "a police state apparatus with fascistic overtones." Having been allowed to witness GVN police "interrogation" sessions, Karnow is authorized to testify that sus-pects were "often tortured." No improvement, the Thieu regime was "an authoritarian, single-party state" (Olson and Roberts), a "single-party, authoritarian, bureaucratic rule" dependent on "the support of a foreign power" (Turley). In its last years, Hess declares, the GVN was going backward, and "political surveillance and control was even more exten-sive than under the Diem government."[12]

Ready enough to quarrel over details, the GVN sympathizers fail to unite against this indictment. Lomperis depicts Diem as an "autocratic Confucian" and is troubled by Thieu's "considerable energy . . . in politi-cal repression." Lewy minces no words in labeling the GVN a "lawless and repressive regime." And even Joes grants that the government came to resemble a "Latin American dictatorship, arbitrary without being ef-fective" and that its handling of prisoners "often left a great deal to be desired."[13]

Saigon and the Peasants

Four textbook surveys provide details on landlessness and usury in the countryside and eight indicate that the Viet Minh's pre-1954 land reform had been effective and that Diem's corresponding efforts brought meager benefit to the rural poor and were politically disastrous. Herring judges that the regime "did little" to satisfy peasant land hunger. Hess, Lewy, and Moss specify that only 10 percent of tenants received land from Saigon, and Karnow is even more pessimistic, citing figures from Long An Prov-ince, where fewer than 1,000 out of 35,000 tenants benefited. Young con-cludes that "the overwhelming majority" of peasants "actually suffered" as a result of Diem's policies.[14]

7.2 The U.S. and South Vietnamese governments
The South Vietnamese government enjoyed greater support from the U.S. government than from the Vietnamese population. Chairman Nguyen Van Thieu, President Lyndon B. Johnson, and Prime Minister Nguyen Cau Ky salute during the playing of the U.S. and Vietnamese national anthems during welcoming ceremonies at Guam's International Airport, Agana, March 20, 1967. NARA, NWDNS-306–SSM-8K(2). War and Conflict no. 388.

The pro-GVN camp does not contest these judgments. Lewy remarks that Diem's land reform was "virtually inoperative," and Joes estimates that it "caused even more damage" than the cancellation of village elections. Lomperis ignores the subject but later suggests that Thieu's land-to-the-tiller reform in 1970 was the first occasion when "Saigon developed an effective program" in this area.[15]

More than any other survey, Lewy's book emphasizes class struggle in South Vietnam, especially in the countryside. He frequently notes the ravages of landlordism and the plight of tenants. "The demand for land ownership became a demand for an end to peonage and for personal freedom," he declares. So it is not surprising that he regards the land-to-the-tiller program as the most positive initiative in the history of the GVN. Within three years, it virtually eliminated tenancy, with the result that "the power of the landlords over rural life had been seriously weakened and a beginning made in changing the perception of government as simply the protector of the rich and the powerful." Redistribution of land stimulated "a new wave of prosperity," and related community development efforts, bustling markets, and an expanding school system reinforced an impression that progress was being made. [16]

Joes and Lomperis follow Lewy on this score, and at least mildly optimistic passages on roads opened, bridges repaired, schools and health clinics built, and increasing rice production appear in Herring, Moss, and Olson and Roberts. But most of the surveys do not buy land-to-the-tiller as a turning point. Lewy's own skepticism is palpable. For example, where Joes celebrates progress in Army of the Republic of Vietnam (ARVN) capabilities, Lewy joins the other survey authors in reserving judgment. ARVN leadership "came from the middle and upper classes of South Vietnam's urban society and had great difficulty in relating to their own soldiers, who were primarily of peasant origin," and to the rural population. The consequent mistreatment of civilians was "reinforced and aggravated by the reliance on heavy weapons," an "addiction" that showed no sign of slackening as the war went on. All in all, Lewy conveys a sense that land-to-the-tiller was only a first step. Victory on the battlefield would not be forthcoming unless Saigon brought about a redistribution of power throughout society.[17]

To sum up, the surveys make clear the GVN's antidemocratic practice and estrangement from the peasant majority. Most readers of these books will not be tempted by a betrayal-of-an-ally interpretation of the war, with Saigon leaders as innocent victims. Even the authors who sound the betrayal chord in their discussions of the catastrophe that befell the regime in 1975 are troubled when reviewing the record for the earlier period, and their most authoritative champion, Guenter Lewy, sharply criticizes the elitism of the regime.

Puppets Who Pulled Their Own Strings

This near consensus on the performance of the GVN still leaves unanswered the question of responsibility. Were Saigon leaders unworthy allies who thwarted good faith efforts by the United States, or were they simply following orders from Washington? Or is a more complex image required, to characterize "puppets who pulled their own strings"?[18]

The surveys underscore American responsibility for the spotty GVN electoral record. Among the most anxious of the survey authors to blame Saigon, Karnow highlights inattention and naïveté on the U.S. side ("What the Americans failed to understand was that [Diem's] mandarin mentality could not accept the idea of even minority resistance to his rule"). Others are tougher on Washington. According to Herring, "the U.S. government and the American mission in Saigon did little to promote democracy, or even political reform, until South Vietnam was swept by revolution." U.S. policymakers got exactly what they had sought—in the words of Olson and Roberts, "an anticommunist government in Saigon—democratic or not." Lewy suggests that the Americans should have pushed harder for "political and economic reform," whereas Lomperis adds that unconditional U.S. aid left Diem free to discount the taxpaying public. Joes is the only author who thinks the Americans were too critical rather than not critical enough of Diem's antidemocratic policies.[19]

The textbooks treat the ruthless face of the GVN in a more evasive fashion. Young is the most insistent on U.S. culpability and pinpoints the role of Michigan State University in training "the forces of repression" employed against opponents of the Saigon government. She is the only author to explore this affiliation.[20] When it comes to the anti-Communist denunciation campaign, torture, and concentration camps, the other surveys blame Diem.

Human rights violations perpetrated by Thieu and abetted by the United States are also not much connected to Washington. CIA and GVN involvement in the heroin traffic goes virtually unnoticed, and tiger cages do not loom large, save in Lewy, who insists—not one of his better moments—that they were more spacious than antiwar activists claimed. Characteristically unwilling to ignore the issue but hard-pressed to fend off critics, he lapses into Orientalism with the suggestion that abuses may have been due to the South Vietnamese "low regard for human life and suffering."[21]

With respect to Diem and the peasants, the survey treatments fall again into a blame-it-on-Saigon mode. Six discussions of Diem's land reform make no mention of the Americans, and several of the others claim that they were prodding Saigon in the right direction. Herring declares that Diem acted on the land question only at "American insistence," Hess claims that grudging gestures at reform were undertaken "under pressure from the U.S.," and Lewy says that the program began with "American support and advice" but was not carried through by the Vietnamese. Karnow notes that Diem "brought in prominent American experts like

Wolf Ladejinsky, who had planned successful land reforms in Japan and Taiwan, but he spurned their advice." Disputing these views, Young describes the GVN initiatives as "Ladejinsky's land reform program" and suggests that Washington got the policy it desired.[22]

Balance Sheet on the GVN

Analysis in the surveys of relations between Americans and Vietnamese is complex and unfinished, but this collective endeavor clearly demonstrates the inadequacy of received paradigms. Advocates of the betrayal-of-an-ally view constitute a minority, and even they run out of patience when reviewing the record of Saigon abuses. Blame-it-on-Saigon exerts more influence, especially when it comes to Diem's repression and class-based land program, and Young performs a service by insisting on U.S. involvement, even in the ugliest GVN practices. Still, all survey authors place at least some of the blame for disaster in South Vietnam on the United States. Finally, a notion of the GVN as a puppet regime has not worn well, as the texts make clear that Diem and Thieu were not mere mandatories of their foreign sponsors.

To sum up, interaction between Saigon and the Americans is a story of differing degrees of power but also of joint responsibility in determining the course of events. No account can leave out the preferences and actions of the Vietnamese, which in turn were influenced by regional, ethnic, and generational tensions within the Saigon milieu. Turley makes a beginning at engagement with these issues when he posits a difference between the founding fathers of the GVN and the Young Turks who supplanted them. He sees Thieu as part of "a new elite—younger, more career-oriented, and more susceptible to U.S. influence by comparison with the mandarin Francophiles it displaced." But Thieu's closeness to the Americans cut both ways. While making him "more susceptible" to outside "influence," it also allowed for a shrewder understanding and opened new possibilities for the Vietnamese. Not even in his most grandiose flights could Diem have imagined intervening in U.S. presidential politics, as Thieu did in 1968 and 1972. Here and elsewhere on the subject of the GVN, there is more to be said. [23]

A Litany of Resistance to Foreign Domination

In defending Saigon, Joes speaks of "an admittedly corrupt government with at least some of the institutions and mechanisms of democracy and capable of further democratic evolution," which he contrasts with "a totalitarian state" of the North, "explicitly contemptuous of all the political values of the American people." Lomperis concludes his commentary on the GVN record by affirming that "there was still more freedom in the South than in the North," and he adds that South Vietnam was "less prosperous" after the war, when it was ruled by the Communists, than "in the days of Nguyen Van Thieu." Lewy agrees that the GVN can be judged only with reference to the DRV. "A totalitarian state like Communist North Vietnam, possessing a monopoly of indoctrination and social control, was bound to display greater military morale and unity than a fragmented and barely authoritarian country like South Vietnam." To pursue the inquiry, one must turn to survey treatments of the North.[24]

A Cold War interpretation of the Democratic Republic of Vietnam holds sway in the three pro-GVN texts. The opening of Lewy's book, situated in 1950, is constructed to imply coordinated Communist aggression in China, Korea, and Vietnam. The author appears to accept Washington's claim that the Viet Minh's battle against the French "was more than a mere colonial war." Joes asserts that U.S. policymakers reacted rationally when "Ho Chi Minh openly declared himself a loyal adherent of a self-proclaimed monolithic and expansionary world Communist movement." Lomperis says that "it was really impossible to disguise the essential foreignness of the Communist ideology."[25]

Elsewhere in the survey, one encounters frequent references to Hanoi leaders as Vietnamese patriots. A "great man" treatment of Ho Chi Minh, with the emphasis on his nationalism, is common. In the words of Herring, "The Vietnamese Revolution was in many ways the personal creation of the charismatic patriot Ho Chi Minh." Critical distance is perhaps signaled when Turley declares that, "As popularly told, Vietnam's history is a litany of resistance to foreign domination." But in most of the surveys the point is affirmed without irony. As Olson and Roberts put it, "Vietnam was for the Vietnamese, not for anyone else, and that passion had driven Ho Chi Minh throughout his life."[26]

Some of the books that stress Ho's patriotism also take note of Vietnamese Communism. It would be "naive" to obscure this aspect, Olson and Roberts warn. Comparing the Viet Minh to other independence movements in Southeast Asia, Moss declares, "Only in Vietnam did the struggle for home rule also become a struggle for who should rule at home." Such formulations recall the notion, proffered by the left wing within the antiwar movement, of the Vietnamese resistance as a social revolution.[27]

The August Revolution

The balance among these conceptions shifts as the surveys trace the history of Vietnamese Communism, beginning with the August Revolution of 1945. Joes argues that the Communist seizure of power in that year was an "elitist movement," resembling "a coup much more than the great revolutions of history." Moss presents a different emphasis, with the Viet Minh harnessing "the vast energies" of the population," leading to "a remarkable merging of a people and a movement" and allowing "the Vietnamese people" to reclaim "their national identity."[28]

Other treatments occupy a space between these interpretive options. A number of passages focus on Viet Minh agency and portray the masses as instruments of party leadership in a way that tilts toward the "coup" version: "the Vietminh opportunistically filled the vacuum, occupying government headquarters in Hanoi" (Herring); "the Viet Minh called for a national insurrection, and its political cadres and army moved southward" (Hess); "the time had come to grab power" (Karnow); "the Communists decided to seize the moment . . . the party decided to strike" (Lomperis); "the Vietminh leaders had the crowd marching through the streets of Hanoi" then "staged similar people's rallies" in other cities (Olson and Roberts). Other formulations make the event sound more like a mass movement: "the August Revolution swept the Vietminh to power" (Hess); Ho was "racing to keep up with events" (Karnow); "the Communists rode to power on the crest of a popular uprising" (Turley); "thousands of peasants poured into the cities from the countryside, demonstrating their support for the Viet Minh in huge rallies" (Young).[29]

To sum up, with respect to the August Revolution, the Communist foreign Other of Cold War discourse signals its presence, but Vietnamese aspirations, both patriotic and revolutionary, also occupy a prominent place in the survey accounts.

Land Reform in The North

Contrasting images of the North Vietnamese are shuffled in a different fashion as discussion turns to the land reform of 1953–1956. Here the debate is between land reform as an atrocity, fomented by the Communists as part of their drive for power and resulting in an immense death toll; and land reform as an episode in a revolutionary process. Five texts argue that the campaign was not a reaction to genuine social ills but instead grew out of the authoritarian politics or ideology of Communism, with catastrophic results: 50,000 to several hundred thousand executions (Lewy and Joes); "epic disaster" (Lomperis); "disaster" (Olson and Roberts); "atrocities throughout the country" and "thousands" of deaths (Karnow).[30]

On this issue the latter two texts abandon their earlier focus on Vietnamese patriotism and switch to a lurid view of the enemy. Karnow transforms Ho Chi Minh from a man of "gentle temperament" into an ideologue who was personally responsible for a bloodbath. The disjuncture is equally stark in Olson and Roberts. "He was just a wisp of a man," they declare in introducing Ho. But in 1954 "he set out on a misguided crusade" leading to a torrent of "accusations, lies, informants, and a neighbor-against-neighbor atmosphere," in which "thousands" died and "tens of thousands more" were placed in labor camps. Both deny that landlordism was an issue in the North (such an idea was "insane," Karnow avers) and therefore imply that the exercise did not have any legitimate purpose. On this point Karnow and Olson and Roberts are close to Joes and Lomperis, who insist that land reform was, in Lomperis's words, an "imperative of Communist ideology" rather than a response to a real problem.[31]

Three of the texts see land reform as a flawed but successful campaign to satisfy peasant land hunger. Hess speaks of "errors"; Moss, of "many abuses and atrocities," "thousands" of deaths, and "a residue of bitterness and distrust" in the countryside; Young, of a campaign that "frequently left villages not transformed, but deeply embittered." In contrast, Hess cites "substantial results," including distribution of land to 2 million peasants and increased rice production. Moss also notes that 2 million country dwellers received land and adds that "a new class of landowners composed of middle peasants strongly supportive of the Hanoi regime took control of the villages." Young agrees that the campaign "deepened popular support for the government."[32]

To sum up, the foreign Other does not win this round, but it fares better in the land reform phase of the debate than in discussions of 1945, whereas social revolution struggles to hold its ground, and Vietnamese patriotism, unable to gain a purchase on the evidence, retreats toward the sidelines.

The Air War Against the DRV

During the period from 1956 to 1965, the DRV virtually disappears from the surveys. Olson and Roberts constitute an extreme case. After land reform, "political life in North Vietnam settled down," they remark, then

7.3 North Vietnam

The politics and society of North Vietnam are presented in confusing and unclear ways in U.S. textbooks, making it very difficult to understand how people chose their allegiances. Here farmers near the Chinese border plow a rice paddy. Dematteis, *A Portrait of Vietnam,* 19. Used by permission.

drop the topic for good. Young mentions but does not explore both "rewards" and "severe problems" in the industrial sector and "serious problems" with agricultural cooperatives. Turley comments on the cooperatives by way of a flashback during discussion of the air war, but more with reference to their role in defending the country than in production. Elsewhere the political and economic systems developed in the North and the health and education policies of the DRV are ignored. Cultural life under the new regime is neglected, too, save for the "hundred flowers" controversy, briefly noted by Turley and Lomperis.[33]

When North Vietnam reappears at the beginning of the air war in 1965, a number of the authors are unabashedly admiring. Herring speaks of "great ingenuity and dogged perseverance"; Hess asserts that the Vietnamese "proved remarkably resilient in responding to the damage and in defending their country"; Olson and Roberts evoke their "cooperative spirit"; and Turley salutes a "well-founded pride" in "collective action when threatened." Turley is the most probing, as he considers both patriotic and revolutionary sources for Vietnamese resistance. To be sure, the war effort relied on peasant cooperatives created by the new government a few years before. But these institutions "were based on the communities to which almost all Vietnamese felt a primordial attachment" and drew on an ageless and "unremitting struggle with nature," as well as on "two millennia of conflict with China."[34]

Quoting Brian Jenkins, Maclear singles out the patriotic aspect (Hanoi leaders "made history work for them"), and Karnow takes a similar tack, with the view that bombing "rekindled their nationalistic zeal, so that many who may have disliked Communist rule joined the resistance to alien attack." Herring, Joes, Lewy, and Turley agree that air attacks helped the DRV solidify mass support, with Turley specifying that it accelerated the mobilization of Catholics, minorities, and women behind the war effort. Discussion elsewhere, even if it does not make the connection explicit, is couched in an idiom recalling earlier passages on the Viet Minh and Vietnam's history of resistance to foreign domination.[35]

Exception made for the passages from Turley noted above, these treatments are more descriptive than analytic and do not weigh the relative contribution of Vietnamese patriotism or the Vietnamese revolution in determining the success of the war effort. On the other side of the debate, for Lewy and Joes, the concept of "totalitarianism," connoting both moral bankruptcy and mass-based dynamism, serves a dual function by placing the Communists beyond the pale and also explaining their success. But Lewy has nothing to say about political or any other institutions in the DRV, and neither does Joes, whose reference to "the familiar machinery of the totalitarian state" is no more than a rhetorical gesture. Lomperis is just as cavalier, and he does not pursue the comparison he proposes between North and South.[36]

To sum up, survey treatments of North Vietnam are cursory. Joes and Lewy do not try to prove that the DRV was totalitarian, and rival claims that it was revolutionary are undocumented. The patriotic aspect is addressed more fully, but passages in this register are essentialist and, in the last resort, take refuge in a great-man evocation of Ho Chi Minh. Given this lack of content, it is impossible to measure the "foreignness" of Vietnamese Communism. North Vietnam remains the terra incognita of the Vietnam War.

Invisible History of the Vietnamese

The surveys are not helpful in addressing the social history of the Vietnamese in the era of the Vietnam War. The problem is apparent in treatments of the people of the GVN, beginning with the refugees who moved from North Vietnam to South Vietnam after the Geneva Accords. The surveys are uncurious about the refugees. Lomperis says nothing about them; Herring, Lewy, and Maclear do not explore their motivation; and the other texts are content to note that they were, in Karnow's words, "fiercely anti-communist." Even Joes, the most sympathetic, pauses only to affirm that they were fleeing "ever further southward, ever away from Communist control."[37]

Several texts execute a swift transition from the thoughts of the refugees to the schemes of those who sought to encourage their flight. Moss's account jumps from "Catholic peasants" who "were uncertain and fearful about life under the Communists and voted with their feet," to propaganda and psychological warfare authored by the Catholic Church, American and French officials, and the Diem administration, which induced "reluctant villagers to flee." It was "not an entirely spontaneous folk movement," he concludes. Hess ("blunt propaganda slogans"), Maclear (CIA "scare tactics"), Turley (refugees "egged on by U.S.-supplied leaflets"), and Young (intelligence operative Edward Lansdale-inspired rumors of U.S. atomic bomb attacks on the DRV) strike a similar note.[38]

Readers would not be tempted to attribute much sophistication to the refugees. Herring, Hess, Karnow, Maclear, Turley, and Young credit watchwords such as "Christ has gone to the South," "the Virgin Mary is going South," and "God has gone South," and these authors as well as Moss and Olson and Roberts stress the leadership of parish priests and the northern Catholic hierarchy. The patronizing undercurrent in such passages is made explicit when Olson and Roberts refer to refugees as "gullible peasants." Karnow's rejoinder to the effect that the subjective impetus must have been more weighty than any external prodding seems plausible. Yet even in this sensible passage Karnow cedes the floor to the Americans, in the

7.4 Catholic refugees

The mass exodus of Catholics from North to South Vietnam in 1954, a huge social transformation, is poorly explained in U.S. college texts. Here the USS *Montague* accepts refugees who
began their voyage on a smaller French ship. NARA, NWDNS-80–G-644449, War and Conflict no. 386.

form of CIA pacification specialist Edward Lansdale's self-serving commentary on the migration, rather than to the Vietnamese who were doing the migrating.[39]

A phenomenon of undeniable significance, this movement of almost a million people remains a mystery that no one seems interested in exploring, some because they would not welcome any softening of the anti-Communist moral of the story, others because their notion of Vietnamese as puppets makes further inquiry seem superfluous. The failure to explain is apparent when one considers that hundreds of thousands of Catholics stayed in the North. To account for these choices, one would have to probe more deeply into the thoughts and experiences of the refugees and of their coreligionists who remained at home.[40]

A similar indifference is apparent as the surveys consider what happened to the Vietnamese in the Saigon milieu in the following years. Several texts note in passing that the war changed the society of South Vietnam. Young refers to Harvard University political scientist Samuel Huntington's defense of an "American-sponsored urban revolution," achieved as firepower and defoliation drove the peasantry from their villages. Turley says the war stimulated "a cityward migration" that proved to be "largely irreversible," Hess declares that it "shattered much of the traditional social structure," and Karnow argues that the United States, "motivated by the loftiest of intentions, did indeed rip South Vietnam's social fabric to shreds." In the words of Olson and Roberts, "American forces destroyed the peasants' way of life."[41]

This transformation is not much considered in the texts. Herring and Moss have little to say about the topic, and in the absence of interviews with refugees, neither does Maclear. In an almost flippant passage, Olson and Roberts remark that Saigon "had become a city of prostitutes, pimps, black marketeers, petty thieves, drug dealers, assassins, orphans, refugees, deserters, Viet Cong, terrorists, and opportunists." Hess strikes a more poignant note, affirming that, "Family life disintegrated as young men and women, tempted by the lure of making easy money from the Americans, abandoned filial loyalty and became part of the booming economy that served the American military." Karnow addresses the topic in almost Victorian tones, claiming that, "for young women in particular, the primrose path to relative riches was irresistible."[42]

For their part, Lewy and Joes refuse to endorse a modernization achieved by force and indeed are among the most insistent of the authors in criticizing an indiscriminate U.S. firepower that, in Joes's words,

7.5 and 7.6 Saigon and Southeast Asia transformed

In 1966 Saigon was still a sleepy little town where bullock carts were an important mode of transportation. By the end of the war, when it was renamed Ho Chi Minh City, life there had been transformed. Economic pressures and the war in Vietnam pulled women throughout Southeast Asia into sex work in bars that catered exclusively to U.S. servicemen, like this one in Olongapao, Philippines. U.S. textbooks do not explore questions of responsibility for those changes. USIA/NARA photo #417, NWDNS-306–MVP-25(1) and Saundra Pollock Sturdevant and Brenda Stoltzfus, *Let the Good Times Roll* (New York: New Press, 1992). Used by permission.

"caused tremendous loss of life and property among Vietnamese civilians." Both are convinced that the war had to be won by protecting, not displacing, the villagers. These two authors do not support "forced draft urbanization," to use Huntington's term, but fail to make clear that this policy brought about a fundamental change in South Vietnamese society.[43]

A related neglect is evident as the writers shift their attention north of the seventeenth parallel. In discussing the DRV, they are most interested in military planning by Hanoi leaders, especially in 1968, 1972, and 1975, and provide only sketchy references "from the bottom up." Other sources make clear that the war in the North uprooted millions of country people, mobilizing them into the army and sending them to fight in the South. Many of the survivors who came home in 1975 had spent their entire adult lives in the armed forces and were not willing or able to resettle in their villages. On the home front, family and neighborhood routines had been altered, and an administrative apparatus grew up around the state and the Communist Party.

After 1975 it became clear that for North Vietnam the war had been more revolutionary than the revolution and had moved the center of gravity in society from the countryside toward the town, from orally transmitted custom toward the written word, from face-to-face reciprocities toward bureaucratic anonymity. The transformation was just as significant as the "urban revolution" promoted by U.S. firepower in South Vietnam. To be sure, peasants in both North and South must still be reckoned with, but in the 1990s the agrarian order they fought to preserve and enlarge is being called into question. Thirty years of resistance eventuated in a triumph over the United States, but it also unleashed market forces throughout Vietnam, which are now drawing the country into the world economic system.[44]

These issues can be explored only when the focus is placed not on Ho or Diem or Thieu but on the Vietnamese people. In this light, what jumps out is the theme of movement, from the near million who migrated from North to South in 1954 to the millions who marched down the Ho Chi Minh Trail or who were evacuated from cities during the air war or who fled from their homes in war zones below the seventeenth parallel to Saigon or other towns. Perhaps even more numerous are those who stayed home but "moved" socially and psychologically, with profound implications for age, class, and gender relations in the country.

The survey authors fail to address these issues. The 1954 migration, an early mass movement of the Vietnamese, is slighted. Disruptions in the South, affecting relations between women and men and youth and elders, are men-

7.7 Postwar Vietnam
Americans also know little about postwar Vietnam. Here schoolchildren hold up chalkboards
with their answers to a math problem in a rural school in Quang Binh Province. Dematteis, *A
Portrait of Vietnam,* 76. Used by permission.

tioned but not with much sensitivity, as, for example, in Karnow's reference
to "the primrose path." And little is said about changes in daily life in the
North, even by authors who note the revolutionary character of the regime.

Opponents of U.S. intervention borrowed "war crimes" from the World
War II context in order to highlight that atrocities were being committed in
Vietnam, and the conception still serves a purpose in the classroom, where
students of a later generation know nothing about the reality of antiguer-
rilla warfare. It is useful as well in underscoring the magnitude of the change

imposed by war on the people of Vietnam, a mutation that deserves comparison to the enclosure movement in England or forced collectivization in the Soviet Union. U.S. intervention disarticulated South Vietnamese society, and the total war strategy adopted by Hanoi leaders in 1965 reworked the social order of the North. Inattention in the surveys to "forced draft urbanization and modernization" is perhaps occasioned by a failure of political nerve. Whatever the source, this reticence hinders efforts to understand Vietnam's recent history. Social consequences require the attention of future scholars hoping to make sense of the Vietnam War.

Notes

For their criticisms and suggestions, I am grateful to James Hunt and Peter Weiler and also to Laura Hein, Mark Selden, and Tom Fenton, editors of the *Bulletin of Concerned Asian Scholars*.

1. Statement by Larry Rottmann, in Vietnam Veterans Against the War, ed., *The Winter Soldier Investigation: An Inquiry into American War Crimes* (Boston: Beacon Press, 1972), 164.

2. On the link between soldiering in Vietnam and studying Vietnamese history, see Keith Taylor, who writes, "As an American soldier in Vietnam, I could not help being impressed by the intelligence and resolve of the Vietnamese who opposed us, and I asked: 'Where did these people come from?' "; Keith Taylor, *The Birth of Vietnam* (Berkeley: University of California Press, 1983), xv. See also David Marr's reference to his experience as a U.S. Marine Corps intelligence officer in Vietnam in 1962–1963, in *Vietnamese Tradition on Trial, 1920–1945* (Berkeley: University of California Press, 1981), vii.

3. David Hunt, "Images of the Viet Cong," in Robert Slabey, ed., *The United States and Viet Nam from War to Peace* (Jefferson, NC: McFarland, 1996), 53–61.

4. On the winter soldiers, see Lewy, 313–21; on evidence of war crimes, ibid., chapter 7 ("American Military Tactics and the Law of War"), 223 ff. See the appendix for a full reference to Lewy's book and to the other surveys cited in this chapter.

5. On the winter soldiers and the Vietnam Veterans Against the War, see Young, 255 ff; and also Herring, 266; Maclear, 234; Moss, 349; and Olson and Roberts, 237 and 239. On the "Hué massacre," see Hunt, "Images of the Viet Cong," 54–57.

6. Max Hastings, *The Korean War* (New York: Simon and Schuster, 1987). For an account that places Koreans in the center of the Korean War, see Bruce Cumings, *The Origins of the Korean War.* vol. 1: *Liberation and the Emergence of Separate Regimes, 1945–1947* (Princeton, NJ: Princeton University Press, 1989); and vol. 2, *The Roaring of the Cataract, 1947–1950* (Princeton, NJ: Princeton University Press, 1990).

7. Joes, 145; Lewy, 202, 436–37; and Lomperis from 163.

8. Herring, 59–60, 70; Hess, 59–60, 61, 63; Joes, 42–44, 68; Karnow, 239–40; Lewy, 7–10, 14; Lomperis, 49–50; Maclear, 49–50, 53, 54–55; Moss, 79, 81; Olson and Roberts, 62, 64; Turley, 6, 14–15, 52; and Young, 52–53, 56.

9. Joes, 77; and Lomperis, 103.

10. Herring, 177–78; Hess, 101; Karnow, 466; Moss, 232; and Turley, 104–5. See also Lewy, 94; Maclear, 147; Olson and Roberts, 167; and Young, 184–86. On the 1971 presidential election, see Herring, 269–70; Joes, 143; Karnow, 635–36; Lomperis, 87, 103; and Young, 263–65.

11. Lewy, 94, 189, 218. See also Herring, 254; Joes, 121; Maclear, 259; Olson and Roberts, 255; and Turley, 169.

12. Herring, 69, 71; Hess, 61, 101; Karnow, 243; Lewy, 14, 297; Maclear, 55; Moss,

91–92; Olson and Roberts, 67, 256; Turley, 52, 170; and Young, 56, 60–62. Joes insists that "Diem was as far as can be imagined from the stereotype of the bloodthirsty tyrant" and that there were only thirty-three "nonjudicial executions" during his regime (69). Other texts provide a more substantial body count: 20,000 arrested by 1956 ("and the campaign was subsequently intensified," according to Herring, 71); tens of thousands arrested (Hess, 61; Lewy, 15); 75,000 killed and 50,000 arrested (Maclear, 55); 20,000–75,000 killed and 100,000 arrested (Olson and Roberts, 67); 75,000 killed (Turley, 18, 33); 12,000 executed and up to 50,000 arrested through 1956 (Moss, 92; Young, 56).

13. Joes, 65, 69; Lewy, 95; Lomperis, 50, 96.

14. Herring, 70; Hess, 62–63; Joes, 68; Karnow, 246; Lewy, 14, 94; Moss, 92, 116; Olson and Roberts, 52, 64; Turley, 23, 55; and Young, 57. Herring, Lomperis, and Maclear make no mention of Viet Minh land reform.

15. Joes, 68; Lewy, 14; and Lomperis, 103.

16. Lewy, 186–91.

17. On the land-to-the-tiller program, see Herring, 254; Hess, 119; Joes, 121; Lomperis, 83; Maclear, 259; Moss, 325; Olson and Roberts, 197, 222; and Turley, 135, 170. On the ARVN, see Lewy, 170–71, 181–83; Joes, 66; and also Moss, 296.

18. The "puppet who pulled his own strings" metaphor is cited by Karnow, 251, and Turley, 52.

19. Herring, 69; Karnow, 239; Lewy, 11; Lomperis, 50–51; and Olson and Roberts, 64.

20. Young, 61.

21. Lewy, 297, 287. On the heroin traffic, Moss is the only author to provide a summary of the dossier (332), and he and Young are the only authors to cite the key text: Alfred McCoy, *The Politics of Heroin: CIA Complicity in the Global Drug Trade* (Brooklyn: Lawrence Hill, 1991).

22. Herring, 70; Hess, 63; Karnow, 246; Lewy, 14; and Young, 57. No text indicates U.S. involvement with Thieu's land-to-the-tiller reform.

23. For a discussion of these themes, see Gabriel Kolko, *Anatomy of a War: The Vietnamese, the United States, and the Modern Historical Experience* (New York: New Press, 1994). Because my focus in this chapter is on survey texts of an introductory character, suitable for college courses on the Vietnam War, I do not include Kolko's dense and formidable book in the discussion, even though it is in my opinion the most authoritative treatment of the subject. On Francophiles and Young Turks, see Turley, 103–4. Moss argues that "Thieu's last-minute demurral" with respect to the Paris peace negotiations "may have given Nixon his slim victory" in 1968 (302). For more on Thieu's efforts to help Nixon at that moment, see Herring, 238–39; Hess, 115; Karnow, 600–1; Olson and Roberts, 203; and Young, 233. On "peace is at hand," Thieu's battles with Kissinger, and the election of 1972, see Herring, 277–82; Hess, 131–32; Joes, 117–18; Karnow, 664–66; Lewy, 202–3; Maclear, 307, 310; Moss, 364–65; Olson and Roberts, 249; Turley, 150–54; and Young, 275–79.

24. Joes, 143; Lewy, 438; and Lomperis, 162. For more on the distinctions between authoritarianism and totalitarianism, see chapter 10 ("The 'Evil Empire'") in Abbott Gleason, *Totalitarianism: The Inner History of the Cold War* (New York: Oxford University Press, 1995), 190 ff.

25. Joes, 105; Lewy, 3–4; and Lomperis, 53. The survey authors are virtually unanimous in distancing themselves from the domino theory. Lewy's phrasing (increases in U.S. aid to France were "accompanied by an escalation in explanatory rhetoric and in the importance attributed to a noncommunist Indochina" [5]) is nuanced. Preferring a moral to a spatial definition of the foreign Other, Joes concedes that "in the last analysis the North Vietnamese and Viet Cong were not aliens but compatriots" (68)—without backing away from his conviction that they could and should have been defeated.

26. Herring, 4–5; Olson and Roberts, 5; and Turley, 1.

27. Moss, 15; and Olson and Roberts, 15.

28. Joes, 18; and Moss, 25–27.

29. Herring, 6; Hess, 20; Karnow, 161–62; Lomperis, 33; Olson and Roberts, 22; Turley, 3; and Young, 10. Lewy does not mention the August Revolution, and Maclear only glancingly refers to the event, because his informant, Archimedes Patti, did not get to Hanoi until after the Viet Minh was installed in power (11). Whereas survey authors see French and U.S. interventions as decisive in the formation of the GVN, the texts assign only a marginal role to external actors in the first days of the DRV. On Japanese, Chinese, French, and, most important, American assistance to Ho Chi Minh, see Herring, 6; Hess, 30; Joes, 18–19, 23; Karnow, 149–51; Lomperis, 33; Maclear, 11; Moss, 24; Olson and Roberts, 21–22; and Young, 10. No one cites any involvement by the USSR or other representatives of international Communism in the events of 1945.

30. Joes, 33; Karnow, 241; Lewy, 16; Lomperis, 51; and Olson and Roberts, 51.

31. Karnow, 133, 240; Lomperis, 51; and Olson and Roberts, 5, 51.

32. Hess, 64; Moss, 85; and Young, 50–51. Herring, Maclear, and Turley say nothing about the aims and results of land reform. All three note that "heavy-handed measures," in Herring's words, were employed during the campaign, while also questioning claims that a "bloodbath" took place. See Herring, 73–74; Maclear, 54; and Turley, 19.

33. Lomperis, 51; Olson and Roberts, 52; Turley, 19, 90–91; and Young, 50, 345.

34. Herring, 162; Hess, 92; Olson and Roberts, 156; Turley, 91–92, 95.

35. Herring, 165; Joes, 112; Karnow, 473; Lewy, 391–92; Maclear, 245; and Turley, 96.

36. Joes, 139.

37. Karnow, 238; and Joes, 32.

38. Herring, 56; Hess, 58–59; Karnow, 238; Maclear, 50; Moss, 77; Turley, 11; and Young, 45.

39. Herring, 56; Hess, 59; Karnow, 238; Maclear, 50; Moss, 76; Turley, 11; and Young, 45. The reference to "gullible peasants" is found in the first edition of the Olson and Roberts text (62) but has been deleted from the 1996 version of the book (63).

40. According to figures cited by Louis Wiesner, 457,000 Catholics (about 40 percent of the total in the North) remained in the DRV; see Wiesner, *Victims and Survivors: Displaced Persons and Other War Victims in Viet-Nam, 1954–1975* (New York: Greenwood, 1988), 17. For a local study of Catholics who did not go south, see François Houtart and Geneviève Lemercinier, *Hai Van: Life in a Vietnamese Commune* (London: Zed Books, 1984). In France, generations of republican historians of the French Revolution wrote slightingly of counterrevolutionary peasants, judged to have been manipulated by their parish priests and the church hierarchy. But then came Paul Bois, who showed that the "republican" communities of the West were "docile," whereas their "right-wing" neighbors had been in 1789 the most militant and class-conscious peasants in the region; and Maurice Agulhon, who argued that the eighteenth-century "white" engagements of villagers in the southeast helped to explain their emergence as "reds" in 1848. When the refugees of 1954 are treated more respectfully, perhaps an equally complex analysis of their motives and behavior will emerge. For more, see David Hunt, "Peasant Politics in the French Revolution," *Social History* 9 (1984): 277–99.

41. Hess, 102; Karnow, 454; Olson and Roberts, 163, 255; Turley, 103; and Young, 177.

42. Hess, 102; Karnow, 455; and Olson and Roberts, 255.

43. Joes, 109.

44. Vietnamese literature has opened the way toward an appreciation of wartime changes in the North. See Le Luu, *A Time Far Past*, trans. Ngo Vinh Hai, Nguyen Ba Chung, Kevin Bowen, and David Hunt (Amherst: University of Massachusetts Press, 1997).

Appendix

Texts considered in this article include the following:

George Herring, *America's Longest War: The United States and Vietnam, 1950–1975* (New York: Knopf, 1979, 1986, 1996).

Gary Hess, *Vietnam and the United States: Origins and Legacy of War* (Boston: Twayne, 1990).

Anthony James Joes, *The War for South Viet Nam, 1954–1975* (New York: Praeger, 1989, 1990).

Stanley Karnow, *Vietnam, A History* (New York: Penguin, 1983, 1984, 1991, 1997).

Guenter Lewy, *America in Vietnam* (New York: Oxford, 1978).

Timothy Lomperis, *The War Everyone Lost–and Won: America's Intervention in Viet Nam's Twin Struggles* (Washington: Congressional Quarterly Press, 1984, 1993).

Michael Maclear, *The Ten Thousand Day War, Vietnam: 1945–1975* (New York: Mentor, 1986).

George Moss, *Vietnam: An American Ordeal* (Englewood Cliffs: Prentice Hall, 1990, 1994, 1998).

James Olson and Randy Roberts, *Where the Domino Fell: America and Vietnam, 1945–1990* (New York: St. Martins, 1991, 1996).

William Turley, *The Second Indochina War: A Short Political and Military History, 1954–1975* (New York: Mentor, 1986).

Marilyn Young, *The Vietnam Wars, 1945–1990* (New York: Harper Collins, 1991).

* * *

Combining anticommunism with a defense of U.S. policy, Guenter Lewy's *America in Vietnam* launched the Vietnam War survey genre in 1978, in terms that reappear in studies by Timothy Lomperis and Anthony James Joes. Lewy devotes many pages to combating (and with surprising frequency echoing) the antiwar case. His book is the strongest of the "right-wing" texts.

George Herring's *America's Longest War* followed on the heels of Lewy's study. Buttressed by dense and original research, Herring develops a critique of U.S. policy couched in the low-key idiom of the diplomatic historian. Revised to incorporate recent scholarship and with graphics added, a third edition in 1996 signals the resolve of the author and publisher to defend the book's place as the most frequently assigned text on the war.

Studies by Michael Maclear and Stanley Karnow were written in the early 1980s to supplement made-for-TV documentaries produced in Canada and the United States. Interview-driven, Maclear's work contains interesting passages, but suffers from the limits of its sources. Karnow's treatment is more realized, but still depends too much on what the author saw and who he talked to. It ranked second in influence behind Herring's book in a 1993 review of the most frequently cited texts in college courses on the war. [1]

Among recent survey authors, Gary Hess, George Moss, and James Olson and Randy Roberts are closer in critical outlook to Herring and Karnow than to Lewy. Hess's book contains many impressive passages, but is among the least noticed of the texts. Moss's treatment, which seems to have sold well (a third edition was published in 1998), is almost twice as long as Herring's book, but is similar to it in shape and argument. Unburdened by footnotes, Olson and Roberts offer piquant anecdotes and thumbnail sketches of major personalities.

Alone among survey authors in drawing on Vietnamese language sources, William Turley respectfully attends to the guerrillas, a strategy that gives his presentation a "left" tone, one that is heard again from Marilyn Young. Now out of print, Turley's study is the shortest of the texts and is alone in beginning in 1954 rather than 1945. Young's *The Vietnam Wars, 1945–1990* is the most readable of the surveys and the closest in spirit to the antiwar movement.

Among survey authors, Herring, Lewy, Moss, and Young spend the most time discussing the U.S. side, well over half of the text in each case, and Herring and Young have the most insight to contribute on the subject. Lomperis and Joes pay less attention to the Americans, with Joes not getting around to examining Washington policy until 1963. Hess also deals rapidly with the United States, in part because he pays more attention than do the other authors to Laos and Cambodia. Also assigning the Americans a minority role in the narrative is Turley, the only author to devote the same amount of space, around 20 percent in each case, to the DRV, the GVN, and the NLF.

Many of the surveys are critical of U.S. intervention. Young condemns the perpetrators of War crimes, and, while other authors hesitate to indict American policy in systemic terms, they do make clear that the Vietnamese were brutally treated. Karnow claims that the United States was "motivated by the loftiest intentions," but one sees little of such excuse-making elsewhere in the surveys. On the prowar side, Joes lashes out at the bad faith of "Free World" leaders, and the case Lewy constructs on their behalf is strikingly ambivalent.

Lewy, Lomperis, and Joes are the most sympathetic of the authors to the GVN and the toughest on the North Vietnamese. On the Saigon regime, Herring, Hess, Lewy, Moss, and Turley weigh in to good effect, while Lomperis stays in a "nation-building" register, and Joes pities the victims of a "satanic" communism. Turley is thoughtful on the DRV, while other authors are content to talk about Ho Chi Minh and strategy debates in Hanoi. Turley and Young are the only authors to analyze the functioning of the NLF and to take their distance from the "Hué massacre," a cold war construct developed by the U.S. Mission in Saigon to establish that the guerrillas were guilty of the war's most blame-worthy atrocity.[2]

Notes

1. According to a survey conducted in 1990–1991, when the "second generation" of surveys (Joes, Hess, Moss, Olson and Roberts, Young) was just appearing, Herring ranked first among survey authors (58 mentions out of 8 respondents), compared to Karnow (46), Turley (11), Moss (7), Olson and Roberts (7), Lewy (2), and Maclear (1); see Patrick Hagopian, "Report on the 1990–1991 Survey of Courses on the Vietnam War" (Fairfax, VA: Indochina Institute/George Mason University, 1993).

2. For more on survey treatments of the NLF, see Hunt, "Images of the Viet Cong."

Part III
Politics of the Classroom

8
The Continuing Legacy of Japanese Colonialism: The Japan–South Korea Joint Study Group on History Textbooks

Kimijima Kazuhiko
(translated by Inokuchi Hiromitsu)

The Origins of the Study Group

Japanese textbook treatments of war and colonialism have been a highly politicized issue within Japan since 1945, but they did not become a major source of diplomatic conflict with Asian nations until 1982, after government officials tried to use the textbook certification system to mute the critical tone of textbooks. The government of the republic of Korea was particularly critical of depictions of Japanese rule of the Korean peninsula. One important response to that controversy was the creation of the Japan–South Korea Joint Study Group on History Textbooks, which subjected the issues of war, citizenship, and imperialism to cross-national study. The joint research by Japanese and Korean scholars on Japanese textbooks offers new perspectives on the issues and illustrates the difficulties of achieving historical consensus.[1]

The joint study group originated in 1989, when Kanazawa University professor Fujisawa H)ei received a letter from Yi T'ae-yLng, a South Korean historian. Yi, then president of Honam University, is currently head of the Korea International Textbook Research Institute. The two had had no previous contact. Yi mentioned having read Fujisawa's *Doitsu-jin no Rekishi Ishiki—Ky)kasho ni miru Sens) Sekinin* (German Awareness of History:

Responsibility for War as Represented in Textbooks) in Germany. (In his book Fujisawa allocated considerable space to the treatment of German-Polish exchanges on history textbook development.) Yi then visited Fujisawa and proposed holding a joint Japanese-Korean study project of history textbooks following such a model of exchange. In the summer of 1990, Fujisawa visited South Korea and met several researchers in order to organize the study group. Because the group was established just after the Korean president's visit to Japan, it drew considerable media attention.[2]

Initially, the purpose of the study group was to examine the descriptions of modern Japanese and Korean history in the history textbooks of each country. But because it seemed important to consider first the way the aggressor depicted its own aggression, the study group decided to begin by looking at Japanese history textbooks for high schools (Japanese scholars concentrated on textbooks on Japanese history only, whereas Korean scholars also examined world history textbooks). It was decided, primarily because of time constraints, that the study group would not review Korean history textbooks, which are written by committees within the government and directly sponsored by the state. In this the underlying situation differs from that in Japan, where several textbooks exist on the subject. In Korea all students study from a single history textbook.

The group was organized without the direct involvement of either the Korean or Japanese government. From the beginning, about thirty people participated, including historians of modern Japan and modern Korea, scholars of history education and education, high school and middle school teachers, textbook editorial staff from publishing houses, and graduate and undergraduate students. My own involvement was as one of the organizers of the study group on the Japanese side, and at the international meetings I reported on the Japanese textbook system and analyzed depictions of Japanese-Korean relations in high school textbooks on Japanese history.

In preparation for the international meeting, the participants from Japan held their own study meeting once a month, and the participants from Korea met several times as well. The international Japanese–South Korean study group meetings were held a total of four times, twice in each country, from the spring of 1991 to the fall of 1992. Each international meeting was open to the public and attracted about 100 people. The discussions explored key historical controversies in Japanese-Korean relations and their depictions in school textbooks.[3] The Japanese scholars often found themselves at odds with their Korean counterparts, even though, unlike some right-wing Japanese scholars, they agreed in general that the history of Japan's relations with Korea was mainly one of Japanese aggression and Korean resistance.

A Preliminary Lesson

The first lesson the study group learned was that Korean scholars did not have accurate knowledge about the Japanese textbook screening system and that Japanese scholars were unaware of some of the exchanges that took place after 1982 between the two governments regarding textbook content. The lesson began in the first international meeting, with a presentation by Pak Sŏng-su of the Academy of Korean Studies. His "On the Depiction of Korean-Japanese History Represented in Japanese History Textbooks" greatly surprised the Japanese scholars who were present. Pak first reminded the audience of twenty-four biased passages in Japanese textbooks that had been pointed out in 1982 by the Korean Committee on Compiling National History (a governmental agency that decides the official history of the Republic of Korea and is responsible for compiling the state history textbooks). The South Korean government had demanded that the Japanese government correct nineteen items, and the Japanese government had subsequently announced that fifteen of them had been corrected and that the remaining four items were "under review" (horū).

The surprise was not over the items the Korean Committee on Compiling National History had pointed out, since those had been well known, given their substantial coverage by the Japanese press at the time, but over the Japanese government's announcement of "correction and review." None of the Japanese scholars had heard of this "announcement" by the Japanese government. Moreover, it was difficult for the Japanese scholars to believe that the Japanese government could have corrected the fifteen items, since, given the way the textbook screening process in Japan works, it has only indirect control of any textbook content.

One example was a reference to Japan's 1910 "annexation of Korea." The Korean scholars thought that after their protests the textbooks had been revised by the addition of the phrase "suppressing the fierce resistance of the Koreans." It would have been impossible, however, for the government to make such a change—or any change—across the board to the texts of all twenty-some high school textbooks on Japanese history. Japanese textbooks, which are state-approved but not state authored, vary in their writing styles, wording, and emphasis, reflecting the values and perspectives of individual authors. Furthermore, quite aside from the content involved, such a "forced uniform change" would have caused a huge social controversy. In this sense, the statement by the chief cabinet secretary, Miyazawa Kiichi, that the Japanese government would take responsibility for correcting the descriptions was just a quick political cover.[4] His statement, which was intended to resolve diplomatic tensions with

South Korea and China, was thus criticized by textbook authors in Japan (even though they were also arguing for the same correction).

After the second international study group meeting, the Japanese scholars requested clarification from the Northeast Asia Division of Japan's Ministry of Foreign Affairs. According to a Foreign Ministry document of July 1, 1984, the division had reported the results of the annual textbook screening twice, in 1983 and 1984, to South Korea's Department of Foreign Affairs. Specifically, it had compared the 1983 and 1984 textbooks with 1982 versions and then reported the changes in the depictions of Korea. The Northeast Asia Division explained that since it had only identified the changes (that had already been made public by the Ministry of Education) and reported them to the South Korean government, there had been no need for a press release in Japan.

The question, then, became how the South Korean officials had interpreted the report. As far as I can speculate, the report of Japan's Ministry of Foreign Affairs was probably discussed in a joint meeting of the Korean Department of Foreign Affairs and Department of Education. Somehow, by the time the information was reported in Korean newspapers, the "changed parts" became "announcement of corrections," and the unchanged ones, which were for that reason not included in the Japanese ministry's report, became the "items under review."[5]

Although some aspects remained unresolved (such as how Japan's Ministry of Foreign Affairs explained the nature of its report to the Korean government), the situation suggested that Korean scholars had not fully understood Japan's textbook screening system. If Korean scholars had had a detailed knowledge of the Japanese textbook screening system, they certainly would have questioned the accuracy of the newspaper report when it first appeared. Both Japanese and Koreans realized that they had to clear up these simple misunderstandings if they wanted to concentrate on substantive differences.[6]

The Issues Raised by Korean Scholars

One of the most important issues raised during the four international study group meetings was that of the conceptualization of the historical relations between modern Japan and Korea.

The Contemporary Debate over the Conquest of Korea (Seikan ron)

The second international study group meeting considered textbook representations of modern Japanese-Korean relations. In one presentation, Japanese historian Katō Akira of Jōetsu University of Education referred to the famous 1873 Japanese official debate over whether or not to conquer Korea. Several leaders of the new Meiji government, including Saigō Takamori, had insisted that the Meiji government should immediately attack Korea, even though the Meiji government had established power in Japan only five years earlier.

The Korean researcher and professor at Sōngsin Women's University Yi Hyŏn-hee countered that the idea of conquering Korea was already well established in the Edo period, when such famous early-nineteenth-century thinkers as Kumazawa Banzan and Andō Shōeki were "representative advocates" of the idea and when major advocates for reform of the feudal system, such as Hayashi Shihei and Yoshida Shōin, also "explicitly argued for the legitimacy of the idea of invasion."

Yi traced the origins of the Japanese desire to invade Korea to the ancient myth, recorded in the *Nihon Shoki* (written in 720), that the legendary Empress Jink) had conquered Korea. He also noted the prevalent Japanese view that in the fourth and fifth centuries A.D. the Mimana governmental area, which was part of the ancient Japanese kingdom, was located in the Korean peninsula. Finally, moving from legend to established fact, Yi noted that Toyotomi Hideyoshi had invaded Korea in the sixteenth century and that late Edo thinkers had thus viewed invasion as part of a "recovery of lost territory." Yi concluded that after Hideyoshi's invasion Japanese intellectuals, who were strongly influenced by the ideology of the warrior class, not only celebrated the idea of conquering Korea but also argued that Korea was inferior and despicable. In short, he criticized Kat)'s description of the 1873 debate as a modern development by exposing its deep historical roots.[7]

Katō also met with resistance when he argued that the debate over invading Korea, the 1875 Japan's military provocation against Korea near Kanghwa Island (which institutionalized extraterritorial rights for Japan in Korea), and the conclusion of the Japanese-Korean Friendship Treaty on terms highly favorable to Japan should also be understood, in part, "in the light of the international context of the advancement of Western powers to Asia." A listener from the floor countered by saying that world historical contexts could not be the cause of Japanese invasion and that by blaming the Western powers Japan escaped accountability for its colonialism. Most of the Korean scholars situated the early Meiji debate on conquering Korea within the larger sweep of Japanese history. They agreed with Yi in tracing the beginnings back to ancient myth, and they viewed current problems in the Japanese-Korean relationship as extensions of that history.

It is important for Japanese scholars to recognize that most of their Korean counterparts see all of Japan's policies on Korea as "the continuation of ideas of conquering Korea" that began much earlier in Japanese history. Taken to its extreme, however, such an interpretation would lead Korean scholars to the argument that Japanese are essentially invasive, with the almost unavoidable result of reinforcing very strong anti-Japanese feelings among the Koreans. This tendency is certainly the legacy of Japan's modern colonial rule of Korea, and it might also have the danger of ruling out any major reconsideration of Japanese-Korean relations in the future.[8]

Views of Japan's Twentieth-Century Wars

Discussion of World War II centered on differences in conceptualizing the scope of the war and in establishing "responsibility for the war." In Japan recent debates over this point have focused on the years between 1931 and 1945. Progressive historians have come to conceptualize the Asian theater of World War II as the "Fifteen Years' War" (the term is also used in some school textbooks). The "war" is viewed as a series of wars beginning with the Japanese invasion of the northeastern part of China (Manchuria) in September 1931 and ending with the Japanese surrender to the Allied Powers in August 1945. The progressives argue that (1) the Japanese invasion of northeastern China was the cause of full-scale war with China; (2) deadlock in the war with China was the chief reason for the Japanese invasion of Southeast Asia; and (3) the invasion of Southeast Asia triggered the Japanese war against the United States and the United Kingdom. In short, the conception of these battles as a single fifteen-year war both provides a coherent explanation and recognizes Japan's war responsibility.

In contrast, some conservative Japanese who wish to underplay the Japanese invasion of China and Southeast Asia for the sake of their larger claim that the war pitted Asian liberation movements against Western imperialists have generally treated this fifteen-year history as if it were composed of a series of unrelated incidents: The Japanese advanced into northeastern China in 1931 (and the conflict ended), the Japanese advanced into the rest of China in 1937 (and the conflict was settled), and the Japanese entered the war against the United States and the United Kingdom in December 1941 (and this war "ended" in 1945). This framework helps hide the essential nature of the war—that it was a continuous and ever-widening war with Japanese invasion as its root cause.

The Korean scholars in the study group, however, posed a series of penetrating questions that challenged the idea of a fifteen-year war: How do the Japanese conceive of "accountability for Japan's colonial rule of

Korea"? And how does the "Fifteen Years' War" relate to that colonial rule? They criticized the concept of the Fifteen Years War as a Chinese-and-U.S.-centered view of history that slights the colonization of Korea. From the Korean perspective, the war that ended in August 1945 was either a seventy-year war that began with the Kanghwa Island incident of 1875, a fifty-year war beginning with the Sino-Japanese War (1894–1895), or, possibly, a forty-year war beginning with the Russo-Japanese War (1904–1905). At the end of that war, Japan made Korea into a protectorate and five years later, in 1910, annexed it as a formal colony. The Korean scholars, citing the example of the Hundred Years' War in European history, contended that the term "war" is not limited to periods of continuous, full-scale fighting. In sum, the central point of the Korean argument was that Japan and Korea were at war at least from the time of the 1894–1895 Sino-Japanese War and that even the progressive Japanese scholars had considered the events of that period only as "resistances," not a "war" [between nations].

In fact, in the Korean high school history textbook, anti-Japanese resistance during the Sino-Japanese War is described as organized by the "Tonghak farmers' army." Korean resistance to Japan after the Russo-Japanese War is similarly described as the anti-Japanese war of "righteous armies" (*ŭibyong*).[9] From this perspective, Koreans fought the war of "righteous armies" for fifty-five years, beginning in 1895. The same textbook also comments that the provisional Korean government (*Taehan Min'guk Imsi Chŏgbu*), established in exile in Shanghai, continued the anti-Japanese War after the March First Independence Movement of 1919 was crushed within Korea. That movement was joined by the anti-Japanese struggle on the part of Koreans in Manchuria. The provisional government declared war on Japan when the Pacific War broke out (in December 1941), and in the final stage of the war planned a military operation to recover Korea but did not carry it out before Japan's surrender.[10]

In the study group, Chŏng Chae-jung, a professor at the City University of Seoul, argued this very point. He stated that the anti-Japanese war in Korea intensified during the 1930s and 1940s, and he linked it to the Korean independence movement in Manchuria. He also stressed the December 1941 declaration of war on Japan by the Korean provisional government in Shanghai. Chŏng's contention was that Japan was at "war" with Korea throughout the years 1931–1945 and that the "responsibility for war" should be termed "accountability for colonial rule."

By contrast, though Japanese textbooks have increasingly included terms such as the "righteous soldiers' movement" *(gihei undō)* or the "righteous soldiers' struggle" *(gihei tōsō)* to describe the Korean resistance to Japanese rule, they have never treated Korea in that period as a separate country waging a "war" for autonomy. Moreover, there are many more textbook descriptions of Korea in the period between the 1873 "conquer Korea" debate and the 1910 "annexation" of Korea than there are of Korea between 1910 and its 1945 "independence." Japanese textbooks seem to imply that the disappearance of the independent nation-state of "Korea" in the years 1910–1945 means the erasure of Korea as a nation.

The Korean conceptualization of the war poses serious questions for modern Japanese historians, who have not thought in terms of the concept of a fifty-year war or a "forty-year Japanese-Korean war." When Japanese historians refer to the Japanese responsibility for the war, they implicitly assume the subject is the Fifteen Years' War, which was fought mainly with China. Moreover, they have not adequately thought through the relationship between the colonial rule of Korea and the Fifteen Years' War. Thus, Japanese historians were not able to respond to the Korean scholars' challenging questions.

Taking those questions seriously requires that Japanese modern historians reexamine the entire framework of existing studies of the Asia-Pacific War. Perhaps Japanese scholars need to study and discuss among themselves the implications of this critique for all aspects of Japanese history (since no individual historian can address it completely) before engaging in further discussions with Korean scholars on equal terms. Although Japanese textbooks of recent years have allowed more space for the discussion of the Japanese invasion of Korea and colonial rule, no textbooks yet have responded to, or been written from, this perspective.[11]

Study of Japanese Who Were Sympathetic to Korea

Fujisawa Hōei, the central Japanese figure in the study group, pointed out that some Japanese were critical of Japan's colonial rule of Korea and sympathized with Korea. Korean textbooks, he suggested, should refer to those people so that Koreans as well as Japanese could recognize their existence.

Takasaki Sōji, a professor of Tsuda College, made similar claims. For example, at the second joint study group meeting in Korea, Takasaki reported on Japanese intellectuals' responses to the colonization of Korea by focusing on the attitudes of socialists, Christians, and humanists (specifically, Kōtoku Shūsui, Uchimura Kanzō, Yanagi Muneyoshi, and Makimura Hiroshi). He discussed their responses to three specific historical events:

8.1 Righteous army rebels defy Japan
Most Japanese texts today do chronicle the history of anti-Japanese resistance in Korea after the Russo-Japanese War but do not present the struggle as an early stage of a sixty-year war between Japan and Korea, as do Korean textbooks. Institute for the Study of Korean Independence Movement, ed. *Independence Memorial Hall Exhibition Catalogue*, Seoul: ISKIM, 1991, 58. Used by permission of the Independence Hall of Korea.

the "annexation" of Korea, the March First Independence Movement, and the independence movement of 1931–1945.[12] Takasaki, though candidly acknowledging the shallowness of modern Japanese intellectuals' views on the issue of Japanese colonialism, argued that it should nevertheless be noted that even in the darkest days some Japanese supported the Korean independence movement and attempted to ally with it. He expressed his wish that Korean people support current Japanese efforts to surpass their predecessors in promoting anti-imperialist views and activities.

The Korean scholars sharply rebutted this position. For example, Kim Sŏng-il of Dong-kuk University insisted that the brutality of Japanese colonial rule cannot in any way be offset or justified by emphasizing the existence of a few Japanese sympathetic to Korea. Kim criticized each individual Takasaki had brought up and argued that not even the most conscientious Japanese of the period actively worked to end colonial oppression. Rather, prioritizing the national interest over individual thought and interests had been the essence of the presurrender Japanese mentality.[13]

The Korean view was summarized in the words of the moderator, Yi Wŏn-sun, professor emeritus of Seoul National University: "It is possible to understand [the point of the Japanese argument], but it is difficult

for Koreans to accept it [and include such references in the textbooks]."
Yi had long promoted exchange in the field of history education. He understood both Korean and Japanese sensitivities on this point. From the perspective of promoting Korean-Japanese friendship, he knew the significance of writing about the existence of Japanese sympathetic to Korea. Nevertheless, pointing to the very few Japanese critics of colonialism, he held that other Japanese had evaded responsibility for colonial rule, and so arguments of this kind would not convince many Koreans.

Of course, many of the Japanese participants understood the Korean point of view. How to frame Japanese-Korean friendship, however, remains a major challenge for progressive educators in Japan attempting to teach modern Japanese-Korean relations. These educators have emphasized three areas of study in turn: the history of invasion, the history of resistance, and the history of solidarity.

The history of invasion, which extends from the modern Japanese invasion of Korea to Japanese colonial rule, has been a central focus. Teachers report two shortcomings of this approach, however. The first is that it tends to disregard the agency of Koreans, in that Korea is simply treated as an object to be invaded and dominated. The second is that teachers have found that because colonial rule was so violent and cruel, more than a few students came to dislike history after the lessons on the invasion. Students frequently made comments such as "Again?" or "Too much!"

The curricula for the history of resistance were developed in response to these criticisms. This second area focuses on Korean bravery in resisting Japanese rule in order to gain independence. This approach teaches not simply the historical events of the other country but also the importance of defending one's nation against invasion. But the educators reported problems with this approach, too. After teaching the history of invasion and resistance, teachers found that the following questions often arose: "Did Koreans and Japanese ever overcome their hostile relations or the dynamic of invasion and resistance?" "Will it ever be possible for the people of the two countries to develop friendly relations in the future?"

Thus, Japanese educators recast the lessons as the history of solidarity, which offers a basis for future solidarity and friendship by collecting historical data showing that some people in the two countries understood and helped each other. Teachers found that this approach helped their students recognize the people of Korea as fellow human beings.[14]

Although Korean people might argue that emphasizing a history of solidarity tends to justify the Japanese invasion, it nevertheless has provided a crucial point for history education in Japan in its attempt to pro-

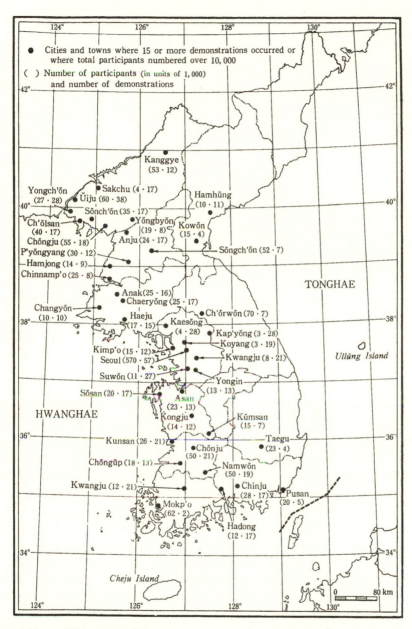

8.2 Map of Korean resistance

Many Japanese textbooks include graphics like this map that demonstrates the scale of Korean protest against Japanese rule in 1919. Korean sources claim that over 2 million people directly participated. *New History of Korea* by Ki-baik Lee, translated by Edward W. Wagner, © 1984 by Edward W. Wagner. Reprinted by permission of Harvard University Press for the Harvard-Yenching Institute.

mote a better understanding of Korea and to build friendship between the countries. In that sense, this approach cannot simply be overlooked. Japanese-Korean friendship must be developed through efforts on both sides, and the success of such efforts depends on how the two countries come to understand each other's present situation and history.[15]

Criticism That Japanese Textbooks Perpetuate the Emperor-Centered View of History

Korean scholars at the second study group meeting repeatedly pointed out that Japanese textbooks perpetuate the "emperor-centered" and "colonialist" view of history that was prevalent during the war. Japanese scholars, however, wondered what kind of description or what specific historical view these terms indicated.

In 1976 Yi Wŏn-sun gave a lecture on this very point, one that still serves as a good reference for the discussion.[16] Yi argued that history textbooks under Japanese colonialism were written from an imperial perspective, to "foster the character and attitude of conquerors and to educate Japanese people that Japan had progressed to the extent that it had by extricating itself from Asia *[Datsua shisō].*" Specifically, in the case of Korea, "the emperor-centered history attempted to explain, in a historical and rational manner, that Korea was an object to be invaded and conquered." It also "attempted to deny the historical autonomy and creativity of the Korean people, while it created a historical image that all of Korean history was determined and fostered by forces and cultures in the Chinese continent, and was after all advanced by external powers. It represented Korea as having a stagnant character with no volition of its own."[17] In my opinion, no Japanese history textbooks today explicitly expound such a view. The question, however, is whether those attitudes are still embedded within specific descriptions.

In the study group, Pak Sŏng-su pointed out that the old idea of the Japanese imperial state—that Japan "annexed" Korea in order to develop the civilization of Korea and protect it from colonization by Russia—survives in present-day Japanese textbooks that still depict Japan as contributing to Korea's autonomous modernization. Cho Hang-nae of Sungmyŏng Women's University expressed similar concern, though provided no concrete examples showing that distorted images are currently being implanted in Japanese students' minds through textbook descriptions of Korea.[18]

The Korean scholars' criticism was disappointing to the Japanese historians because they had already made substantial efforts since 1945 to

8.3 Happy Asian children in the Japanese empire
During the war the Japanese presented the subjugation of Korea and other Asian countries in idealized images of boys united under Japanese command in a Pan-Asian battle against the evil West. Koreans are particularly critical of any postwar remnants of this fantasy in Japan. Kuboi, *Nihon no shinryaku sensō*. Used by permission.

critique and abolish the imperialist ideology and ethnocentrism in historical studies, and many Japanese historians believed that they had overcome those views. Suddenly they were asked to confront the fact that a large number of Korean scholars, whose country experienced extreme forms of colonial rule, saw these Japanese efforts as insufficient. Japanese researchers and educators need to recognize that elements remain in current textbooks that remind Koreans of the emperor-centered view of history. These include the terms used to describe particular historic incidents (e.g., "annexation"), the evaluation of historic events, and the overall organization of topics in the textbooks. The history of Japanese-Korean relations needs to be reexamined from this perspective, too.[19]

The Study Group's Achievements: Deeper Understanding of the Japanese Textbook Screening System and Joint Discussion of Textbooks

The study group ended after two years, disbanding in March 1993, and the discussions of the meetings were summarized in a book. Thereafter, members moved on to pursue their own studies of textbooks and to exchange views in more depth individually. The study group both produced much of value and raised many issues, some of which were left unresolved. Below I explore two of the major achievements.

The first achievement was a significant increase in the understanding of the Japanese textbook screening process that is fundamental to the Japanese textbook production system. As discussed earlier, the Korean scholars could have recognized the errors of the 1984 newspaper report if they had had an accurate picture of the Japanese system. The information Koreans receive on the Japanese textbook screening system tends to be by way of explanations delivered by the Japanese Ministry of Foreign Affairs or the Ministry of Education, or by the Japanese mass media, and those sources have often been not only insufficient but also inaccurate. By the end of the study group's forums, however, the Korean scholars had developed a deeper understanding of the screening process than they had previously held, and the Japanese scholars had learned much about the Korean system. Their mutual understanding established a strong basis for subsequent discussion.

The second notable achievement, perhaps more important than the first, was the opportunity to examine Japanese high school history textbooks through both Japanese and Korean eyes. There are currently several routes of academic exchange available between Korea and Japan, but previous exchanges had been primarily for research purposes. The study group was the first to have its members read specific textbooks together line by line.[20]

In the study group, Korean scholars did comment on specific points in Japanese high school textbooks on Japanese and world history that they considered biased. For example, Pak Sŏng-su praised the Japanese history textbooks but also offered several criticisms. He discussed two textbooks published by the Jikkyō Shuppan press, *Kōkō Nihonshi* (Japanese history for high school) and *Nihonshi* (Japanese history), and assessed them as generally "well written" in terms of the Japanese-Korean relationship. But he criticized the description in these textbooks of the massacre of Koreans in Japan just after the great Kantō earthquake of 1923. Pak pointed out that the racist significance of the massacre was obscured because the books failed to differentiate between the mass killing of Koreans and the politically motivated murders by police of the Japanese anarchist Osugi Sakae and a group of labor organizers in the Kameido district of Tokyo.

Although Pak noted approvingly that Jikkyō Shuppan's *Nihonshi* is the only textbook that refers to the Cheam Chapel massacre of 1919, he found fault with the last sentence in the caption of one of the book's photographs.[21] Pak saw the line, which reads, "This is the photograph of a new chapel built in 1970, funded by Christians in Japan and others," as part of an attempt to offset and so justify the Japanese invasion with talk of Japanese donations.

Past Korean criticism often took the right-wing, militarist textbook *Shinpen Nihonshi* (New edition history of Japan), published by Hara Shobō Press) as its target, typically resulting in the comment that "Japanese textbooks are as awful as this" or "all Japanese textbooks are the same." By contrast, Pak's specific criticisms of the "well-written" Japanese textbooks are timely and very useful. Japanese historians and educators should be prepared for more such criticism, based on the close reading of actual texts, and should respond to it in a serious and sincere manner.[22]

Remaining Tasks and New Problems: The Need to Study Korean Textbooks

The study group did not analyze Korean textbooks, perhaps one of the most important tasks it omitted. For the moment, however, I present some of my own observations on Korean textbooks I have researched since 1992. Since the establishment of the South Korean government in 1948, Korean history textbooks have been changed six times in accordance with changes in the national curriculum guidelines. The first two sets of guidelines, adopted in 1954 and 1963 and written under Presidents Syngman Rhee and Park Chung Hee, respectively, coincided with adoption of the state-certified textbook system. Under that system several existing textbooks were retained for each subject. The major catchwords at that time were "anti-Communism" and "anti-Japan."

In the third period beginning in 1973, President Park Chung Hee proposed "education with nationalism," and the state took on the responsibility of writing history textbooks (this system continues to date). History textbooks during this period emphasized that the Japanese invasion was the major historical factor disrupting Korea's potential for development.

The fourth curriculum guidelines, implemented in 1981, stressed continuities in Korea's autonomous development despite Japanese invasion and colonization. It described Korean modern history as the history of antifeudalism and anticolonialism and portrayed the history under Japanese rule as the history of an anti-Japanese war for independence.

The 1987 textbook written to meet the fifth round of curriculum guidelines, presented modern Korean history as an age of autonomous development in politics, economy, and thought. The colonial period was seen as the "period when Korean national identity developed" and "the time of the Korean national independence movement." Although nationalism was heavily promoted, the significance of the Japanese invasion was muted and the anti-Japanese tone significantly reduced.

Textbooks based on the sixth curriculum guidelines were put into use in March 1996 and 1997. These textbooks carried on the basic perspective of the fifth curriculum guidelines, with additional emphasis on the national independence movement of the colonial period. These most recent textbooks for the first time included a description, albeit a short, simple one, of the comfort women. The passage, which reads, "Women were also taken in the name of volunteer corps and victimized as comfort women of the Japanese military," appeared in a section entitled "Japanese Imperialist Policies of Exterminating the Korean Nation." Within Korea, however, some argued the passage was not detailed enough.[23]

Nationalism was still a central theme, as it is also for the seventh guidelines, scheduled to be implemented in March 2000. Overall, recent Korean textbooks tend to underscore the nation's autonomous development and to play down the impact of Japanese invasion and rule. Korean textbooks now stress the fight for independence rather than the suffering caused by Japan's oppression.

This position has not necessarily eradicated the old anti-Japanese one, however. For example, the current Korean history textbook says that all autonomous historical activities of Koreans were suppressed. The history of Japanese invasion and oppression has hardly been forgotten in Korea, nor will it be in the future, even if (as it appears) it is no longer central to

8.4 History of resistance
Korean texts now stress Korean autonomy and resistance more than oppression by the Japanese. Many Japanese texts also include this photograph of female students rallying during the March First Independence Movement of 1919. Institute for the Study of Korean Independence Movement, ed., *Independence Catalogue*, 99. Used by permission of the Independence Hall of Korea.

Korean history textbooks. Other areas of Korean culture also demonstrate the persistence of the earlier position. On August 15, 1987, Koreans opened the Independence Memorial Hall, a huge museum in Ch'onan that some Koreans call a "center for anti-Japanese education." If researchers wish to understand the descriptions of modern Korean history in Korean textbooks, it is important that they recognize the existence of the two positions: one spotlighting Korean agency and resistance to Japan, the other emphasizing Korea's victimization by Japan—and that they understand the at times conflicting meanings the two views represent.[24]

Perspectives on Resident Koreans in Japan

Another topic relevant in both Japan and Korea is the 680,000 resident Koreans in Japan today. In the study group, the issue of resident Koreans in Japan surfaced again and again, but for the most part, without any fruitful results, since the study group had limited its discussion to historical events before 1945.

The subject came up in the first international study group meeting when I gave a report introducing some Japanese students' negative responses to the teaching approach that foregrounds the history of Japanese invasion of Korea. A resident Korean scholar in the audience reacted strongly, expressing his disappointment with the report and reiterating that Japanese students must recognize the fact of Japanese invasion of Korea. Resident Koreans in Japan naturally expect Japanese to acknowledge not only the treatment of Koreans during the colonial period but also the discrimination against resident Koreans that has continued since then.

In the second study group meeting, the Korean scholar Kim Sŭng-il referred to the issue, but from the Japanese scholars' point of view he seemed to regard the issue of resident Koreans in Japan as a matter to be solved only by resident Koreans themselves. In the fourth meeting, Sakai Toshiki of the Tokyo University of Liberal Arts reported on the way the issue of resident Koreans in Japan had been addressed in Japanese history education. Sakai proposed the need for diversity in the education of resident Koreans along with the traditional approach that emphasized an ethnic consciousness, one that typically included the practice of encouraging the use of one's "real" ethnic name. As an increasing number of Koreans who were "naturalized" to Japan wish to retain their ethnic identity as "resident Koreans" instead of totally abandoning their Koreanness, resident Koreans currently do not maintain a single ethnic identity as "Koreans." For these reasons, Sakai argued that the creation of a pluralist society is a common goal of Japan and Korea. In response, however, Kim commented that the cultural and ethnic consciousness of resident Koreans would be influenced by the balance of national power between Japan and Korea.[25]

It appeared that in general Koreans in Korea were not very interested in Koreans in Japan. Although Japanese scholars viewed Japanese as primarily responsible for solving those issues, they also hoped Korean scholars would understand the issues of resident Koreans in Japan. This wish, however, did not seem to be fulfilled, from what I saw of the responses of Korean scholars and audience.[26]

Is a Common Korean-Japanese Textbook Possible?

The study group did not resolve the question of whether it would be possible to create a common textbook for both countries. On this point Korean scholars were divided. Pak Sung-soo insisted on the need to strive for a common textbook (in his words, "It is worth pursuing even if it takes 100 years to develop"), whereas Yi Wŏn-sun thought the task impossible. Many Japanese participants, too, considered it impossible, given the many institutional differences between textbook systems, differences in the or-

8.5 Forced assimilation

During the colonial period schools themselves became a highly politicized battleground. Koreans were forced to adopt Japanese names and learn in Japanese rather than in Korean. This photo, which appears in several Japanese textbooks, however, shows a deceptively peaceful and familiar scene to Japanese schoolchildren. Satō, ed., *Asahi Rekishi Shashin Riburarii,* vol. 2, 191. Used by permission.

ganization of the history textbooks, and above all differences in the interpretation of history between the people and scholars of the two countries.

I am inclined to agree that a common textbook is impossible, at least for now, for several reasons. First, as I mentioned, Japanese and Korean history textbooks are very different in their organization of knowledge and topics. In Japanese history textbooks, discussion of Korea appears mainly in political and diplomatic histories. Analyses of modern diplomatic history, moreover, generally focus on Japan's relations with Europe and the United States first, then China, and last Korea.

In contrast, in the Korean history textbooks, Korea's relationship with Japan is central. The description of the period under Japanese rule concentrates on Japanese oppression, even in the economic and cultural realms—for example, the textbooks discuss anti-Japanese literature and anti-Japanese music in their sections on cultural history. In sum, Korean textbooks cannot narrate modern Korean history without extensive reference to Korea's relation with Japan, whereas Japanese textbooks treat Korea as peripheral. There seems to be no easy solution for the differences involving the relative historical importance of each nation for the other, and these discrepancies carry over directly into textbooks of the two countries.

The second reason I see such a textbook as impossible has to do with the textbook production systems in Japan and Korea. Japan uses a state screening and certification system and supports about twenty history textbooks at the high school level; Korea uses a single state-authored history textbook. This distinction constitutes a significant barrier to work on a common textbook. A third reason is that there is a clear difference in the approaches in history research in the two countries. Although it may be possible to overcome disagreements in interpretation and conceptualization in history studies through scholarly exchanges, it will take time before the gap can be bridged.

Having said this, I maintain that the attempt to create a common textbook and examination of the content of existing history textbooks can be separate projects. The study group was able to conduct focused discussions on the issue of historical facts and on the ways in which the two sides connected with each other. In the course of the discussions, we gained a clearer sense of the future tasks of history education and history studies. For these reasons, the project should continue. By jointly analyzing the textbooks of both countries, researchers will be able to begin to clarify the historic relationship between Japan and Korea, choose common themes for study, and deepen the understanding between the people of the two nations.[27]

Notes

For the romanization of Korean names, I followed the McCune-Reischauer method, except for some commonly known names in English (e.g., Syngman Rhee). The translator would like to thank Nozaki Yoshiko and Sylvan Esh for their assistance in translating the article and Son Gwang-rak and Bruce Cumings for their help in romanizing Korean names.

1. The study group was not the first attempt at dialogue on the issue. An earlier Japanese-South Korean textbook dialogue occurred in the late 1960s as a response to a call in 1965 from UNESCO headquarters, when Japan's domestic UNESCO committee and Korea's preparatory committee agreed to establish a History Education Conference. However, the conference was postponed indefinitely because the textbook lawsuit by

Ienaga Saburō triggered a political conflict over textbooks on the Japanese side. Dialogue in this area reopened only in the mid-1980s.

2. See Fujisawa Hōei, "Nikkan Rekishi Ninshiki no Rakusa o Umerutameni" (Bridging the gap in historical views between Japan and Korea), in Nikkan Rekishi Kyōkasho Kenkyūkai (Japanese-South Korean History Textbook Research Group), ed., *Kyōkasho o Nikkan Kyōryoku de Kangaeru* (Examining textbooks through Japanese-Korean collaborative efforts) (Tokyo: Otsuki Shoten, 1993), 12–13.

3. Three books have been written in Japanese as a result of the conference: Kimijima Kazuhiko and Sakai Toshiki, *Chōsen/Kankoku wa Nihon no Kyōkasho ni Dō kakarete iruka* (How Korea/Koreans are represented in Japanese history textbooks) (Tokyo: Nashinokisha, 1992); Nikkan Rekishi Kyōkasho Kenkyūkai, *Kyōkasho o Nikkan Kyōryoku de Kangaeru*; and Kankoku Kyōkasho Mondai Kenkyūjo (Korean Textbook Problems Research Group), ed., *Kan/Nichi Rekishi Kyōkasho Shūsei no Shomondai* (Various issues regarding Korean-Japanese history textbook revision) (Seoul: Peksan Charyowŏn, 1994). See also Kimijima Kazuhiko, *Kyōkasho no Shisō: Nihon to Kankoku no Kingendaishi* (Textbook perspectives: modern and contemporary history of Japan and Korea) (Tokyo: Suzusawa Shoten, 1996).

4. For more on the Miyazawa statement, see Kimijima, *Kyōkasho no Shisō*, 163–64.

5. One of the references in Pak's presentation was an article from *Chŏson Ilbo* (a major Korean newspaper) of July 1, 1984.

6. Although it is possible to say that the Ministry of Education attempts to change depictions in textbooks, it is difficult to say that the ministry forces changes. The relationship between the screening system and how it is actually administered is very complex. See Kimijima, *Kyōkasho no Shisō*, 35–40.

7. Yi Hyŏn-hee, "Kaikō (1876) Zengo no Kannichi Kankei: Seikanron to Kōkatō Jōyaku" (Korean-Japanese relations around the opening of ports of 1876), in Dainikai Nikkan Gōdō Rekishi Kyōkasho Kenkyūkai (Second Japanese-Korean Joint Study Group Meeting on History Textbooks), in *Shudai Happyō Ronbun* (Presentation papers) (September 28, 1991). See also Kimijima, *Kyōkasho no Shisō*, 31–32.

8. See Kamishima Ryūichi, "Dainikai Nikkan Gōdō Rekishi Kyōkasho Kenkyūkai" (The Second Japanese-Korean Joint Study Group Meeting on History Textbooks), in Nikkan Rekishi Kyōkasho Kenkyūkai, *Kyōkasho o Nikkan Kyōryoku de Kangaeru*, 102, and Hikaku Rekishi Kyōiku Kenkyūkai (Comparative History Education Research Group), ed., *Ajia no "Kindai" to Rekishi Kyōiku, Zoku "Jikokushi to Sekaishi"* ("Modernity" of Asia and history education, a sequel to "History of One's Own Nation and World History") (Tokyo: Miraisha, 1991), 16. Also see Kimijima, *Kyōkasho no Shisō*, 31–32, 78–79.

9. The "righteous armies" were local armies consisting mainly of peasants led by the *yangban* class (former government officials or landlords) and local intellectuals in order to resist the Japanese invasion through military struggle. At the time of the Sino-Japanese War and the Russo-Japanese War, many groups of righteous armies united and fought in organized ways.

10. In the course of the March First Independence Movement of 1919, while Korea was under Japan's colonial rule, several separate groups of Koreans in various places such as Seoul, Siberia, Manchuria, and Shanghai attempted to establish a provisional Korean government. In April 1919, the organizers of these groups gathered together to establish the provisional Korean government in Shanghai, outside the reach of Japanese authorities, where it was easy to develop diplomatic relations with many countries. The provisional government adopted a republican form of organization, and Syngman Rhee became the first prime minister. Although it organized secret operations in Korea, it attempted to restore its sovereignty primarily through diplomatic means. Kim Kyu-sik, who stayed in Paris, was secretary of foreign affairs. In spite of some difficulty caused by

internal power struggles, it continued the independence movement and declared war on Japan when the Pacific War broke out.

11. Chŏng Chae-jung, "'Jugonen Senso' to Chōsen/Chōsenjin" ("The Fifteen Years' War" and Korea/Koreans), in Daisankai Nikkan Gōdō Rekishi Kyōkasho Kenkyūkai (Third Japanese-Korean Joint Study Group Meeting on Historic Textbooks), *Kenkyū Hōkokusho* (Research report) (March 28, 1992). See also Kimijima, *Kyōkasho no Shisō*, 32–33, 79–83.

12. Takasaki Sōji, "Kindai Nihon ni okeru Hanshokuminchi no Shisō to Kōdō: Chōsen no Baai" (Anticolonialist thought and action in modern Japan: the case of Korea), in Dainikai Nikkan Gōdō Rekishi Kyōkasho Daitōronkai, ed., *Shudai Happyō Ronbun* (September 27, 1991).

13. Kim Sŭng-il, "Nihon ni okeru Hansen/Hanshokuminchi Undō to Zainichi chōsenjin" (Japanese antiwar and anticolonialism movements and Koreans in Japan), in Dainikai Nikkan Gōdō Rekishi Kyōkasho Kenkyūkai, ed., *Shudai Happyō Ronbun*.

14. See Mera Seijirō, "Nihon Kindai no Jūdaina Ketten no Jikaku to sono Kokufuku eno Iyoku/Tenbō o, Kodomotachi to tomoni: Nihon Kingendai shi Kyōiku no Ichikadai" (Making self-conscious efforts with children to cultivate the desire to overcome the crucial weak points of modern Japan), in Nishikawa Masao, ed., *Jikokushi o Koeta Rekishi Kyōiku* (History education beyond one's own nation) (Tokyo: Sanseidō, 1992).

15. See Kimijima, *Kyōkasho no Shisō*, 68–74.

16. Yi Wŏn-sun, "Nihonshi Kyōkasho ni Mirareru Kankokushi Kankei Kijutsu ni tsuite (Kōen Yōshi)" (Regarding the depiction of Korean-history-related items in Japanese history textbooks [lecture summary]), *Kan* (Korea) 56 (September 1976): 91. This paper was included in Yi Wŏn-sun, *Kankoku kara Mita Nihon no Rekishi Kyōiku* (Japanese history education from the perspective of Korea) (Tokyo: Aoki Shoten, 1994).

17. In Japan the historian Hatada Takashi and others have criticized this as the "view of history that sees Korea as a dependent nation" (*Chōsen taritsusei shikan*) or the "theory of Korea as a stagnant nation" (*Chōsen teitaiseiron*).

18. Pak Sŏng-su, "Nihon no Rekishi Kyōkasho no 'Shinshutsu'shikan o Hihansuru: Jingo Gunran kara Nisshin Sensō made" (Criticizing the "advancement" view of history in Japanese history textbooks: From the military rebel of Jingo to the Sino-Japanese War), in Dainikai Nikkan Gōdō Rekishi Kyōkasho Kenkyūkai, *Shudai Happyō Ronbun* (September 27, 1991), and Cho Hang-nae, "Ronichi Sensō (1904) zengo no Kannichi Kankei" (Korean-Japanese relations around the time of the Russo-Japanese War), in ibid.

19. See Kimijima, *Kyōkasho no Shisō*, 78–79.

20. *Nihon Kyōkasho ni Detekuru Kankoku shi no Naiyō no Kentō* (Examination of the content of Korean history represented in Japanese textbooks), authored by the Korea Education and Development Institute and published in 1987, is the closest to such a project. However, although it discusses Japanese elementary, junior high, and high school history textbooks, it does not provide specific references to titles of textbooks or page numbers.

21. In Japanese the incident is called Teigan Kyōkai Jiken. This incident was one example of severe repression of the Korean independence movement. As part of the March First Independence Movement, some Koreans demonstrated near Suwon City on April 5, 1919. On April 15, Japanese police and military searched for the leaders, and at the village of Cheam-li they confined twenty-one Christian villagers in the chapel and burned them to death. They also killed two village women and burned the village. They then killed six Ch'ondogyo (a popular religion) in a neighboring village because Christians and Ch'ondogyo believers worked together for independence.

22. See Kimijima, *Kyōkasho no Shisō*, 41–45.

23. See Kimijima Kazuhiko, "Chūgaku/Kōkō no Rekishi Kyōkasho Kijutsu" (On de-

pictions of high school and junior high school history textbooks), in "Chūgakkō Shakaika Kyōkasho Mondai" Tokubetsu Iinkai (Special Committee on "the Issue of Middle School Social Studies Textbooks"), ed., *Ima, Rekishi no Shinjitsu o: Kyōkasho de Oshieru "Jūgun Ianfu"* (Truth in textbooks now: Teaching "comfort women" with textbooks) (Tokyo: Adobantejisaba, 1997), 57.

24. For more details, see Kimijima, *Kyōkasho no Shisō*, 56–62, 135–53.

25. Sakai Toshiki, "Daiyonkai Nikkan Gōdō Rekishi Kyōkasho Kenkyūkai" (Fourth Japanese-Korean Joint Study Group Meeting on History Textbooks), in Nikkan Rekishi Kyōkasho Kenkyūkai, ed., *Kyōkasho o Nikkan Kyōryoku de Kangaeru*, 137–38; also see Kim Sŭng-il, "Nihon ni okeru Hansen/Hanshokuminchi Undō to Zainichichōsenjin."

26. See Kimijima, *Kyōkasho no Shisō*, 35.

27. See ibid., 83–84.

9

The Power of Selective Tradition: Buchenwald Concentration Camp and Holocaust Education for Youth in the New Germany

Gregory Wegner

Recent developments in the new Germany reveal serious, unresolved conflicts over the legacy of the Holocaust. The *Historikerstreit*, the heated debate among German historians initiated in 1986 over the meaning of Hitler and the Third Reich, continues unabated and has spread beyond academic circles. The philosopher Jürgen Habermas of the Frankfurt School sparked one of the great flashpoints in this controversy with his insistence that the viability of German democracy demanded a continuing and open confrontation with the Nazi past. He attacked the revisionism of neoconservative historians, including Ernst Nolte, Andreas Hilgruber, Joachim Fest, and David Irving, and their attempts to relativize the Holocaust with the claim that Auschwitz did not stand alone but assumed a position in history as merely one of a long line of similar atrocities and mass murders ranging from Stalinist purges to the crimes of the Pol Pot regime in Cambodia. Moreover, Habermas questioned the revisionist assertion that the Third Reich did not deliberately establish a genocidal dictatorship but carried on the war for the singular purpose of preventing the Communist domination of Europe.[1]

More recently, the debate over the legacy of the Holocaust entered another contentious phase with the publication of Daniel Goldhagen's book *Hitler's Willing Executioners: Ordinary Germans and the Holo-*

caust (1996). Goldhagen, a young professor of government and social studies at Harvard University, sparked controversy among historians when he claimed that anti-Semitic hatred, nurtured in the soil of Christianity, was *the* central cause for the Holocaust and that such hatred was imbedded in German culture. Goldhagen attacked the cherished assumption that most Germans were guilty only of obedience to authority. The German persecution and murder of Jews, he firmly insisted, was first and foremost a matter of choice, not simply a question of obedience to the regime. Like many other institutions under the fascist process of *Gleichschaltung* (coordination of all aspects of institutional life under the state), he argued, the churches participated in an already deeply rooted German tendency toward "eliminationist anti-Semitism."[2]

The battle over historical interpretations of the Nazi past continues unabated in the United States and Germany. The thesis proposed by Goldhagen came under withering criticism by a host of historians, including Christopher Browning, a highly respected American historian of the Third Reich. Although he did not discount the role played by anti-Semitism in the rise of the Nazi state, Browning emphasized obedience to authority as a critical development leading to the Holocaust. Browning forcefully contended that the "demonization" of an entire people with the charge of anti-Semitism "explained nothing." Goldhagen received a somewhat more positive reception in Germany, including a prestigious book award at the Frankfurt Book Fair, but his work also came under considerable fire in German academic circles as well. Prominent German historian Eberhard Jäckel accused Goldhagen of advancing "primitive stereotypes" while making wholly inaccurate contrasts between anti-Semitism in Germany and developments in Italy and Denmark.[3]

Academics are not the only Germans to have had profound differences of opinion over the meaning of Hitler in modern German history since the unification process began in 1989. Although Neo-Nazi splinter groups collectively account for only a tiny minority of the German populace, they are impossible to ignore. The severe economic dislocation and rising unemployment accompanying German reunification, especially evident in the five eastern German states of the newly expanded Federal Republic of Germany, continued in the wake of increased right-wing, Neo-Nazi violence against foreigners and stepped-up recruitment efforts among skinhead groups.

When Neo-Nazi youth in Solingen, a city in the Ruhr Valley, murdered five Turks in the summer of 1993, they demonstrated that xenophobic violence was not exclusive to the eastern German provinces. During the

9.1 Cover of *Hitler* by Friedemann Bedürftig and Dieter Kalenbach
The authors of this graphic-format textbook attempt to explain why Hitler and the
Nazis were able to gain power in interwar Germany. *Hitler*. Used by permission.

first nine months of 1993, militant nationalists and Neo-Nazi groups in
the Federal Republic were responsible for an estimated 1,480 attacks on
foreigners, a rate twenty-two times the level reported a decade earlier.
Holding together many of the Neo-Nazi groups are the Nazi ideological
remnants of racism and anti-Semitism directed against those deemed en-

emies of the German state. Symbolic remembrances of the dead who represent a culture outside a definition of the new German citizen acceptable to Neo-Nazis also became targets of destruction. Ignatz Bubis, the head of the Central Council of German Jews, reported that eighty Jewish cemeteries were desecrated in Germany in 1992, almost as many as were defiled between 1926 and 1931.[4]

While Neo-Nazi violence has subsided somewhat in the Federal Republic since 1997, renewed discussions in the new capital of Berlin over how to memorialize the victims of the Holocaust took on a tone of frustrated irresolution. Even German officials who agreed that the Holocaust was a terrible chapter in German history remained split over how their society could even begin to address that tragic story through a monument at all. At the center of the controversy was the chosen design for a monument, which called for 4,000 concrete columns set down over about 60,000 square meters between Potsdamer Platz and the Brandenburg Gate, in the heart of Berlin. Severe reservations about the design led to the conclusion that education rather than remembrance alone should be at the heart of the project. Thus, by the end of 1998, Germans learned about the proposed establishment of a new school for religious studies combined with a large research library on the Holocaust representing an active way to remember the victims of Nazi tyranny. The institute would support theological research on Judaism, Christianity, and Islam, all three Biblical traditions that came under Nazi oppression. This form of active remembering can connect the past to the present and remind observers "that the suffering was not restricted to the Jewish community."[5] Among more recent developments are plans by Michael Naumann, the state minister for cultural affairs, for the integration of a "genocidal watch" institute charged with investigating causes of genocide as well as opening dialogue over how to prevent the growth of genocidal movements.[6]

Teaching History and the Oppression of the Recent Past

The exceedingly complex process of confronting the dark legacy of the Holocaust as well as the Cold War in the new Germany is now expressed through the term *Vergangenheitsbewältigung*, or confrontation with the past. As in many other countries, the task of interpreting and preserving historical legacies for the presumed benefit of the young falls heavily on German schools. A recent experimental history curriculum project on the Holocaust for German secondary schools reflected the sensitive nature of the issue. The Federal Center for Political Education in Bonn sponsored a

9.2 Teaching about bigotry
Although Germans have engaged in several highly publicized debates on anti-Semitism and the Holocaust, none has centered on textbooks, which now are typically highly critical of the Third Reich. This image depicts persecution of critics of the Nazis, especially religious and intellectual leaders. Carl von Ossietzky, a Nobel Peace Prize winner, journalist, and Jew (prisoner 562) represented everything the Nazis hated. He died under torture on May 4, 1938. *Hitler,* p. 89. Used by permission.

pilot project beginning in 1990 involving more than 900 pupils from tenth-grade classes in two German states.

The stated purpose of the entire curriculum project was to help teenag-

9.3 Explanation versus glorification

The text of *Hitler* quotes from speeches by Hitler, Goebbels, and other Nazis so that schoolchildren will understand exactly what they had said. Critics worried that some students would glorify rather than repudiate what they learned. Here Hitler decries the "cancer of democracy" and vows to "pull out Marxism, root and branch." *Hitler*, 88. Used by permission.

ers in the new Germany develop a better understanding of the causes of Nazism. Underlying the program was the assumption that a historical investigation of the Third Reich would contribute toward a renewed dialogue among the young concerning the moral implications of the Holocaust. The project used a comic book called *Hitler*, based on a book of the same title by author Friedemann Bedürftig with artwork by Dieter Kalenbach. Included in the work were quotations from speeches delivered by Hitler, Joseph Goebbels, and other Nazi figures, interspersed with color-pencil drawings of the Nazi rise to power, the torture of Jews and political opponents in the concentration camps, and blood-drenched depictions of the war. (See Figures 9.1–9.4.) The center also developed a series of large colored posters; one showed scenes of Hitler surrounded by adoring, blond young Germans and another showed the Nazis burning books.[7] After schools began asking for the curriculum of the pilot project, the Center for Political Education produced 5,000 copies of a teaching package to support the comic book, including color slides and posters.

Suddenly, however, following an alert from the Israeli embassy, the center halted distribution in the fall of 1993 because of fear that the curriculum might be misused, especially by youth with tendencies sympathetic to Neo-Nazi ideology and those seeking to recruit them for active membership in Neo-Nazi groups.[8] The intended purpose of the curriculum, to build a deeper understanding about the rise of Nazism and its great potential for the destruction of democratic societies, came into conflict with an unintended consequence. Committed Neo-Nazi youth could see in the richly illustrated comic art central to the text a means to glorify the Third Reich. The struggle to legitimize what schoolchildren should or should not know about the Third Reich in the new Germany involves what Raymond Williams called building a "selective tradition," or an "intentionally selective version of a shaping past and a pre-shaped present, which is then powerfully operative in the process of social and cultural definition and identification."[9] The experimental curriculum produced by the Federal Center for Political Education was part of a selective tradition legitimized by Bonn for educating German youth about the Holocaust. Although initially approved, then censored and withdrawn by the government of Helmut Kohl in 1993, the program was eventually reinstated in late 1995 with stricter guidelines for access by teachers and academics and the introduction of a second edition.

Omissions in teaching the young about the history of their nation are central to this process of ideological formation. The reunification process triggered by the collapse of the East German state in 1989 had a profound influence on the social and cultural definition of legitimized school knowledge about the Third Reich. The Cold War had provided a powerful example of how ideology shaped two selected historical traditions in divided Germany, which in turn influenced what was said or not said about the complicity of corporate interests in the use of forced labor in the concentration camps. In East Germany the Marxist-Leninist authors' collective that wrote the state-sanctioned history textbook for the polytechnical secondary school, *Geschichte 9* (History 9), published by Volk und Wissen in 1987, had interpreted anti-Semitism and the mass murders in the concentration camps as logical extensions of an evil fascist regime. The authors, Wolfgang Bleyer and Gerhard Hass, were not content with simply rendering a chronological account of the Nazi boycott of Jewish shops, the Nuremberg Laws, Kristallnacht, the expropriation of Jewish property, and the Wannsee Conference of 1942, which framed the Final Solution under the SS. Marxist-Leninist views of both history and the immorality of capitalism provided the authors with the ideological foundation for establishing a certain cause-and-effect relationship. They saw the use of forced labor in the concentration camps by corporate interests as a crucial part of the Holocaust narrative. The same monopoly capitalism that helped Hitler rise to power was also a dominant force in making mass murder possible. German industrial combines, many of which existed long before Hitler, "enriched themselves from the misery and deaths of the camp inmates" (*bereicherten sich am Elend und Tod der Gefangenen*). Many of them erected factories utilizing masses of forced laborers in or near the concentration camps with the full cooperation of the SS.[10]

The material in East German texts on corporate complicity in the Final Solution was often quite detailed. In one example, beneath a photograph showing the railroad entry gate to Auschwitz-Birkenau, Hass informed the readers of *Geschichte 9* that I.G. Farben had constructed a chemical factory in this, the largest concentration camp in the system. An exchange of letters between I.G. Farben and the Auschwitz concentration camp administrator, reprinted in the last edition of the textbook published in East Germany, revealed negotiations for the use of 150 female inmates by the chemical company for a series of experiments, ostensibly for the development of sleeping pills. The letters included an exchange in which I.G. Farben complained that the price of 200 marks per person was too high and that they would pay only 170. Soon after I.G. Farben received the inmates, the SS was informed that the first round of experiments had ended successfully and that all the "objects for experimentation" were dead. I.G. Farben then requested a meeting with the SS in Auschwitz to transfer yet more inmates for other lines of experimentation.[11]

This kind of evidence, used here morally to condemn the complicity of some German industrial concerns in the Nazi policy of mass extermination, is rarely if ever found in secondary school history texts of reunified

9.4 The Holocaust in history
Analyzing the place of the Holocaust within German history is the greatest challenge for German educators. This discussion of the gas chambers points out that prisoners had to be forced to do the inhuman work of unloading the bodies. The text goes on to comment that the smoke from the Auschwitz ovens could be seen from 30 kilometers away and that "many suspected, few knew, and none said" what was happening there. *Hitler,* 174. Used by permission.

Germany. (Nor has this issue been explored in textbooks published in the United States. And it is interesting to note that General Motors and Ford Motor Company came under renewed investigation for their alleged involvement with the Nazi regime through forced labor.[12]   The evidence supporting the traditional East German interpretation of history is still visible in other places, however. For example, in the Buchenwald concentration camp, a small and unobtrusive sign marks the site of the forced labor camp run by Siemens Corporation, a major electrical contractor under the Third Reich.

The two selective East and West German traditions differed as well in their depictions of those who resisted Hitler. Yet in an important omission, the East German guidelines for the *Abiturstufe*, a course of study for those preparing for the graduation exam, mentioned nothing about the persecution of Jews and the concentration camps. The same document, by contrast, places a great weight on the heroism of the Soviet and German Communist resistance movements. [13] After reunification, German youth were offered a new pantheon of historical heroes from the era of the Third Reich and the struggle against fascism for German youth from the newly integrated eastern states. Gone was the singular emphasis on the resistance of the Red Underground and the Communist heroes who defied the Nazis. The traditional western German models for civil courage under the oppression of the Nazi dictatorship, such as the upper-class and Christian dissenters among the White Rose, Bishop Clemens Graff von Galen, and the Stauffenberg Circle, are prominent in the current history textbooks published for eastern and western German youth.

The reunification of Germany meant that monopoly capitalism, the central thesis espoused by East Germany to explain Hitler's rise to power, remains delegitimized and therefore expunged from the history curriculum for the schools of the new Germany. One curricular result of this ideological transition is that the role of the corporate state in the forced labor camps remains downplayed.[14] Both East and West German communities initiated Holocaust education programs in their own unique ideological ways. The ideological differences over the meaning of the past in divided Germany, especially the Holocaust, was profound. Even with this great rift in thinking, both sides held a certain faith in the power of education to transform character in order to create a more just and tolerant society. This is the substance and source of the contradictions inherent in the moral assumption behind the education program at Buchenwald. For much of human history, the behavior of many generations has rejected the notion that we have "arrived" at this kind of society. Perhaps reflecting a strain of idealism in Western thought, some German educators share a certain optimism that young people studying the Holocaust at places like Buchenwald will participate in building a society based on a greater sense of social justice than that of the previous generations.

Buchenwald as a Place for Youth to Confront History

Textbooks, though valuable in explaining shifts in the legitimization of historical knowledge, represent only a part of the larger problem of meaningfully engaging young people in an examination of the Holocaust and the Third Reich. In perhaps no other place is the potential for history curriculum innovation more promising in the new Germany than in the concentration camps, the actual sites where Nazi efficiency and the brutal policy of mass murder reached a fateful climax. Buchenwald concentration camp, located near the city of Weimar in the province of Thüringen, has moved to the forefront of Holocaust educational innovations by instituting a *Jugendbegegnungsstätte* (JBS), a place where youth confront history.

The research I report on in this section examined the context and scope of Holocaust education as practiced by teenagers and their teachers at Buchenwald, as well as the selected traditions upon which the Buchenwald program is based. The *Historikerstreit* and the more recent Goldhagen controversy, heightened Neo-Nazi activity, and the social and economic tensions surrounding the new Germany are part of the larger context for the investigation. Moreover, these elements intersect culturally with the goals and purposes of Holocaust education in Buchenwald. During the study, I served as a participant-observer with a group of fourteen German youths from Weibelfeldschule, a school in Dreieich (Kreis Offenbach), located in the western German province of Hessen. The group gathered for a five-day history seminar on the Holocaust held at Buchenwald in June 1993.

The program at Buchenwald attempts to present a localized means of innovative curriculum within a specific historical and social context. Buchenwald symbolizes a double legacy that cuts across not only the Third Reich but also the Cold War. The camp, opened by the Nazis in 1937 for political prisoners, eventually became the site for 250,000 inmates from thirty-five countries. Among the more than 50,000 people who died at Buchenwald were more than 15,000 Soviet citizens, an estimated 10,000 Jews, and an undetermined number of homosexuals, Gypsies, German Communists, Jehovah's Witnesses, and Christian clergy—victims of shooting, hanging, torture, beatings, starvation, and illness. As it did in other camps, such as Auschwitz and Sachsenhausen, the SS conducted gruesome medical experiments on some prisoners at Buchenwald and forced others either to work in adjoining factories producing articles for the war effort or to mine and haul heavy rock and stone from the nearby quarry.

After its liberation by the U.S. Army and General George Patton's tanks in April 1945, the camp eventually came under the control of Stalin and

9.5 The different lessons of Buchenwald
This famous picture can be read, in the West German tradition, as the story of the Allied liberation of the Jews (Elie Wiesel is lying on one of the rear bunks) or, in the East German tradition, as the story of self-liberated slave laborers. The caption, presumably written by the photographer, Private H. Miller, supports both readings: "These are slave laborers in the Buchenwald concentration camp near Jena; many had died from malnutrition when U.S. troops of the 80th Division entered the camp" (1945). NARA, NWDNS-208–AA-206K(31), War and Conflict no. 1105.

the Soviet occupation army, who maintained it as a prison camp. By 1950 about 10,000 prisoners had died at the hands of the Soviets from sickness and starvation in a special camp organized within Buchenwald. Many of the inmates were Hitler Youth functionaries, lower- and mid-level members of the Nazi Party, and others opposed to the Soviet occupation. Mention of the Soviet camp remained strictly forbidden in East German schools and society during the Cold War. East German history textbooks and visitor guides for Buchenwald during those years scrupulously omitted any discussion of the postwar camp.[15]

German students coming into Buchenwald today step into a memorial that not only recalls the horrors of the Nazi concentration camp but also calls to mind a selective tradition of history propaganda practiced by East German educational authorities during the Cold War. In contrast to its capitalist neighbor to the west, East Germany initiated a new history curriculum only several weeks after the war that placed heavy emphasis on the study of fascism and the Third Reich with the purpose of preventing a resurgence of fascism in the future.[16] After its opening as a memorial in 1958, Buchenwald eventually became part of a large and well-developed system of *staatlich verordnete anti-Faschismus* (state-sanctioned antifascism), a form of political socialization for youth and adults. Central to this brand of East German antifascism was the preservation of selective historical memory for future generations, a practice common to many political cultures. As noted earlier, for its part West Germany practiced a version of history propaganda in neocapitalist form by holding up those figures deemed heroic in the struggle against Nazism, like the White Rose and the Stauffenberg Circle, none of whom were among the eastern pantheon of resistance fighters from the Red Underground.

To East German authorities, the brave deeds and the spirit of resistance embodied by camp inmates from the Red Underground in the concentration camps became part of the acceptable cultural definition of heroism. Those inmates from Buchenwald who had stood beyond the ideological pale of East German socialism, such as Jews, generally received much less attention or were forgotten altogether in the official history curriculum of the German Democratic Republic (GDR). This development was also reflected in the way history was interpreted in the exhibits and written materials created for camp visitors during the Cold War. There were many visitors to Buchenwald: At the age of thirteen, thousands of East German youth joined the ranks of the Free German Youth each year, taking the oath of Buchenwald, in which they pledged their efforts in preventing fascism from assuming power in the world again. The oath was often taken at Ettersberg Memorial, constructed by the GDR on a scenic hillside near the camp during the late 1950s. The propaganda implication behind this endeavor was that the "real" antifascists resided in the East, whereas the Neo-Nazis had simply found a new home in the imperialist power of the Federal Republic under the protective wing of the cosmopolitan United States.[17]

Buchenwald as Teaching Model

During the mid-1980s, several years before the fall of East Germany, important changes were already evident in the teaching methods used at

The Buchenwald Oath

We, the men of Buchenwald, Russians,
Frenchmen, Poles, Czechs, Slovaks, Germans,
Spaniards, Italians, Austrians, Belgians, Dutch,
English, Luxembourgers, Rumanians, Yugoslavs,
and Hungarians, fought together against the SS,
against the Nazi criminals, for our own
liberation. We had a common ideal. Our cause is
just—it must win. In many languages we
conducted the same hard struggle, a struggle rich
in victims This struggle is not yet ended. Nazi
flags are still flying! The men who killed our
comrades are still alive! The men who tortured us
sadistically are still free! We therefore swear
before the world on this barrack square, this site
of fascist horror: We shall only end our fight
when the last criminal has been brought before
the tribunal of the nations!

Our slogan is the destruction of Nazism with its
roots! Our aim is the construction of a new world
of peace and liberty! We owe this to our
murdered comrades and those they left behind. As
a sign of your readiness to take part in this fight,
raise your hands and repeat:

We swear!

21,000 men and boys raise their hands and repeat:

We swear!

9.6 Buchenwald oath

Buchenwald to engage young people in the study of the Third Reich.
Propaganda in the service of the established order still assumed a central
role, but new didactic initiatives became more evident among the educators administering camp programs. The idea of organizing Buchenwald
as a place to provide youth with an opportunity to confront the past more
directly was inspired in part by the peace education program begun in the
late 1970s called Aktion Sühnezeichen (an active program representing a
sign of atonement for the past), used at Auschwitz in Poland.[18]

The collapse of East Germany in 1989 and the proposal by a historical commission in 1991 to change the ideological perspective of the Buchenwald memorial offered a strong impetus for reconceptualizing the pedagogical approach of the camp. A report filed with the commission noted the importance of generational timing in the work of educators at Buchenwald:

> The changed experiential horizons of youth, at this point a third postwar generation without a direct witness to the era of National Socialism or an immediate connection with the postwar years, necessitates new methods in the museum-pedagogical work of the memorial. The confrontation with the historical place or the identification of past events alone is no longer sufficient. Only in association with sensible, solid historical-political education will it be possible for young people to feel sadness, repulsion, or compassion in this place as well as to understand its history. Buchenwald as a place of human suffering and human greatness, next to its meaning as a place of commemoration, must be increasingly understood as a place of learning.[19]

The notion that learning about the past invariably connects to contentious issues of the present represents a critical pedagogical assumption underlying the entire experimental approach at Buchenwald. The study of the Nazi period in the camp claims the dominant instructional emphasis in the JBS program. In an attempt to interrelate important historical themes for study, the curriculum considers contemporary social tendencies toward racism, xenophobia, the acceptance of violence in everyday life, and various forms of extremism.[20] In this way Buchenwald symbolizes something more than a mere geographical location in German history, and its meaning is linked to contemporary social and political developments.

A profound moral assumption in the pedagogical program at Buchenwald seemingly contradicts much of human history. Even though the behavior of many generations testifies to the contrary, the Buchenwald teaching model, like the Hitler curriculum, holds forth a daunting but optimistic challenge to teachers and students interested in exploring possibilities for the creation of a more tolerant and just society. Studying the Holocaust "on site," that is, in concentration camps where the Nazi evil took on its darkest forms, may encourage young people to rethink their own cultural assumptions and raise critical questions about the conditions that made Nazism possible for their grandparents' generation. In the informational pamphlet published for JBS Buchenwald, the ideas of "confrontation, understanding, and preservation" *(Begegnung, Begreifen, Bewahren)* are articulated within several different but related experiences. In the view of JBS director Helmut Rook, students in Buchenwald confront many things: history, the actual place where the events happened, the city of Weimar with its contradictory and varied past, other students from different backgrounds and viewpoints who are committed to study history and contemporary society (*Beschäftigung mit der Geschichte und Gegenwart*), and "their own reflections about guilt and responsibility."[21] Translating these notions of confrontation into meaningful connections between past and present in Buchenwald therefore remains one of the greatest challenges for both the education staff in the camp as well as visiting teachers and their students.

Buchenwald as a teaching model integrates a series of learning activities. One such activity began during August 1990, in the form of work camps organized in Buchenwald by the Service Civil International (SCI) for twenty young people from eastern and western Germany, the Soviet Union, and the United States. The students in this group initiated an exploratory archeological dig to unearth the detention cells of the central office for the SS. In what the local press termed "the track of history," the students emphasized through their careful excavations the importance of preserving artifacts from the daily lives of prisoners who once lived in the camp. Silverware, cups, combs, buttons, and metal bowls taken from the ground in and around the building took on new significance as mute witnesses to the world of oppressor and victim. That this kind of archeology might promote a greater understanding among members of the group was not lost on a nineteen-year-old medical student from Boston: "I am in Europe for the first time. We are working together—Russians, Germans, and Americans—and have much time to talk with each other. During the excavations, I ask myself how much history is in the ground and what the past will still yield."[22]

Also significant to the students was that this special security building once imprisoned prominent opponents of the Nazi regime, including the Protestant theologian Dietrich Bonhöffer, who remained there a short time before his transfer to Flossenberg and his execution. During their efforts, the students insisted that this site memorialize the courage and heroism of the "Christian-conservative opposition" to Hitler from July 20, 1944.[23] Perhaps without realizing it, the group imposed its own ideological meaning from the West over this piece of ground and its relationship to modern German history. Only a few years before, under the aegis of the Cold War, such an interpretation would have been wholly unacceptable to the regime of Erich Honnecker and its ideological canonization of the Red Underground.

The power of archeology to open new levels of meaning for the study of history extended to a series of other programs in Buchenwald. From January to November 1991, some sixty-five student groups comprising

1,347 youth visited the JBS.[24] Another work camp set up by SCI with the help of students from Germany, France, the Soviet Union, and Bulgaria in the summer of 1991 excavated the foundations of Block 46, the site of the infamous SS medical experiments. Later, teenagers from Baden-Württemberg and Thüringen joined young people from the Soviet Union and Hungary to unearth the area in and around the former train station, the original arrival point for thousands of prisoners condemned to Buchenwald. As before, the students unearthed artifacts from the daily culture of the prisoners, in particular silverware and pieces of clothing; they did so within a historical context previously established through extended tour of Buchenwald and research on focused historical problems conducted in the camp archives. Several Soviet students, for example, dedicated themselves to the examination of camp life for Soviet prisoners under Hitler and Special Camp II established by Stalin in 1945.[25]

The public debate over the role of Buchenwald as memorial and museum became part of the impetus for the establishment of a two-day seminar in Oberhof for students from Hessen and Thüringen in June 1991. At the top of the agenda was the theme of neofascism and hatred directed against foreigners in the new Germany. The students called for the preservation of Buchenwald as a site for the study of the Holocaust, as well as a place for intercultural learning.[26]

Buchenwald and the Youth from Weibelfeldschule

The earlier youth projects undertaken by the JBS constituted an essential context for my experiences in Buchenwald during June 1993 with fourteen students and their two teachers from Weibelfeldschule, structured as a *Gesamtschule*, a comprehensive school through the tenth class, or age sixteen, that offers pupils a flexible curriculum and more experimentation in instruction than does the traditional *Gymnasium*. The comprehensive schools remain most popular in Berlin, Hamburg, Bremen, Lower Saxony, North Rhine–Westphalia, it garners the least support in Bavaria and Baden-Württemberg.

The initial idea for the school's involvement in the Buchenwald project came from a teacher at the school, George Harnischfeger, after he visited Buchenwald in 1992 with a group of educators attending a conference on the pedagogy of the memorial sites. The prospect of organizing a school project that would engage students in historical research and would enable them to live in the camp for one week and exchange viewpoints with students from the five newly integrated eastern German states or from

9.7 The Buchenwald cell of Pastor Paul Schneider
The students were most deeply moved by the life and death of this Protestant pastor,
who openly defied the Nazis both before and after his arrival at Buchenwald. Archive
of the Memorial Site Buchenwald. Used by permission.

foreign countries provided the original motivation for the program.[27]
Unfortunately, the weeklong project did not afford students the opportunity to meet with their peers from either eastern Germany or abroad, which
resulted in a rather narrow base of interaction. This illustrated the problem of scheduling school groups at JBS to ensure broadened discussion

and work networks beyond the students' immediate community circle. More important, rising tensions between eastern and western German teenagers symbolize the ongoing and tortuous process of unification in the new Germany, and this factor offers at least a partial explanation why initiating this kind of interaction proved difficult during the early 1990s.

The lack of a genuine interaction between youth from east and west was not the only difficulty facing the teachers from Dreieich. Harnischfeger and his colleague, E. Dürr, faced tough competition in their attempts to recruit students for the Buchenwald program. The project at JBS represented one choice among seventy elective projects offered to students during the summer of 1993. Choices included bicycle touring, judo training, and self-defense for girls, a first-aid course, AIDS education, calligraphy, badminton, silk and glass painting, Asian culinary arts, and puppetry. Many of the projects were fully enrolled. Such was not the case with the program advertised as "Experience History: A Week in JBS Buchenwald with a Day Trip to Weimar." Fourteen students enrolled for the Buchenwald project, though the original target had been set for twenty.[28]

The publicity announcement informed prospective participants that they would "work, study, research, and write reports actively associating history and the present" under the theme of "persecution against the Jews, antifascists (German Communist and Social Democrats), Sinti and Roma (Gypsies) and Christians." The teachers stress the contemporary nature of this investigation by insisting that the persecution theme be conceived in its historical context and in connection with the "real problem of present-day xenophobia, which only recently had become part of a new orientation in the historical writing of the Federal Republic."[29] With this perspective on Buchenwald, Harnischfeger and Dürr proceeded far beyond the predominant history textbook approaches to the Third Reich, many of which omit any real discussion of the *Historikerstreit* or fail to draw relationships between the racist and prejudicial assumptions underlying Nazi ideology and much of the xenophobia in the Federal Republic during the post–Cold War era.[30]

The students arriving at Buchenwald from the Weibelfeldschule stepped into an environment heavily reinforced with the geographical significance of place. The JBS is headquartered in a building once used as apartments for SS personnel. Students lived, conducted discussions, formed work groups, and wrote research reports in the rooms of this building under the guidance of their teachers and the JBS director. One room contained an impressive collection of historical works on the Third Reich, including many documents and diaries written by both the SS oppressors and the victims, reproduced from the camp archives. To set the tone for Buchenwald as a place of learning *(Lernort)*, JBS director Helmut Rook provided students on their first day with an "evolving history" of the camp and its triple legacy under the Nazis, the Soviets, and the East Germans.

The following day opened with the documentary film *O Buchenwald*, produced in 1984 for the concentration camp memorial. The film examined the economic and political developments leading to the rise of German fascism and the horror of the Holocaust, along with a concise overview of Buchenwald within that historical context. This cinematic teaching resource, as one *Gymnasium* educator from Essen observed, prepared visitors emotionally and intellectually for their visit to the camp.[31] The vast majority of students from Weibelfeldschule agreed that the somber film, timed at the beginning of the week, provided a much-needed context for their subsequent work, although three class members objected to what they insisted was an overemphasis on the Red Underground. Here was a definite sign that some students were able to articulate their understanding of Buchenwald as not only a place for Nazi persecution and mass murder but also the site for the practice of history propaganda under the former East German government. The same kind of critical thinking did not extend to an awareness of history propaganda as practiced by the Federal Republic. Only one student expressed suspicions that ideological biases in history instruction that flourished under the Honnecker regime also extended to the Federal Republic before and after 1989 as well.[32]

Rain delayed for two days an archeological investigation to find artifacts from the everyday lives of prisoners from the grounds located at an SS dump site. The delay actually served the project well because it gave students more time to tour the grounds of the camp under the direction of excellent guides and to visit the historical exhibits and permanent art collection in the former storehouse and disinfection buildings. A large, scale model of the camp, located in the gatehouse, gave the students a sense of time and place before they stepped into the broad expanse beyond the gate, which was marked with the cynical slogan *"Jedem das Seine"* (variously translated as "To each his own" or "Each person to himself").

Touring the camp that day with German teenagers two generations removed from the Third Reich left me with powerful impressions about how the concept of place, when given appropriate historical context, can provide meaningful opportunities in the teaching of history. Without realizing it, the young people from Weibelfeldschule became my teachers in a most direct way. Certain parts of the camp elicited powerful emotions in members of the group. The detention quarters attached to the gatehouse held twelve cells that

9.8 Main gate at Buchenwald
This slogan, "To each his own" (*Jedem das Seine*) is just as cynical but in a different way from the more famous declaration at Auschwitz: "Work makes you free" (*Arbeit macht frei*). Archive of the Memorial Site Buchenwald. Used by permission.

had housed a variety of political prisoners and Soviet prisoners of war. Several members of the group expressed shock and sorrow at the sight of the memorial cell honoring Protestant minister Paul Schneider. The clergyman had openly defied the Nazis from the pulpit and later, after being arrested by the Gestapo, arrived in Buchenwald. Shortly thereafter, Schneider refused to remove his prisoner's hat during morning muster as a sign of respect to the flag of the Third Reich. Put into solitary confinement, the clergyman bravely called to his comrades beyond the cell bars to remain faithful in their struggle against the Nazi menace. His exhortations led to a swift execution that same day.

The somber mood established at the detention cells extended to another place of execution, the former horse barns, in which thousands of Soviet POW's were shot through the neck soon after their arrival from the railway station. By now, students were asking questions related to a host of issues, including the reasoning the SS used for the method and place of execution, why their grandparents' generation could allow such horrors to take place, and what this could mean for their own personal understanding of Nazi Germany in modern history. Spirited discussions continued between the young people and JBS director Rook and their teachers. The discussions suddenly ceased as the group stepped down into the basement of a building attached to the crematorium structure, one of the darkest and most haunting places in Buchenwald.

Mass hangings of up to twenty prisoners at a time occurred here. The massive meat-hook devices used for the hangings, lined up neatly across the walls, and large drainage holes in the floor, used to collect the blood and excrement, proved so graphic and revolting that several students left the room shortly after arrival. One student could be heard to ask "why?" over and over again as we proceeded to the upstairs room, where corpses were sorted and certain body organs and valuables, including gold from teeth, were removed. Continuing to the final stage in the brutally efficient Nazi process of mass murder, the group examined the crematorium and the ovens constructed under special German industrial patents. Experiences such as these contributed mightily to the historical context established for the communal discussions between teachers and students after the evening meal.

The brief time and emotional intensity of the Buchenwald teaching model demanded a written means for students to articulate their own knowledge and understanding about the Holocaust and the legacy of the camp. In preparation for a presentation to the community at a school festival, students formed two-person research groups to examine a historical topic of their choice. The resulting research papers, after editing by the teachers and two student editors, appeared in a publication compiled by the class. The choice of topics revealed wide-ranging but related interests:

- children and youth in the concentration camp
- daily life in the camp
- the "Song of Buchenwald"
- from the train station to the barracks: the way of the prisoners in the camp
- medical crimes
- the camp bordello
- Ilse Koch: the "beast of Buchenwald"
- execution and sentencing
- who were the instigators?

In a method reminiscent of the pedagogy of W.H. Kilpatrick, a professor from Columbia University who became well known for the development of the project method, the German students completed much of their written research in work groups that took on the responsibility of determining the scope and function of their efforts.[33] With a good share of the Buchenwald archive at their disposal, the young researchers were able to read diary accounts from SS officers and surviving prisoners and peruse statistical evidence and other SS documents about various aspects of camp life. The research endeavor, one of numerous learning experiences crammed into five days, constituted the first foray into archival research for the students. They were pleased to assume responsibility for their research and enjoyed the scope of opportunities to find answers to their questions abut the place of Buchenwald in the history of the Holocaust.[34]

The city of Weimar, treasured by many for its unique place in the literary history of Germany and remembered as the political symbol of the ill-fated Weimar Republic, became another kind of historical laboratory for the youth from Dreieich. Moving from the intensely emotional tone of the previous day in the camp, the students took an extended "alternative tour" of the city. The splendid castle art gallery, Goethe's summer home, and a walking tour of sites linked to the literary history of Weimar provided a much-needed emotional respite from what one student called the "shocks, tears, sadness, and frustration" many of her peers felt in confronting the dark revelations of Buchenwald.[35]

In this different setting of Weimar, the students discovered once again, however, the weight of the recent past. In a park memorializing Ernst Thälmann and the antifascist resistance movement, a local guide informed the group about a heated debate among Weimar citizens over the fate of the park, which had been constructed by the East German government. One group wanted the statue kept on the original site, whereas others thought it best to remove it to Buchenwald concentration camp, where Thälmann was executed. Yet another group wanted the statue destroyed, since it represented a reminder of Germany's Communist and East German past. That this controversy remained unresolved reminded the young people of the problematic nature of the reunification process and its relationship to interpretations of history.

On a social level, these same young people experienced an even stronger reminder of the arduousness of the task of German reunification. At one point during the day, the students split into groups to visit parts of the city on their own. The two teachers found themselves acting as security guards when resentful eastern German teenagers from Weimar taunted and verbally threatened some of the western German students. The fear of physical attack was real and not unexpected when viewed within the context of rising economic tensions associated with increasing joblessness in eastern Germany. Although the tense interaction passed without any clashes between the groups, the situation illustrated why history seminars in Buchenwald usually do not combine teenagers from eastern and western Germany.

Later the program was reorganized so that the kind of east-west dialogue originally envisioned did take place.

A report published by Buchenwald authorities in 1995 recounted some critical changes in this relationship. During the summer of 1993, two school classes from a *Gymnasium* in Erfurt and Bettinaschule in Frankfurt am Main joined in a research project at Buchenwald exploring the persecution of Jewish communities in Hessen and Thüringen as well as the concentration camp. The work began with research in the archives of their respective sites and towns on the local persecution of Jews and their fate. The pupils from the two German provinces then joined for additional research on Jewish life at Buchenwald with the aid of camp archives. The groups shared the results of their research while discussing the implications of this kind of historical oppression for understanding racism in present-day German efforts toward reunification. Historical research of this nature will not by itself fully address the complex problems associated with reunification. Not the least of these are social psychological elements engendered from decades of political socialization during the Cold War. A courageous dialogue over the dual legacies of the Third Reich and the Cold War may be a healthy place for German youth to start as the twentieth century draws to a close.[36]

By 1999 these tensions also had subsided somewhat with the gradual improvement of economic life in the east. With slowly increasing enrollments, the JBS at Buchenwald is enjoying some success in organizing history study groups with pupils from formerly divided parts of Germany. This does not suggest in any way that the social psychological divide no longer exists. What we witnessed on the streets of Weimar offered a profound and humbling reminder that reunification is a process that goes far beyond the interactions of the generation currently in positions of political power. School-age youth, especially in eastern Germany, have felt the sting of reunification on a variety of levels; their counterparts in the west groan under the weight of heavy taxes to restore the infrastructure in eastern Germany.

The "divided memory" of the Nazi past, to use Jeffrey Herf's phrase, is sometimes superseded by more pressing issues—such as basic human survival.[37] The Weimar incident reminded me of a guest teaching opportunity with *Gymnasium* students in eastern Berlin at Treptow a week before I departed for Weimar. The faculty asked me to teach a closing session on the lessons of the Holocaust to the upper-level students. In the middle of the class, a very angry young woman asked why we were studying the Holocaust when both parents of many students had recently lost their jobs and were struggling to find enough food just to feed their families.

9.9 and 9.10 German high school students conducting an archeological dig at the Buchenwald garbage dump, 1993 and their discoveries
This former SS garbage dump revealed artifacts of prison life. The students unearthed buttons, spoons, a shoe horn, combs, dentures, prisoner ID disks, a penknife, a coin purse, a condom (for use in the camp brothel where some of the women inmates were imprisoned), electrical wires, tops from beer bottles, and a razor. Gregory Wegner.

This, too, is a brutal part of reunification history, aspects of which overshadowed our work at Weimar.

The day after the visit to Weimar, the students continued their project work for eventual presentation before the community at Weibelfeldschule. This ambitious undertaking included the production of a videotape of the Buchenwald concentration camp with student voiceovers, the publication of a school newspaper reporting on the exhibits at the camp museum, the preparation of a photography project on the artifacts from the displays relating to Soviet Special Camp II, and the creation of posters depicting student impressions of the permanent collection of Holocaust art. Late that day several students joined their teachers for a tour of nearby Ettersberg Memorial honoring the antifascist resistance against Hitler—the same place where young people in the former East Germany took the oath of Buchenwald and completed the civic ritual marking their admission to the Free German Youth.

Significantly, not one of the pupils had any previous knowledge or understanding of the place and its historical importance for East Germany. The reactions of former East Germans over the meaning and importance of this oath to the state are mixed. Recent research suggests that the *Jugendweihe*, the former civic ceremony conducted by the East German state to induct thirteen-year-olds into adult membership in the political community, continues in parts of eastern Germany for largely social reasons. Some citizens from the east cherish the social interactions with family and friends that the *Jugendweihe* affords. The political oath-taking passed away, but not the social traditions and the tradition of atheism that remain part of eastern German identity in some communities.[38]

The teaching model described in this essay represented one option from among a wide range of pedagogical possibilities. Certain elements of historical learning remained conspicuously absent in the Weibelfeldschule program in Buchenwald. One visiting group of students from Erfurt and Czechoslovakia, for example, visited the Jewish cemetery in Erfurt. Other JBS programs included discussions with survivors of Buchenwald from the Nazi era. In early 1999 Rook and the JBS planned a special commemoration for April marking the fifty-fourth anniversary of Buchenwald's liberation. Students and Holocaust survivors from across Europe joined several veterans of Patton's army for a series of ceremonies and presentations.[39]

Although JBS Buchenwald offers many possibilities for teaching models, educators with recent experience there agree that the archeological digs seem to be a particularly potent method for drawing young people into what Siegfried Wolf called, "an immediate relationship with history." This kind of learning, Wolf insisted, "cannot be prescribed."[40] From the perspective of the students, the archeological dig, called "We Dig Up History" (*Wir graben Geschichte aus*), held the most meaning of any teaching activity associated with the entire project week. In a wooded area not far from an SS settlement and a short distance from the camp proper, the students unearthed a former SS dumping site for unwanted articles stripped from inmates after execution and a multitude of other items from daily camp life. The layers of soil covering the somber reminders of the camp's fifty-year legacy yielded eyeglasses, buttons, shoes, pieces of dishware and clothing, bottle fragments, shaving utensils, a penknife, a Singer sewing machine, a coin purse, beer bottle caps, electrical conduits, and prisoner identification tags. Digging up artifacts from the daily lives of prisoners brought history to life in a way that was not possible through other methods of teaching.

One student asked about a piece of round plastic he found at the site. The object turned out to be a prophylactic condom of the sort that favored prisoners received from the SS for visits to the camp brothel, a subject of one of the students' research projects. After initially expressing disbelief at his teachers' explanation, the student made the connection between archeology and the archival research his peers had completed days before.

In the collection of research essays, one of the student editors captured the intellectual curiosity of her class and the difficulty of trying to deal with a past that remains largely unresolved in the new Germany:

> It is not simple to write about our experiences. All of us are trying to make sense of our thoughts and from this to understand and comprehend what we have seen and experienced. We did not come to the camp to see only the terrible, the hideous, and the gruesome and then ignore the importance of everyday life under this impression of fear. We are in Buchenwald so that we can understand what happened here between 1937 and 1945. What did the prisoners feel? How could the SS people carry out over a period of years so many terrible and such gruesome deeds? These are questions that move us.[41]

Interviews with the students in the research groups revealed their struggle in trying to articulate not only the meaning of what happened in Buchenwald under the Nazis but also the legacy of the camp and its implications for the contemporary problems of xenophobia and racism in the new Germany. One of the original purposes of the week was to draw a relationship between these elements of past and present. The students showed their common concern that declining economic conditions in the new Germany, a major factor supporting the rise of Nazism under Hitler two generations before, would lead to even more persecutions of Turks, Vietnamese, and other foreigners.[42]

The continuing conflict in Bosnia, fueled by ethnic hatred and marked by grim linguistic parallels with the SS vocabulary of ethnic cleansing, was not lost on the students of Weibelfeldschule. In a sobering epilogue to the volume of research essays entitled, "Germany of the Germans?" the students integrated the prose and poetry of two school companions, recent refugees from Bosnia and Eritrea, who recounted the bitter legacy of war and ethnic violence from personal experience.[43] In the view of the student editors and their teacher, the Buchenwald experience raised a multitude of disturbing and unanswered questions regarding dark parallels with the Third Reich and the human propensity for war as a way of dealing with conflict.[44]

Learning and living with the community at JBS Buchenwald for five days demonstrated to me one of the greatest gifts of the camp to members of this young generation of Germans and their teachers. Buchenwald represents a precious historical and cultural treasure where, through active investigation, critical questions about political power, moral responsibility, and the relationship of the individual to the state can be raised within the powerful contexts of place, time, and archeology. It gives students the unique opportunity to go beyond the textbook as they explore the importance of selective traditions in framing legitimized historical knowledge and history propaganda under democracy and dictatorship.

Buchenwald is not the only concentration camp in the new Germany that holds a great potential for sparking renewed and vigorous inquiry among the young about the dual legacy of the Third Reich and the Cold War. Other sites include Sachsenhausen and Ravensbrück in Brandenburg. As in Buchenwald, the educational authorities in these two camps are articulating broadened interpretations of Germany's recent past that diverge sharply from the heavy emphasis formerly placed on the heroic resistance of the Red Underground by the East German state. The implications of this ideological transition are already evident in the changes introduced in the concentration camp museums and in the new plans for expanded museum exhibits relating to the special camps of the Stalinist era.[45] With the change in regimes came a shift in history propaganda. Similar to the debate in Weimar over the future of the Thälmann statue and the city square that bore his name, public discussions continue over the fate of the antifascist memorial sculptures commissioned by East Germany in Sachsenhausen and Ravensbrück.[46]

Buchenwald offers an omnipresent reminder that the success of political and economic reunification in the future is related to a slow but necessary healing of national and international wounds over the dual legacies of Hitler and the Cold War. In the midst of painful transitions in the new Germany, the living memorial of Buchenwald holds promise as a place where Germans, once schooled under the divisive East-West tensions of the Cold War, might continue the arduous dialogue over the meaning of German history since the 1930s. Existing tensions and mistrust between citizens of eastern and western Germany, exacerbated by continuing unemployment problems in the East and periodic outbreaks of Neo-Nazi activism, suggest that building a just and humane nation is indeed a daunting challenge.

Notes

Special thanks to the Research and Grants Committee at the University of Wisconsin–La Crosse for their generous support of this research as well as Helmut Rook, the JBS director at the Buchenwald Memorial, without whom this project would have been impossible; Marina Bock, the head of the *Gesamtschule #2 mit gymnasieler Oberstufe* in Berlin-

Treptow; and teachers George Harnischfeger, E. Dürr, and all of the students from the Buchenwald project at Weibelfeldschule in the Hessian city of Dreieich. This essay originally appeared in an abridged version in the *Journal of Curriculum and Supervision* 10, 2 (Winter 1995): 171–188.

1. See three essays by Jürgen Habermas, "A Kind of Settlement of Damages: The Apologetic Tendencies in German Historical Writing"; "On the Public Use of History: The Official Self-Understanding of the Federal Republic Is Breaking Up"; and "Note: February 23, 1987," all in *Forever in the Shadow of Hitler?* trans. James Knowlton (Atlantic Heights, NJ: Humanities Press, 1993), 34–44, 58–60, 260–62; Andreas Hillgruber, "Jürgen Habermas, Karl-Heinz Janssen, and Enlightenment in the Year 1986," *Geschichte in Wissenschaft und Unterricht* (History in academics and instruction) 12 (December 1986): 725–38; Ernst Nolte, "Between Historical Legend and Revisionism?" in H.W. Koch, ed., *Aspects of the Third Reich* (London: Macmillan, 1985), 17–38; Joachim Fest, "Die Beladene Erinnerung" (Encumbered Remembrance) *Frankfurter Allgemeine Zeitung*, August 29, 1986; Geoff Eley, "Nazism, Politics and the Image of the Past: Thoughts on the West German *Historikerstreit,* 1986–1987," *Past and Present* 121 (1988): 171–208.

2. Daniel Goldhagen, *Hitler's Willing Executioners: Ordinary Germans and the Holocaust* (New York: Knopf, 1996), 383, 484–88.

3. Christopher Browning, *Ordinary Men: Reserve Police Battalion 101 and the Final Solution in Poland* (New York: HarperCollins, 1992), 159–89; Eberhard Jäckel, "Einfach ein Schlechtes Buch" (Simply a bad book), *Die Zeit,* May 27, 1996.

4. Craig Whitney, "Germans Begin to Recognize Danger in Neo-Nazi Upsurge," *New York Times*, October 21, 1993; Wolfgang Gessenharter, "Das Freund-Feind-Denken der Neuen Rechten" (Friend-foe thinking of the new right-wingers), in Christoph Butterwege and Horst Isola, eds., *Rechtsextremismus in Vereinten Deutschland* (Right-wing extremism in united Germany) (Bremen: Steintor, 1991), 62–70.

5. German Information Center, "Bundestag to Settle Debate over Holocaust Memorial,"*Week in Germany*, November 20, 1998, 6.

6. German Information Center, "Minister and Architect Agree on Revised Design for Holocaust Memorial,"*Week in Germany*, January 22, 1999, 6.

7. Friedemann Bedürftig and Dieter Kalenbach, *Hitler* (Hamburg: Carlsen, 1990), 3–28.

8. Craig Whitney, "Germans Halt Comic Book That Backfired," *New York Times*, October 21, 1993.

9. Raymond Williams, "Hegemony and the Selective Tradition," in Suzanne and Alan Luke, eds., *Language, Authority and Criticism: Readings on the School Textbook*, (London: Falmer Press, 1989), 58.

10. Wolfgang Bleyer and Gerhard Hass, *Geschichte 9* (Berlin: Volk und Wissen, 1987), 133, 162, and in the 1988 edition, 168–70, 194–95.

11. Ibid., 1987, 163; 1988, 169.

12. For a penetrating historical study of I.G. Farben and the Third Reich, see Peter Hayes, *Industry and Ideology: I.G. Farben in the Nazi Era* (New York: Cambridge University Press, 1987). See also Morton Minz, "GM, Ford Units Criticized on WWII Role," *Washington Post*, February 27, 1974, and the investigative work of Bradford Snell, assistant counsel to the Senate Monopoly and Anti-Trust Subcommittee, in "GM and the Nazis," *Ramparts* 12 (June 1974): 14–16. The issue arose again in 1998 under a shower of class action suits by Holocaust survivors. See "GM, Ford Deny They Aided Nazis," *Detroit Free Press*, December 1, 1998.

13. Ministerium für Volksbildung (Ministry for Popular Education), *Lehrplan Geschichte: Abiturstufe* (History curriculum: *Abitur* level) (Berlin: Volk und Wissen, 1989), 2.

14. Gregory Wegner, "Ideologischer Wandel beim Unterricht über das Vermächtnis des Dritten Reiches in ostdeutschen Oberschulen" (Ideological Change in teaching over

the legacy of the Third Reich in East German secondary schools), *Geschichte, Erziehung, Politik* 3 (History, education, politics) 3 (March 1993): 171–79; Hans Ebeling, *Die Reise in der Vergangenheit* (The journey into the past) (Braunschweig: Westermann, 1991), 172–78; Peter Alter and others, *Geschichte und Geschehen IV* (History and events) (Stuttgart: Klett, 1987), 118–21. One notable exception to an otherwise sparse treatment of the Communist resistance figures is found in the textbook by Peter Hüttenberger, *Geschichtsbuch* (History book) (Berlin: Cornelsen, 1990), 150–53; German Information Center, *German Society: Holocaust Education in Germany* (New York: GIC, 1999), 1–3.

15. Bodo Ritscher, *Buchenwald: Guide to the National Memorial* (Buchenwald: Gedenkstätte Buchenwald, 1986), 1–26; Bodo Ritscher, *Speziallager Nr. 2* (Special camp no. 2) *Buchenwald* (Buchenwald: Gedenkstätte Buchenwald, 1993), 60–66.

16. Lehrplan für Grundschulen (DDR), 5. bis 8. Schuljahr (Curriculum for East German elementary schools, grades five through eight), 1953, cited in *Zu Fragen der Erziehung im Geschichtsunterricht*, (On questions about education in the teaching of history), ed. Christel Sievert (Berlin: 1955), 174–75.

17. DDR, Ministerium für Volksbildung der Deutschen Demokratischen Republik, *Mahn- und Gedenkstätte Buchenwald: Bild- und Leseheft für Kunstbetrachtung* (Buchenwald as memorial and a place for admonishment: picture and reading booklet for the contemplation of art) (Berlin: Volk und Wissen, 1969), 1–30; Ingrid and Arthur Burghoff, *Erbe als Auftrag: Zur Geschichte der Nationalen Mahn- und Gedenkstätte Buchenwald* (Inheritance as mission: The history of the Buchenwald national memorial) (Erfurt: DEWAG, 1977), 29, 43–46. See also Gregory Wegner, "In the Shadow of the Third Reich: The *Jugendstunde* and the legitimation of antifascist heroes for East German youth," *German Studies Review* 19 (February 1996): 127–46. For a pioneering study of the profound contrasts between the public memory on the Holocaust fostered in East and West Germany, see Jeffrey Herf, *Divided Memory: The Nazi Past in the Two Germanys* (Cambridge: Harvard University Press, 1997).

18. Christa Uhlig, "Auschwitz als Element der Friedenserziehung in der DDR" (Auschwitz as an element of peace education in East Germany), in *Erziehung nach Auschwitz* (Education after Auschwitz), ed. H.F. Rathenow and N.H. Weber (Pfaffenweiler, Germany: Centaurus, 1989), 89–97; Emeryka Iwaszko, "Pädagogische Arbeit mit Jugendlichen im staatlichen Museum Auschwitz" (Pedagogical work with youth in the state museum at Auschwitz), in *Zur Arbeit in Gedenkstätten für die Opfer des Nationalsozialismus: Ein internationaler Überblick* (About work on memorials for the victims of National Socialism: An international overview), ed. Wulff Brebeck (Berlin: Aktion Sühnezeichen Friedensdienste, 1988), 73–84.

19. M. Graefe, "Vorlage zur Diskussion um eine zentrale Bildungs- und Begegnungsstätte auf dem Ettersberg" (Proposal for discussion of an education and meeting center on Ettersburg), *Zur Neuorientierung der Gedenkstätte Buchenwald: Die Empfehlungen der vom Minister für Wissenschaft und Kunst des Landes Thüringen berufenen Historikerkommission* (On the new orientation of the Buchenwald memorial: recommendations of the Minister for Science and Culture from the historical commission of Thüringen). (Weimar-Buchenwald: Gedenkstätte Buchenwald, 1992), 39.

20. Ibid., 40.

21. JBS Buchenwald, *Begegnen, Begreifen, Bewahren: Die Jugendbegegnungsstätte an der Nationalen Mahn- und Gedenkstätte Buchenwald* (Confrontation, understanding, preservation: the JBS at the Buchenwald national memorial). (Buchenwald: Gedenkstätte Buchenwald, 1993), 2.

22. Mario Schattney, "Auf den Spuren der Geschichte" (On the tracks of history). *Thüringer Nachrichten*, August 18–19, 1990.

23. Helmut Rook, ed., *Jahresbericht 1990/91: Die Jugendbegegnungsstätte an der Nationalen Mahn- und Gedenksstätte Buchenwald* (Annual Report for 1990–91: The JBS at the Buchenwald national memorial) (Buchenwald: 1991), 6.

24. Ibid., 2.

25. *Thüringer Tageblatt*, September 24, 1991.

26. *Erfurter Wochenblatt*, June 24, 1991. Note the development of a similar program under the Boston-based group Facing History and Ourselves (FHAO), which conceives Holocaust studies as a way of confronting youth with the reality of racism. FHAO organizer Margot Stern Storm noted that "if you are trying to teach about social justice and democracy, you have to look at how it failed. The whole lesson is to say that history is not inevitable and that the Holocaust could have been prevented." See Erica Simmons, "Facing History in Ourselves," *New Internationalist,* September 1993, 7.

27. Georg Harnischfeger, "Projekt Buchenwald and wie es dazu kam" (Project Buchenwald and how it came about). *Buchenwald: Eine Woche in der Jugendbegegnungsstätte* (A week at the JBS), ed. Sonja Bergström and Dina Keller (Dreieich: Weibelfeldschule, 1993), 2.

28. "Vielseitige Präsentation beim Schulfest: Weibelfeldschule stellte eindrucksvolle Ergebnisse ihrer Projektwoche vor" (Diverse presentation at school festival: Weibelfeldschule presented impressive results of their project week). *Langner Zeitung,* June 25, 1993.

29. George Harnischfeger and E. Dürr, "Projektbeschreibung (Project description) PROWO (Project week) 1993," in Sonja Bergström and Dina Keller, eds., *Buchenwald*, 66.

30. Joachim Hoffman et al., *Geschichtliche Weltkunde: Klasse 9* (Historical world studies) (Frankfurt: Diesterweg, 1990), 98–135; Alter et al., *Geschichte und Geschehen, IV* (History and events, 4) (Stuttgart: Klett, 1991), 78–124, 283–98; Arno Höfer et al., *Lebendige Vergangenheit:* (The living past) *Geschichte 9* (Stuttgart: Klett, 1990), 64–95; Thomas Berger et al., *Entdecken und Verstehen: Von 1917 bis zur Gegenwart* (Discovery and understanding: from 1917 to the present) (Berlin: Cornelsen, 1989), 89–136, 162–83; Peter Hüttenberger et al., *Geschichtsbuch IV* (History book 4)(Berlin: Cornelsen, 1990), 124–59; Hans Ebeling, *Die Reise in die Vergangenheit: 5* (Trip into the past) (Braunschweig: Westermann, 1991), 126–87; Hans Ebeling, *Die Reise in die Vergangenheit: 6* (Stuttgart: Klett, 1991), 123–69. One notable exception to the general omission in textbooks regarding anti-Semitism in Europe during recent years is the booklet written by Jochen Bracker, *Lebendige Vergangenheit: Brennpunkte* (The living past: Burning Issues) *1989/1990* (Stuttgart: Klett, 1991), which accompanies the text of the same name. Bracker included a picture of a defaced Jewish gravestone in France with the caption, "Racism: a European problem" (7). Examples of violence committed against foreigners in the Federal Republic are left out.

31. Peter Kleine, "O Buchenwald" (translated as written in the German) *Geschichte, Erziehung, Politik* (History, education, politics) 2 (1991): 101–7.

32. Group interview, students from Weibelfeldschule, Buchenwald, June 16, 1993.

33. W.H. Kilpatrick, "The Project Method," *Teachers College Record* 19 (1918): 319–35.

34. Sondra Fleck, "Brief aus Buchenwald," in Bergström and Keller, *Buchenwald,* 57–60.

35. Sonja Bergström, "Offene Brief aus Buchenwald" (Open letter from Buchenwald), in Bergström and Keller, *Buchenwald, 55.

36. Gendenkstätte Buchenwald, ed., *Jugendbegegnungsstätte der Gedenkstätte Buchenwald* (JBS at the Buchenwald memorial) (Weimar-Buchenwald: JBS, 1995), 10.

37. Herf, *Divided Memory: The Nazi Past in the Two Germanys.*

38. Gregory Wegner, "In the Shadow of the Third Reich: The *Jugendstunde* and the Legitimation of Antifascist Heroes for East German Youth," *German Studies Review* 19 (February 1996): 127–46.

39. See the account of Peter Kleine, a history teacher from a *Gymnasium* in Essen, for

his comparative observations on Buchenwald as teaching model based on visits in 1980 and 1991 in Peter Kleine, "O Buchenwald," *Geschichte, Erziehung, Politik* 4 (November 1993): 691–95.

40. Siegfried Wolf, "Lernort Buchenwald" (Buchenwald as a place of learning) *Geschichte, Erziehung, Politik* 4 (November 1993): 698–702.

41. Sonja Bergström, "Vorwart" (Forward) in Bergström and Keller, *Buchenwald,* 1.

42. Interviews with students from Weibelfeldschule, Buchenwald, June 16–17, 1993. For a larger interview sample revealing youth attitudes on the problem of reunification associated with school visits to Buchenwald, see a special joint study conducted by Hessen and Thüringen in *Auswirkungen der Besuche von Gedenkstätte auf Schülerinnen und Schüler: Bericht über 40 Explorationen in Hessen und Thüringen* (Effects of visits to memorial sites by school children: A report from over forty explorations in Hesse and Thüringen), ed. Cornelia Fischer and Hubert Anton (Frankfurt: Hessische Landeszentrale für politische Bildung, 1992).

43. Bergström and Keller, eds., *Buchenwald,* 78–81.

44. Georg Harnischfeger, "Wer waren die Täter" (Who were the perpetrators?) in Bergström and Keller, *Buchenwald,* 46–50.

45. Ministerium für Wissenschaft, Forschung und Kultur des Landes Brandenburg, *Empfehlungen zur Neukonzeption der brandenburgischen Gendenkstätten* (Recommendations for the new conceptualization of the memorial sites in Brandenburg) (Berlin: Ministerium, 1992), 23–40.

46. Bernd Faulenbach, "Von der Gegenwärtigkeit des Vergangenen: Zur Neukonzeption von Gedenkstätten in der ehemaligen DDR" (From the present of the past: toward a new conceptualization of memorial sites in former East Germany) in *Tagesspiegel,* February 7, 1993.

10

Teaching Democracy, Teaching War: American and Japanese Educators Teach the Pacific War

Kathleen Woods Masalski

National narrative, master narrative, textbook narrative, counternarrative, multiple narratives–the language, though not the ideas behind it, was new to me and to most if not all the high school and college teachers in the audience when our keynote speaker at a National Endowment for the Humanities summer institute in 1994 challenged us to "problematize the national, the master, the textbook narrative . . . to make history messy!"[1]

As social studies and history teachers in the 1970s, 1980s, and 1990s, we learned through personal experience that the teaching of history had been on trial in this country for years. Despite the 1988 declaration by the Bradley Commission on History in the Schools that teachers "should feel free to choose their own emphases and ways of teaching, according to their own teaching conditions, interests, and talents," all veterans of the classroom in that 1994 summer institute audience knew that the commission's statement did not always ring true.[2]

Some in the audience had little choice in the matter. The state, the local community, or the textbook itself dictated the story for the teacher to tell. A number of states had issued ill-conceived guidelines; their brevity or their specificity (sometimes within the same document) frustrated good teachers. At the local level, teachers often faced hostile though some-times well-intentioned special interest groups. There was—and is—a lot of knee-jerk patriotism among parents out there; with each new year, teachers are forced to begin where their students are. And rather than helping teachers, most if not all textbooks put impediments in their way.

The culture wars over the national history standards that raged during 1994 brought the conflict to a head. But teachers of history have always had to struggle with the fundamental questions on which the debate centered: Where and how to begin? What and whom to include? What and whom to leave out? And how to present it?

This chapter deals with textbooks and the teaching of history. If we agree with an underlying premise of this book (see chapter 1) that "schools and textbooks are important vehicles through which contemporary societies transmit ideas of citizenship and both the idealized past and the promised future," then it is worth our while to ask how social studies teachers in America's classrooms treat textbooks and the controversies that surround them.

Why Textbooks?

For all the talk of alternative means of instruction, the conventional textbook remains the core and often the sole teaching tool in most American history classrooms.[3] In their 1987 publication, *What Do Our 17-Year-Olds Know?* Diane Ravitch and Chester E. Finn Jr. reported that 80 percent of American students use a history textbook at least twice a week.[4] A National Assessment of Educational Progress study of history courses (conducted in 1994 and published in 1996) confirms that the single most important tool used by teachers in the classroom is the textbook. Almost half the students had teachers who reported using textbooks on a daily basis. Sixty-two percent of the students in fourth grade and 23 percent in eighth grade had teachers who reported that they never or hardly ever used primary historical documents in their teaching.[5] For fifteen years, I, too, used textbooks to teach American history in junior and senior high schools.

In *America Revised*, Frances FitzGerald wrote, "History textbooks for elementary and secondary schools are not like other kinds of stories. . . .They are essentially nationalistic histories . . . written not to explore but to instruct—to tell children what their elders want them to know about their country."[6] The textbooks told my students who they were and how they fit into our nation's story of its past. The books also told them what to think about themselves as citizens of a nation and their relationship with others in that nation and in the world.

I used textbooks in my history classes for a variety of reasons, but not for most of the ones James Loewen suggests in his 1995 *Lies My Teacher Told Me: Everything Your American History Textbook Got Wrong*. Loewen states that many history teachers don't know much history.[7] He goes on to say that "most teachers do not like controversy" and that "it is hard for teachers to teach open-endedly. They are afraid not to be in control of the answers, afraid of losing their authority over the class."[8] But I graduated from college with a B.A. in history, was certified to teach history in at least three states, and spent many summers in institutes and seminars studying subjects related to the courses I was teaching. I thrived on discussion and controversy, and my approach to teaching rested on the idea that in any classroom the teacher is the number one student.

So why did I use textbooks in my American history classes? In part because they were there; I inherited them. They also offered me, as they do other teachers, a convenient means of organizing a course. They promised me the security of knowing that I was "covering the waterfront" (as Loewen put it), that my students would not be disadvantaged on state or nationwide tests.[9] I also saw that textbooks satisfied the needs of students who were absent for any period of time and who wanted to know, "Did I miss anything?" but didn't want to spend hours after school making up the time missed in class. (The assumption behind the question offended me because it implied that nothing much happened in class, which was simply not the case.) Finally, with five courses and three or four preparations every night, both I and the students used textbooks in American history courses to survive.

At the same time, although I used textbooks, I supplemented them with additional readings, films and slides, and outside speakers. By doing so, I mediated and sometimes challenged the texts. I assigned other readings (case studies, biographies, diaries, novels, and songs, for example) or showed films (both American and foreign) or used lessons developed by creative colleagues in the field precisely because they cast doubt on the claims made by textbooks. Like all other teachers, I made key political decisions behind the closed classroom door.

I also transformed the way that students looked at the texts themselves. Many of my students held to the widely accepted idea that history consists of what textbooks present as fact. Yet I wanted my students to see textbooks as more than collections of facts, as books that vary a good deal from one another, that are written by ordinary human beings, and that, like the students' own work, have strengths and weaknesses.[10] I wanted my students to use textbooks as tools for learning about the process of history, about how history is written. So together we examined our textbooks, both as historical documents and as secondary sources of evidence. We devoted the first several days of history classes to deconstructing our textbooks.

In most years, students in my American history classes had two different textbooks. Lewis Paul Todd and Merle Curti's *Rise of the American Nation* (later *Triumph of the American Nation*) was a constant; it was one of the most popular texts in the 1980s, and I used it for its chronology and broad coverage. *Promise of America* by Larry Cuban and Philip Roden, in contrast, was one of the so-called inquiry or discovery texts that came out of the 1970s. With its thematic approach to the past, it dealt more deeply with a limited number of issues in American history. Although I supplemented them with case studies, biographies, stories, and documents, these textbooks were our "primary sources."

Deconstructing the Textbook

To introduce the study of history, I asked students how they thought the textbooks on their desks had come into being and how they had come to be on their desks. In the discussions that followed, students came up with their own ideas about authors, publishing companies, state and local adoption bodies, and teachers. I asked them to think about the components of the textbooks (titles, covers, graphics, narratives) and whether there were other ways to organize and present the material included in their texts.

The class divided into small groups to complete a number of assignments that I had prepared. I asked my students to:

- Think about the titles. What was the reader supposed to think or feel about the subject or country presented? What words in the title invited a particular response?
- "Read" the covers. What did the colors and pictures say about the book and its contents? What did they promise would be on the inside? If people were represented, who were they? If the focus was a symbol, what did that symbol represent?
- Get to know the authors. This was key. Textbooks are nearly always written in a distant, magisterial tone, discouraging students from questioning any of their assertions.[11] How many were there? Were they pictured? What were their ethnic or racial backgrounds, their ages, sex, education, disciplines, fields of study? From where did they come, what part of the country? How might each of these factors have influenced the way an author told a story? Did it matter that some had died before the date of publication? Why were their names still listed?

- Learn about the publishing companies. How long had they been in the business? Were they subsidiaries of a larger company? To which (and how many) states did they sell their textbooks? And what difference did it make?[12]
- Check the dates of publication. How did the time something was written affect historical interpretation? Did the gap between the event and the time the textbook was written make a difference? Does a recent publication date necessarily signal a book with up-to-date content?[13]
- Look at the tables of contents. How were the texts organized: chronologically or thematically? How might the organization of a text affect a reader's view of history?
- Survey the indices. Were any types of people and groups more heavily represented than others? Approximately what percentage of names in each index were those of minorities (sometimes difficult to ascertain)? Of women? Was there significance to the percentage?
- Examine the graphics, the photographs, paintings, illustrations. How were women and minorities portrayed? The rich and the poor? What country or countries appear in the optical center of the world maps?

The students and I concluded that in producing history textbooks historians and educators (and their publishers) make choices about what to exclude and what to include—and how to present what they choose to include. I encouraged students to think about who owns history and whose knowledge schools teach. We talked about what the authors and publishers saw as important for American youth to learn about their country and about the world.

With this introduction we had begun to explore some of the aims and structure of the course. For example, a major theme covered by most American textbooks is the diverse groups of people from many cultures that have made up and are still changing our society.[14] I wanted the students to think about how they as individuals and as members of a group fit into each textbook's version of the history of this country. Like thousands of other teachers across the country, I invited students to question their textbooks, for the practice of questioning and debating "received truth," as in textbooks, is where citizenship really develops, not from the content of the national story passed down. To do so, students had to understand that textbook history, like all history, is not "the truth," but a version of the past written by historians on the basis of analysis and evidence.[15]

Throughout the school year, I used similar strategies to focus on the textbook as a source of evidence. Other teachers had published their ideas on that subject, and I found them enormously useful. In the early 1980s, for example, when funds for textbooks were especially tight, several articles appeared in *Social Education*, a professional journal for social studies teachers, advocating creative use of textbooks. The authors of these articles offered suggestions to counteract the limitations of textbooks.[16]

One approach I culled from that series had students creating a time line from the information in a textbook chapter. The purpose was to ascertain what the authors of the textbook deemed significant in a given period, to prod students into thinking about the perspectives of the authors. Were the events and people on their time lines important to political, social, economic, or military history? What were the authors' frames of reference? I often asked students to create time lines for the decade preceding our study, to enter key events for each of the years. The disagreements among them vividly illustrated how firsthand observers can honestly differ on the relative importance of key events.

I recently demonstrated a variation of the time-line activity for a group of American middle and high school teachers who had participated in a three-week summer institute on postwar Japan. Prior to my presentation, I created a time line by gleaning important events that occurred during the past fifty years from chapters in *Japan in Modern History*, which is published in Tokyo.[17] As I read quickly through the relevant chapters, I jotted down important events in the appropriate slots on the time line. I had perhaps thirty entries, nearly all of which (not surprisingly) related to Japan's political, military, or economic history as opposed to its social or cultural history.

I divided the teachers into small groups and asked them to strike out the five entries they saw as least important to Japan's recent past and to substitute five others they thought deserved mention. I was not sure what to anticipate in the way of deletions, but I was pleased with many of the choices. I overheard one teacher explain that had he not participated in the summer institute, he would have deleted the 1964 Tokyo Olympic Games from the "textbook" time line. Others in the group admitted that they, too, had been unaware of the importance of the Olympics and the International Exposition of 1970 to postwar Japan, to the millions of Japanese who had taken great pride in their country's hosting both events.

I expected the teachers to substitute milestones related to Japan's recent social and cultural past for more traditional events associated with the country's political history. I thought that as teachers they might list some of the educational reforms introduced during Nakasone Yasuhiro's administration in the 1980s, or perhaps some of the films by well-known director Kurosawa Akira. They did not disappoint me. In addition to one or two educational reforms and films, a few groups added Ōe Kenzaburo's Nobel Prize for Literature in 1994 and the Equal Employment Law of 1986 that—on paper at least—gave Japanese women more rights in the workplace. Several of the items that the teachers added to the time lines represented Japanese purchases of American real estate and equities. But for the most part, the teachers, like the Japanese textbook writers, opted for conventional political, military, and economic entries.

Although the activity wasn't as successful as I had hoped (I wanted more exchange, more dialogue), I think it made its point. In an attempt to connect the question with the time-line activity, I had titled my presentation "Who Owns History?" I wanted to drive home that those who construct time lines, whether textbook authors, teachers, or students, control the reader's impression of what is important in a given period. I'd like to think that the teachers in the room that day have since adapted the activity to meet their classroom needs.

Other suggestions from the series in *Social Education* encouraged me to help students approach graphics (charts, graphs, diagrams, and maps) with a critical eye. Throughout the school year, I asked them to explain how "the definitions presented, the categories established, the type of graphics chosen, the scale selected, and the artistic license used in choosing colors" prejudiced the final results of the graphic.[18] On occasion I asked them to redesign charts or graphs in the textbook, using the same information, to make the impression more favorable to one country or people represented. Converting to a pie chart from a bar graph or reversing colors on a map had the potential to change the reader's interpretation of the information presented.

One activity I especially liked used maps. American history textbooks often present U.S. expansion into the Pacific by labeling the date of acquisition of a U.S. territory, trust, or protectorate. In contrast, maps of imperial Japan in American texts frequently attach Japan to its Pacific territories with large red arrows. Using transparencies and the overhead projector, I removed the arrows from Japan (labeling its territories with the dates of acquisition) and drew red arrows connecting the United States with its domain. I then asked students to

10.1 Global maps
Graphs and maps display the assumptions of textbook writers and publishers. Japanese maps put Japan at the center of the world just as American ones locate the U.S. East Coast at the geographic center. Map by Christopher Tassava.

explain how the changes that I had made altered the messages of the original maps. They caught on quickly.

Key to critical thinking in social studies is the ability to distinguish between fact and opinion. I designed a rather simple exercise to help students recognize the differences between statements of fact and expressions of opinion. When studying the reasons for Japan's surrender at the end of World War II, my students and I read selected paragraphs in textbooks (and translations of textbooks) written in the Soviet Union, Japan, and the United States. Using Ray A. Billington's list of "five forms of nationalistic bias," we looked in the following excerpts from three texts for bias by inertia (the failure of textbook writers to keep abreast of current scholarship), bias by omission (inappropriate selection of facts, leading to distortion), bias by cumulative implication (giving only one side of a many-sided story), bias in the use of language (use of derogatory terms as well as subtle nuances of language), and bias by unconscious falsification (the inability of authors to divorce themselves from the national milieu in which they have been reared): [19]

> After Nazi Germany and its allies in Europe had been defeated, and Germany had signed the act of unconditional surrender on May 8, 1945, the Soviet Union, true to its pledge to the USA and Great Britain, entered the war against militarist Japan in autumn 1945, to put an early end to the Second World War. In a short but overwhelming operation, the Soviet army routed the one-million-strong Kwantung Japanese army, located in Manchuria and aimed against the USSR. Thus, the Soviet Army made the decisive contribution to Japan's complete defeat as well.[20]

* * *

> The Japanese government ignored the Potsdam Declaration. Consequently, the U.S. dropped the atomic bomb on Hiroshima on August 6 and on Nagasaki on August 9. Also the USSR, ignoring the Japan-USSR Neutrality Treaty, declared war against Japan and began to invade Manchuria. Finally the Emperor decided to accept the Potsdam Declaration despite the opposition of the military, and notified the Allied side on August 14.[21]

* * *

> In authorizing the atomic bombing of Hiroshima, President Truman knew that he had made an extremely grave decision. He had given the order only after days of conferring with his key military and political advisers. His decision was made to force Japan to surrender immediately and thus to save the lives of hundreds of thousands of American troops. Despite the devastation of Hiroshima, the Japanese failed to surrender. On August 8 the Soviet Union declared war on Japan. On August 9 the United States dropped a second atomic bomb. This one destroyed the city of Nagasaki. On August 10 the Japanese government finally asked for peace.[22]

Perhaps because some of the biases in the paragraphs above were so obvious, this exercise was a student favorite; the students were particularly amused by the bias of omission in the Soviet and American accounts. As we know, bias of omission can occur outside textbooks, as well. An editorial from the February 17, 1998, issue of *New York Times*, "Teaching Myths and History," criticized South Africa, Russia, France, and, of course, Japan for being uninterested in puncturing inaccurate but cherished national myths in their textbook writing. It did not mention the United States.

In recent years some American textbooks have been edited to challenge certain of our myths (the repositioning of Columbus is a good example). Publishers scramble to meet the demands of states and districts to which they sell large numbers of textbooks.[23] As a result, today's teachers must pay attention to features that were not included in textbooks in

10.2 Japan surrenders, September 2, 1945
The Japanese surrender, like all important historical events, is taught very differently in various countries even though there is no disagreement as to the basic facts. NARA, NWDNS-111–SC-210626, War and Conflict no. 1362.

years past. Some teachers complain about American textbooks today (for one thing, they are simply too big), whereas other teachers find them better than ever. In response to teachers' past complaints, the publishing companies have included skill-building activities to help students understand historical readings, think critically, and explore historical evidence. They have more color, more historical documents, more charts, more graphs . . . more everything. But how much have the narratives changed? And how many of the new American history textbooks evaluate their content as national narrative? Every textbook reflects a point of view, and we and our students must approach all texts, including this one, with caution.

Going Beyond the Textbook

Teachers know that students benefit from careful, in-depth study of historical events: "Memorable insights are to be gained from longer, closer looks at selected episodes, and all the more so by the deft use of primary sources, which have the power to draw students into the historical moment itself. . . .Closer looks are necessary so that students will not fall into some of the tempting traps opened by the superficial sorts of chronology-without-interpretation that many textbooks present."[24] The same strategy works well with teachers in professional development courses. Summer institutes with scholars in the field offer excellent opportunities for teachers to go beyond the textbook—to explore the complexities of critical moments in history, to take longer, closer looks at selected episodes in our or another nation's distant or recent past. The summers between 1980 and 1989 that I spent learning about American women's history, about Daniel Shays, Japan, India, and Russia and the Soviet Union were among the most intellectually exciting experiences of my teaching career. Indeed, they enabled me to draw my junior and senior high school students into the historical moment itself.

After I left the classroom in 1990, I took a position at the Five College Center for East Asian Studies and began organizing summer projects for teachers. I led study groups to Japan and coordinated the efforts of several faculty of the Five Colleges in western Massachusetts to work with primary and secondary school teachers in summer institutes and seminars. The fiftieth anniversary of the war in the Pacific prompted several of us to embark on a project with teachers eager to go beyond the textbook version of one of the formative events of the twentieth century.[25] Our goal was to broaden knowledge about the Pacific war among secondary school teachers and to stimulate them to think about their goals and strategies for teaching about that war in both American and Japanese schools at century's end.

The project included a four-week summer institute, "The War in the Pacific: Experiences and Legacies" for American teachers; an invitation to Japanese teachers to join in that summer institute for one week and to attend a regional social studies conference in the United States the following spring; and a seminar in Japan in 1994 for some of the same American and Japanese participants. It required that educators and scholars from each nation share their insights and findings with scholars and educators from the other nation.[26]

The overriding goal of the project was to broaden perspectives on both sides of the Pacific by presenting various points of view on topics that have consequences far beyond the boundaries of the two nations: the perennial questions of war and peace, of human nature in its many guises, of the search for meaning in both personal and national history. Another goal was to bring together Japanese and American teachers to explore their views on textbook coverage of the war and on the treatment of war on the home front.

In framing the institute, we followed several general principles:

- that primary sources are of particular value for the study and treatment of history. For example, we used selections from Studs Terkel's *Good War: An Oral History of World War II* and Haruko Taya Cook and Theodore F. Cook's *Japan at War: An Oral History*. Both books provide interviews with startlingly diverse people. Teachers might select excerpts for their students to compare not just what happens in them but how they are presented: in what voice, what tone, what setting, what context.
- that American students should read not only about the American experience and interpretations but also about Japanese (and other) experiences and interpretations. So in counterpoint to Norman Mailer's *The Naked and the Dead* and Paul Fussell's *Wartime: Understanding and Behavior in the Second World War*, we studied *Requiem for Battleship Yamato* by Yoshida Mitsuru and *City of Corpses* by Ota Yoko. We chose these texts because they were written by individuals who were directly affected by the war in the Pacific and who had survived it.
- that "study the historian" is the fundamental task for all who seek to gain some measure of personal control over the learning process. We provided teachers with biographical information on all the authors they encountered and focused on the relation between the authors' lives and their testimony or interpretation.

The institute engaged American teachers in intensive reading about the war, from both the American and the Japanese side and, to a lesser degree, from other perspectives. This was important because textbooks tend to focus on the conflict between the United States and Japan only; offering other viewpoints forced us to listen to the voices and to see the faces and bodies of, for example, Chinese and Koreans. The reading was split about evenly between firsthand accounts and historical treatments. We examined records related to the war, including President Franklin D. Roosevelt's papers: personal letters, proclamations, and diplomatic exchanges. We studied excerpts from a collection of policy documents translated and edited by Nobutaka Ike entitled *Japan's Decision for War: Record of the 1941 Policy Conferences*. And we read two narrative texts, *Eagle Against the Sun: The American War Against Japan*, by Ronald Spector, and *The Pacific War: 1931–1945*, by Ienaga Saburō. (Although some of the teachers had used Spector in their classrooms, few knew the Ienaga text before that summer.)

Further, the institute featured presentations by scholars and other experts specializing in various aspects of the Pacific War. Speakers included Institute director Richard H. Minear (history, University of Massachusetts) and other faculty from our local institutions (for example, a historian of China, Jonathan Lipman of Mount Holyoke College, and a specialist in twentieth-century U.S. history, Aaron Berman of Hampshire College), as well as scholars and experts from outside the Five College area, such as historian of Japan Carol Gluck (Columbia University) and Colonel Charles Kades, who had been a leading figure in the U.S. occupation of Japan.

We viewed both American and Japanese films that brought the wartime years alive and demonstrated the uses of history in filmmaking and the uses of film in teaching history. Early in the program we viewed *Pearl Harbor: Surprise and Remembrance* and met with Leslie Mason, associate producer of the film. Later we screened *Tora, Tora, Tora; Biruma no tategoto* (Harp of Burma); *Hotaru no Haka* (Grave of the fireflies); *Family Gathering; World War II: The Propaganda Battle* (from the television series *A Walk Through the Twentieth Century with Bill Moyers*); *Our Job in Japan; Air War over Japan; Hiroshima and Nagasaki;* and *Hellfire: Journey from Hiroshima,* exploring a range of Japanese and American feature films and documentaries.

We also questioned the assumption that only fighting men can produce and analyze the literature of war. We invited Richard Kim, author of *Lost Names*, to join us for a discussion of his fictionalized account of his childhood in Japanese-occupied Korea. And we brought to the participants' attention recent contributions that American women have made in broadening our understanding of what constitutes war literature. Whereas war fiction from World War II written by men tends to center on the combat experience, women's war literature most often highlights the feelings and reactions of both civilians and soldiers to their war experiences. *Obasan* by Joy Kogawa, for example, not only includes sections on life in wartime Japan but also explores the experience of Japanese Canadians. To better understand the meaning of the war in Asia, we read and discussed two works produced in China, *Selected Readings from the Works of Mao Tsetung* and Lu Xun's *Selected Works*.

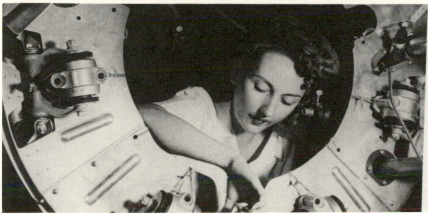

10.3 and 10.4 Civilians and war
Japanese, German, and American texts today all underscore the experience of war on the home front as well as on the battlefield, telling the story from the point of view of civilians as much as from that of soldiers. Some of the war imagery, such as these photos of Japanese and American women taking over heavy industrial production, is very similar in the two countries. Sato ed., *Asahi Rekishi Shashin Riburarii*, vol. 3, 60 and NARA NLR-PHOCO-66127(11). Used by permission.

By the end of the third week of the institute, the teachers had immersed themselves in the war and the issues that surround it, issues that go far beyond those presented in most history textbooks. We knew that what teachers took away even at that point would have an important bearing on their students' knowledge of the postwar world. The teachers already had gathered a wealth of information to supplement their textbooks, plenty of material for problematizing the national narrative and making history messy. But the final week of the institute proved for many to be the most worthwhile component of the project.

Binational Interactions

Massachusetts and Hokkaido had signed a sister-state agreement in February 1990. A year later, I traveled to Sapporo in search of Japanese "partners" to study the war in the Pacific. When I learned via the teachers' union that the local history teachers kept their "unofficial" teaching units on the war in the Pacific at the union headquarters, I knew that my search had ended.

In August 1993 Hokkaido teachers joined the American teachers at Smith College for the final week of the four-week institute. With the help of interpreters, the teachers worked together and lived side by side in a college dormitory. They attended many of the same lectures and discussions and traveled together to the FDR Library and Museum. On the weekend, the Japanese visitors enjoyed home stays with the American teachers.

Prior to their visit, the Japanese teachers had participated in a one-week seminar on the war. The focus of that seminar as well as of the institute at Smith was on content: readings, presentations, films, and discussions. Participants learned about the war itself, about American and Japanese contexts and experiences and legacies, and about those who have interpreted the war for us. In our respective venues, we explored traditional history (the events identified with the war), of course, but also public history (the memory of those events), and engaged in literary analysis and film criticism.

At our request, the American teachers had brought with them the textbooks they use in their American and world history classes. In the closing days of the institute, we took a look at the textbooks' treatments of the war. Using some of the activities described earlier in this chapter, we analyzed the textbook interpretations of various events. Minear had translated excerpts from the most recent Japanese texts and led a session on textbook content and approaches to teaching about the war. Many American teachers were surprised that the narrative included more controversial issues than they had anticipated: forcible expatriation of Koreans and Chinese to Japan and the Nanjing massacre, for example. An eighth-grade teacher who has kept abreast of the textbook controversy in Japan recently expressed surprise that the subject of comfort women appears in eighth-grade texts in Japan. She questioned whether American middle or junior high school textbooks would touch such a sensitive issue.

For their part, the Japanese teachers—who paid little attention to American textbook accounts—were astonished at the easy access American teachers have to primary sources to supplement their textbooks, historical documents available at museums such as the FDR Museum in Hyde Park and the Kennedy Museum in Boston. They complained that they knew of few such repositories available to them or their students in Japan.

Our time together was short, but the evaluations written by the American teachers revealed that the majority saw that time as the most meaningful experience of the institute. On the concluding day, a politically conservative participant wrote, "My one indelible impression of these last four weeks is of Fumie's 'watching' [the video] *Hotaru no Haka* (Grave of the Fireflies) with her hands over her eyes. That told me more about the atomic bomb than I ever wanted to know." Because it is such a powerful video, several teachers from the institute (and others) borrow the center's copy of "Grave of the Fireflies" to preview with their classes when they study World War II. [27]

In summer 1994 the project brought the American teachers back to Smith College for one week and then took twelve of them (and Minear and me) to Japan for a weeklong seminar (including home stay). Hosted by Hokkaido University of Education, the seminar, "Hokkaido and New England: Thinking About Education for the 21st Century," was held at Sapporo Guest House, an ideal place for scholars and teachers to meet and exchange ideas.

The Sapporo seminar featured two main speakers on the war in the Pacific, each of whom criticized the master narrative in his own country's textbooks. One was Minear, who spoke to the question, "How do American schools teach the Pacific war and postwar Japan?" Prior to the seminar, Minear surveyed the twenty-four American teachers who had participated in our 1993 summer institute, many of whom were in the audience in Sapporo. He explained that the teachers teach the war in diverse ways to grades 7 through 12, in English courses, in U.S. history, in world history, and in topics courses, such as law or Asian studies. In most cases, he reported, they have only four to six hours to devote to the war; in a few cases, they have fifteen class hours or more. So there is a wide disparity in context and coverage.

During our institute, Minear told the group, we had spent a lot of time talking about master narrative, the dominant national narrative that comes in part from textbooks. Although he acknowledged the surface variety in American schools texts, he summarized the master narrative in all of them as highlighting "the status quo of the 1920s, Japanese action in China to upset that status quo, slow American response to Japanese aggression, Japan's surprise attack at Pearl Harbor (FDR's 'day which will live in infamy'), Japan's fanatical resistance, Hiroshima, surrender, peace, and friendship."[28]

Minear reported that our teachers were almost unanimous in thinking that American teaching about the war is inadequate and that the master narrative leaves out too much. He argued that teachers need to make history messy, to pose questions that have no easy answers. "If we depend on textbooks," he maintained, "history is not messy. If we depend on sources from one side of the war only, history is not messy."[29]

Fujioka Nobukatsu, professor of education at Tokyo University, lectured on "Problems of Teaching on War and Peace in Japan." Like Minear, he spoke to the issue of national narrative, although not labeling it as such. Fujioka said he was bothered by Minister of Justice Nagano Shigeo's statement in May 1994 that Japan had not fought a war of aggression. He worried that Nagano's statement might suggest to outsiders that Japanese teachers never teach a critical view of Japan's war. To provide evidence to the contrary, Fujioka mailed to principals of 641 junior high schools questionnaires that asked teachers what they regarded as the nature of the war that Japan had fought between 1941 and 1945. He received responses from social studies teachers in 51 percent of the schools, 70 percent of whom said that they viewed it as an aggressive war.[30]

Fujioka's questionnaire also asked the teachers what they teach about the war in the Pacific. He reported that in presenting background to the war, teachers deal with the Great Depression most intensively. In teaching about the war itself, teachers put strong emphasis on the suffering of Japanese people (atomic bombing or the Battle of Okinawa) as well as Japan's acts of aggression, such as the Manchurian incident or the Sino-Japanese War. He used this evidence to argue that "the criticism made by some Asians and Americans against Japan for not dealing with its acts of aggression is totally groundless."[31]

Fujioka also argued that peace education in Japan is highly emotional and at least in part responsible for the Japanese people's unwillingness to fight for their country. He pointed to a Worldwide Value Investigation's interim report, which found that only 10 percent of Japanese respondents answered yes when asked, "Are you willing to fight for your own nation?" By comparison, 85 percent of Korean and 70 percent of American respondents answered affirmatively. Fujioka criticized contemporary Japanese for a lack of patriotism, attributing it in part to a flawed understanding of the Pacific War transmitted through texts and classroom teaching practices.[32] Fujioka has since become a leader of the movement calling

10.5 Texts and the bomb

Japanese and American texts alike suppress the civilian perspective in their imagery of the atomic bombing of Hiroshima and Nagasaki. Texts in both countries show either the mushroom cloud (in this case over Nagasaki) or an aerial view of a flattened city. Very few in either place present images of the victims of the bomb. NARA, MWDNS-208–N-43888. War and Conflict no. 1242.

for Japanese textbooks to present a more "positive" image of Japan. Seeds of that later development were evident in his presentation to us. (See the introduction, Gavan McCormack's and Aaron Gerow's discussion of Fujioka in chapters 2 and 3 of this volume.)

The Japanese teachers' reaction to Fujioka's talk helped to break down the stereotype of Japan as a homogeneous, harmonious society. A number of the teachers vehemently questioned Fujioka's assertions, and something akin to a debate ensued. Angry words were spoken, and voices were raised on both sides. The American teachers were fascinated by the unexpected head-to-head combat.

A Japanese stereotype of Americans may have been destroyed as well. Surprisingly, none of the American teachers challenged Minear openly. Instead, they registered their complaints silently on the evaluation forms. In private one woman wrote, "Please stop the revisionist anti-American slant [that you're putting on] the seminar. In an effort to be balanced, you have tipped the scales to the other side, appearing overly critical of our motives, policies, and actions."[33] Had she said those words aloud, her "performance" might have been much more in keeping with Japanese images of Americans.

On one occasion in Sapporo, when the teachers were not meeting in large group sessions for formal presentations, not attending welcome or farewell parties, not at home with their Japanese hosts (where they probably learned more about the war in the Pacific, the Other, and themselves than they did in any other setting), we all got together to talk informally about curriculum, of how teachers teach about the home front during the war in the Pacific.

By the time the meeting occurred, the group had self-selected. Only twelve American teachers (the original group numbered twenty-four) traveled to Sapporo for the seminar. Eager to learn more about their Japanese counterparts' perspectives on the war, these twelve teachers had invested more than $1,000 of their own money in the trip across the Pacific. The Japanese history teachers who greeted them had already made a commitment to investigate alternative approaches to teaching about their country's and world history by meeting monthly over the previous year with Aiuchi to read in English *A Different Mirror: A History of Multicultural America* by Ronald Takaki and to discuss multicultural approaches to teaching history, especially the history of Japan. Together we focused on textbook interpretations of the war and on activities on the home front.

The Japanese teachers brought with them to that meeting a retired elementary school teacher who had with her a diary from the war years, a record of her experience from January 1, 1943, to February 27, 1945, her first three years of elementary school as a student. Although Hayashi Hisako experienced neither evacuation nor bombing raids and her diary record had little more than 100 words for each day, it captured the atmosphere in Hokkaido during the war and conveyed what life was like for young children. For example, Hayashi and her classmates spent many days collecting wild plants and worms for the war effort. The students dried the plants, which were then ground to powder for food. They put the worms in water to make them regurgitate dirt, then sun-dried them on a board to prepare them for use in antifever medicine. On one occasion, the children's families who lived near the streetcar line were told to evacuate their homes so that the authorities could widen the road as a firebreak. Many buildings were torn down, and Hayashi and others in the class carried the debris to the school to be used as fuel during the long winter. When she learned of Germany's surrender, Hayashi prayed at the family altar every morning, "Please let the divine wind blow soon."

In addition to reading entries from her diary, Hayashi spoke of her feelings during the war as she remembered them. She closed with the words, "I hope that this [my diary] will be one of the resources to bring out the lessons of history more richly, by studying in more depth the methods of indoctrination and the mass communication in the years when children grow naturally into militant girls."[34]

The diary was only the beginning. The Japanese history teachers added other primary sources for the American teachers to use in their classes: a certificate of physical fitness for women, a certificate of war refugee status, and a map of Japanese air raid casualties, among other documents. While the Five College Center for East Asian Studies had the documents translated from Japanese into English, the American teachers searched for comparable items in their local communities. They then built lessons around both. For example, one teacher wrote a lesson featuring the Hayashi diary, a class history from the 1945 yearbook of Worcester (Massachusetts) Classical High School, and a Newton Falls, Massachusetts woman's recollection of her grade school years during the war. Another teacher found a 1944 announcement of a commando course at the high school in her community to use with the Japanese certificate of physical fitness for women. We hope to have these and other lessons translated into Japanese for use in Japan.

At their own expense, eight of the Japanese teachers came with Aiuchi to the Northeast Regional Social Studies Conference in Boston in March 1995 to participate in sessions on teaching about the war in the Pacific and other issues, especially those related to the treatment of minorities. Hosted by their New England colleagues, the Japanese teachers again enjoyed home stays and, this time, visits to American classrooms.

The Japanese and American teachers continued to meet, formally and informally, and discuss related historical and pedagogical issues. As a result of their experiences, American teachers designed pedagogy sessions to introduce their colleagues to the ideas and materials they garnered from (either or both) the institute and seminar. For example, at a full-day program I organized called "The War in the Pacific: Fifty Years Later," twenty teachers from the institute led sessions on topics with titles as varied as "Patriotism Reflected in American and Japanese Art," "Pacific War Literature Around the Rim," "Racism in U.S. and Japanese Cartoons," and "Why Hiroshima: Geography and History."

In their own teaching and in presentations for their colleagues, many of the American teacher participants have in different ways changed their teaching by questioning or adding to the American national textbook narrative. In the past, most had begun their teaching of the war in the Pacific with the bombing of Pearl Harbor. Now they begin their units with maps illustrating European and American expansion into Asia and the Pacific in the nineteenth and early twentieth centuries. Prior to their involvement in the project, few had raised questions about the role of natural resources and other economic factors related to the war effort. Today they ask, Which resources—oil, rubber, coal, steel—were critical? Where were they located? Who had access? And under what restrictions? How strong were the economies of the major actors in the Pacific? They raise additional questions about dropping atomic bombs on Hiroshima and Nagasaki. They ask, "Was the bomb needed to avoid an invasion of Japan?" and "Did alternatives to dropping the bombs exist?"—questions that require going beyond the argument that the bomb would save American lives. The teachers assign readings and films that question the claims of many textbooks.

In other words, these teachers are challenging the traditional narrative on the war in the Pacific. Many are doing so by introducing to their students a wide range of Japanese, American, and Asian sources and perspectives that permit a reassessment of the basic frameworks of the war and subsequent international relations. Teachers comfortable with literature and art use a variety of sources with their students. They share with them the poems of Kurihara Sadako or the comic book *Hadaka no Gen* (Barefoot Gen), for example, publications that show that not everyone on the home front in Japan supported the war effort. They read poems written by kamikaze pilots. They ask their students to write entries in their journals reacting to incidents of Japanese colonialism in Korea as described by Richard Kim in *Lost Names*. Some high school teachers assign Ariyoshi Kinokawa Sawako's *The River Ki* in order to focus discussions on the changing relationship of mother and daughter during the war years. A few use parts of the film *Battle of China* to illustrate Japan's aggression in China. And the film *Hellfire* is a favorite among those who want to show the artists Maruki Toshi and Iri's interpretation of the fate of Japanese, Koreans, and Americans in Hiroshima at the time of the bombing and of Chinese during the Nanjing massacre.

When the Japanese teachers arrived in Massachusetts in 1993, Sasaki Masao, a high school history teacher, spoke before our newly assembled group. He explained that many teachers in Japan approach the history of defeat in World War II as a tale of moral retribution for Japanese aggression in China. "There has been a naive perception shared among [Japanese] history teachers about how to explain the Pacific War in their classrooms, which is to perceive the war as a direct result of Japan's invasion of China. In other words, Japanese teachers have shared a view that describes the Pacific War as the last five years of the Fifteen-Year War, which began in 1931 with the Manchurian Incident, and sees the Japanese invasion of China as the major cause of the United States-Japan War. . . . Japanese teachers have more or less tried to teach their students that Japan's defeat was something like "Heaven's Vengeance" against its cruel activities in invading China."[35] Sasaki's paper supported the standard counternarrative in Japan, one in opposition to the Education Ministry's official, or master, narrative. The project goal was to push teachers beyond both.

To conclude our final follow-up session at Amherst College in March 1995, Nishimura Yoshinori, also a high school history teacher, warned against attaching too much importance to any one cause of the war and giving little attention to others. He asked his audience of American and Japanese history teachers, "Was the war the counterattack of the United States and the Allied Powers against Japan's taking part of China? Was it the struggle for colonies among the advanced capitalist countries? Or did Japan provoke war in order to liberate the colonies from the Western countries? To accept only one of these ideas as a correct one and to exclude the others," he posited, "will surely lead to misunderstanding."[36]

The Textbook Controversy in Japan: Lessons for Americans

When I lived in Japan in 1982–1983, the Ienaga Saburō textbook controversy was at its height. After the Japanese government directed Ienaga to

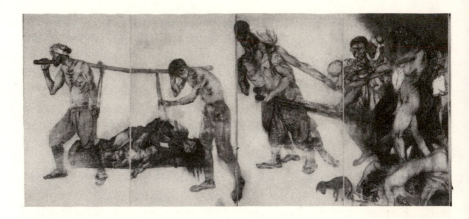

10.6 Atomic bomb victims

This painting by Iri and Toshi Maruki of family members caring for atomic bomb victims was rejected as "too dark" for use in an elementary school textbook, although Osaka Shoseki later published the same image in its junior high school social studies textbook, *Chugaku Shakai. (Social studies for junior high school)*. But should students be protected from horrifying images of war? *The Hiroshima Panels: Joint Works of Iri and Toshi Maruki* (Saitama: Maruki Gallery for the Hiroshima Panels Foundation, 1983). Used by permission.

remove critical language in his history textbook, including insisting that he write of the Japanese army's "advance" into China instead of its aggression in China, of "uprising among the Korean people" instead of the March First Independence Movement, Japan's textbook screening process became a diplomatic problem.[37] I followed the controversy in the English-language press, paying close attention to articles and letters to the editor, which I filed and brought home to discuss in my high school classes in western Massachusetts.

Focusing on the connotations of words such as "aggression" and "advance," my students and I examined our own textbooks for evidence of similar bias. We found that some American textbooks used "sneak" whereas others used "surprise" to describe Japan's attack on Pearl Harbor; we discussed the implication and spirit of each word. Our brief lesson in semantics took us miles toward understanding the power of words and the ability of textbooks to influence their readers. How I could expand that lesson today.

Nearly twenty years later, controversy over textbooks continues in Japan, and Ienaga, now in his eighties, remains at the center of the controversy. As Nozaki Yoshiko and Inokuchi Hiromitsu point out in this volume (see chapter 4), "the ongoing battles over educational content in postwar Japan have been one of the crucial fronts in a long-running struggle over the identify of the nation itself." Their chronology of Ienaga's court challenge to the Japanese government's textbook certification and McCormack's depiction of Fujioka Nobukatsu's efforts to "correct" Japanese history provide excellent lessons for American teachers and students who want to learn more about Japan, about the war in the Pacific—and about ourselves. (At the least, Ienaga's and Fujioka's strong-minded opinions and fierce debates challenge American assumptions of Japan as a harmonious society, without conflict or litigation.)

One lesson brought home to American teachers and students by the textbook controversy is the myriad ways in which international events can influence national narratives, including those in textbooks. Just as pressure from Japan's neighbors in 1982 kept a conservative Japanese government from altering textbook explanations of the role Japan played in the region in the period leading up to the war in the Pacific, international events affected the official narrative at Hiroshima's Peace Memorial Museum. Just prior to the Asian Games hosted by Hiroshima in 1994, the museum added a new wing depicting Hiroshima's role as a military center during World War II after complaints by Asians that the atomic devastation was presented without context. During commemorations of the fiftieth anniversary of the end of the war, protests by Korean comfort women, soon joined by comfort women from the Philippines, Indonesia, Taiwan, and other countries, focused the world's attention on the need for alteration of Japan's dominant narrative.

In contrast to the long and acrimonious controversy over Japanese textbooks, Hein and Selden observe earlier in this volume that other nations have not—at least not yet—commented significantly on American textbook narratives of this and subsequent wars. Will the situation change as the international scene changes? Is it possible, for example, that as Japan grows stronger and more independent, its leaders will ask us to reconsider the Pacific War narrative that appears in most of our precollege textbooks? And what will our response be?

As we use American and world history textbooks with our students, shouldn't teachers and students think carefully about how the words might sound to the ears of our former adversaries? Shouldn't we make-believe that Japanese scholars and students (or Latin American or Vietnamese scholars and students, for that matter) are reading over our shoulders as we teach and learn about the war in the Pacific, war with Mexico, war in Vietnam?

A reviewer of world history texts for the 1993 Columbia University and Association for Asian Studies' National Project on Asia in the Schools found that some of the texts in the study "totally blamed Japanese 'ag-

10.7 National textbooks and the global village
School textbooks around the globe have more and more information about the contemporary world beyond national borders. This famous picture of the 1963 civil rights march on Washington appears in Japanese as well as U.S. textbooks (Source: NWDNS-306–SSM-4D(86)3.)

gression' for World War II. They ignored the problems that Japan faced in the 1930s and the role that the West in general and the United States in particular played in creating them. The statements about Japanese 'aggression' supplemented by Pearl Harbor pictures usually ignored such things as the Triple Intervention, Wilson's veto of the Racial Equality Clause at Versailles, the tariff disputes, and the 5–5–3 disarmament problem."[38] In his study of American history textbooks, Loewen found that eight of the twelve books he reviewed did not include the My Lai massacre in their discussion of the Vietnam War.[39] How will we as a nation react if and when "outsiders" challenge our textbook narrative?

When teachers evaluate a nation's interpretation of its past involvement in wars, such as World War II or Vietnam, we must ask whether the nation won or lost the war under discussion. Losers are far more likely to argue that war goals are not worth the price. In Japan, Pacific War history is often presented as peace education, as is much of the teaching about Vietnam in the United States. If we want to examine Japan's narrative of its role in the Pacific War, we might want to compare it with American explanation for United States actions in the war in Vietnam rather than in World War II.

Study of Fujioka's movement to reinsert patriotic orthodoxy into Japanese texts can help American teachers and students speculate on what might happen when those who want to sanitize history have their way. Fujioka and his Liberal History Group are committed to a far-reaching reappraisal of national history. They want to delete from social studies textbooks any references that might detract from a student's sense of pride in the history of the Japanese nation. Some American teachers may want to compare Fujioka's approach to that of the Holocaust deniers in their world history courses. Yet shouldn't they also ask themselves whether they can find similarities closer to home? Do we Americans sanitize our national past?

Even today most American and world history textbooks fail to question the decision to drop atomic bombs on Hiroshima and Nagasaki, asserting that the bombs were used solely to save American lives. These accounts diverge sharply from the scholarly debates over alternative strategies for bringing the war to a timely conclusion, the ethics of bombing of noncombatants, and the relationship between the atomic decision and the origins of the Cold War. Precisely because the issues have been debated ever since 1945, students need to know about the controversies and the matters at stake.

Some middle school teachers I work with hesitate to use *Hiroshima no Pika*, a Japanese children's book on the impact of the atomic bombings, in their classes because of the artist's graphic images—even though their students see far more graphic images on a daily basis on their television screens at home. Could it be that as we write and teach about our nation's past, we—textbook authors, publishing companies, classroom teachers—like Fujioka, fear taking away our students' sense of pride in the history of our nation? Is this what making good citizens is all about?

There is an added benefit to studying Japan's textbook controversy, one that on the surface may seem insignificant. When American students and teachers study the textbook controversy in Japan, they meet Ienaga and Fujioka, real Japanese people. A teacher in the Five College area asks his students at the outset of each semester to name five Chinese or five Japanese or five Koreans, depending upon the course he is teaching. He says that sometimes the students are able to name five Chinese (if they're into Confucius and Laozi and Zhuangzi and the like), but not usually. Seldom are they able to name five Japanese, except for the occasional war buff, and almost never five Koreans. The point is, he says, that we all know that there are places out there called China, Japan, and Korea, but rarely do we consider that they are made up of individual human beings with both names and real lives. The more Asian (in this case Japanese) faces teachers can give students names for, the better.

If we step back for a moment and look at the larger picture framed by the Ienaga and Fujioka cases in Japan, what can we learn? We see a conservative narrative promulgated by a Japanese government that denies Japan's war of aggression—a narrative that the Ministry of Education has done its best to promote for more than fifty years. Ienaga's court battles and the efforts of many other progressive researchers, teachers, and labor unions produced a far more self-critical narrative. Japan's dominant narrative, modified as a result of the lawsuits, eventually came to include the Nanjing massacre, anti-Japanese resistance movements in Korea, forced mass suicide on Okinawa, and the plight of Asian comfort women. Today we see a challenge to the Ienaga counternarrative, a call for a sanitized version of Japan's history promoted by Fujioka and other like-minded nationalists.

This pattern of reinterpreting history should not be unfamiliar to Americans. As Robert Lerner, Althea Nagai, and Stanley Rothman remind us in their introduction to *Molding the Good Citizen: The Politics of High School History Texts*, "the Founding Fathers intended that education be an instrument in the service of republican virtue. Later activists of the antebellum and Progressive era wanted public education to play a crucial role in creating good citizen-democrats. Starting in the 1960s, new social movements—black civil rights organizations, feminists, peace groups, and environmentalists—sought to change the schools in specific ways to bring about a new social order."[40] In contemporary America, with the renewed emphasis on teacher and student testing, state frameworks, and national standards (although national standards take an explicit stand against any official history), many are crying out for a return to a more "traditional" narrative.

Can we teach about this in American classrooms—about master narratives and counternarratives and challenges to them both? This is what we should be teaching, . . . teaching that history is a process, an argument. We need to help our students realize that history is not what's in the textbook but a process of argument that is shaped by who is making the argument and when and where. As William Faulkner wrote, "The past is not dead. . . . It's not even past."

Notes

Thanks to Laura Hein and Mark Selden for their helpful suggestions and to Richard H. Minear for his continued support of my work with students and teachers.

1. The speaker was Jonathan Lipman (a historian at Mount Holyoke College), one of many scholars in the Five College area in western Massachusetts who has collaborated with social studies teachers throughout New England (and across the country) to bring serious historical thought and controversy into precollege classrooms.

2. Bradley Commission on History in the Schools, *Building a History Curriculum: Guidelines for Teaching History in Schools* (Westlake, OH: National Council for History Education, 1988), 24.

3. Anne Chapman, "The Textbook as Primary Source: How to Wring Novel Benefits from Conventional Texts," *Social Education,* February 1980, 87.

4. Diane Ravitch and Chester E. Finn Jr., *What Do Our 17-Year-Olds Know?* (New York: Harper and Row, 1988), 191.

5. "NAEP 1994 U.S. History Report Card: Findings from the National Assessment of Educational Progress," April 1996 National Center for Education Statistics Issue Brief, available at URL <http://nces.ed.gov/nationsreportcard/y25flk/hrcexec.shtml> (version current March 23, 1999).

6. Frances FitzGerald, *America Revised: History Schoolbooks in the Twentieth Century* (New York: Vintage Books, 1979), 47.

7. James W. Loewen, *Lies My Teacher Told Me: Everything Your American History Textbook Got Wrong* (New York: New Press, 1995), 280.

8. Ibid., 281.

9. My guess is that with the growing emphasis on national standards and state frameworks and guidelines, teachers will look even more to the textbook to provide that security. In fact the chair of a social studies department in western Massachusetts told me that his department chose a particular world history text precisely because the publishing company provided a teacher's manual linking textbook content with the Massachusetts state curriculum framework.

10. Paul Gagnon, *Democracy's Half Told Story: What American History Textbooks Should Add* (American Federation of Teachers, 1989), 27.

11. Ibid., 26.

12. Today I would spend more time discussing the adoption process. At that point in my career, I was unaware of the political clout that the big adoption states, California and Texas in particular, and certain urban districts have in determining textbook content.

13. Copyright laws allow publishers to change only a small portion of a book (including ancillary materials) in order to qualify for a fresh publication update.

14. Gagnon, *Democracy's Half Told Story*, 27.

15. Diane Ravitch, "The Plight of History in American Schools," in Paul Gagnon and the Bradley Commission on History in the Schools, eds., *Historical Literacy: The Case for History in American Education* (Boston: Houghton Mifflin, 1989), 55.

16. The series included suggestions for using pictures as teaching aids, hypothesizing for directed reading, distinguishing fact from opinion, writing editorials, and identifying propaganda.

17. In 1997 the International Society for Educational Information of Tokyo published a two-volume bilingual English and Japanese edition of excerpts from high school Japanese and world history textbooks that are widely used by Japanese students, *Japan in Modern History*. I selected events for my time line from volume 2.

18. Gerald Danzer, "Textbook Graphics and Maps: Keys to Learning," *Social Education*, February 1989, 102.

19. As found in *The Historian's Contribution to Anglo-American Misunderstanding: Report of Committee on National Bias in Anglo-American History Textbooks* (New York: Hobbs, Dorman and Co., 1966).

20. S. Schmidt, K. Tarnovsky, and I. Berkhin, *A Short History of the USSR*, trans. Sergei Sossinsky (Moscow: Progress Publishers, 1984), 234.

21. M. Inoue, K. Kasahara, K. Kodama (and ten others), *Japanese History*, trans. Midori Matsuyama Brameld (Tokyo: Yamakawa Publications, 1984), 292.

22. Lewis Paul Todd and Merle Curti, *Rise of the American Nation* (New York: Harcourt Brace Jovanovich, 1982), 348.

23. For example, many textbooks now have added glossaries in Spanish, concessions to the large-adoption states of Texas and California and an effort to include Hispanic immigrants who are learning about their new country's past.

24. Charlotte Crabtree, Gary B. Nash, Paul Gagnon, and Scott Waugh, eds., *Lessons from History: Essential Understandings and Historical Perspectives Students Should Acquire* (Los Angeles: National Center for History in the Schools, 1992), 18.

25. The planners were Richard H. Minear, professor of history at the University of Massachusetts at Amherst, and myself (codirectors of the summer institute) and Aiuchi Toshikazu, professor of political science at Hokkaido University of Education. The other participants in the Five College Center are Amherst, Hampshire, Mount Holyoke, and Smith Colleges.

26. The institute for New England teachers was funded by the National Endowment for the Humanities. Japan's Ministry of Education provided some funding for Japanese teachers attending the institute. The seminar in Japan was funded in part by grants from the United States–Japan Foundation and Hokkaido University of Education.

27. *Hotaru no Haka* is an animated tale based on the novel by Akiyuki Nosaki. It is the story of a fourteen-year-old boy and his four-year-old sister who become orphans during the U.S. firebombing of Kobe, seek refuge with relatives, but eventually die of starvation.

28. Richard H. Minear, "How Do American Schools Teach the Pacific War and Postwar Japan?" in Aiuchi Toshikazu, ed., *Education from the Pluralistic Viewpoints: Hokkaido–New England Seminar in Sapporo* (Sapporo: Hokkaido University of Education, 1995), 166–67.

29. Ibid., 160.

30. Fujioka Nobukatsu, "Problems of Teaching on War and Peace in Japan," in Aiuchi,

Education from the Pluralistic Viewpoints: Hokkaido–New England Seminar in Sapporo (Sapporo: Hokkaido University of Education, 1995), 172.

31. Ibid., 173.

32. Ibid., 175.

33. Evaluations were anonymous, unless a teacher chose to identify him- or herself.

34. Hayashi Hisako, "Records and Memories During World War II," talk given at Sapporo International Guest House, Sapporo, Japan, July 1994.

35. Sasaki Masao, "The Cause of the Pacific War: Explanation Based on International Relations," paper delivered at Smith College, Northampton, Massachusetts, August 1993.

36. Nishimura Yoshinori, "On Teaching History and the Smithsonian Atomic Bomb Exhibit," paper delivered at teachers' reunion at Amherst College, Amherst, Massachusetts, March 13, 1995.

37. "In 1919, mass movements swept many colonial and semicolonial countries, including Korea. Drawing upon Woodrow Wilson's promises of self-determination, a group of thirty-three intellectuals petitioned for independence from Japan on March 1 and touched off nationwide mass protests that continued for months. . . . At least half a million Koreans took part in the demonstrations in March and April, with disturbances in more than six hundred different places." Bruce Cumings, *Korea's Place in the Sun: A Modern History* (New York: W.W. Norton and Company, 1997), 154–55.

38. Peter K. Frost, "World History Texts: Coverage of Japan," in *National Review of Asia in American Textbooks in 1993* (Ann Arbor, MI: Association for Asian Studies, 1993), 57.

39. Loewen, Lies, 241.

40. Robert Lerner, Althea K. Nagai, and Stanley Rothman, *Molding the Good Citizen: The Politics of High School History Texts* (Westport, CT: Praeger, 1995), 1.

The Contributors

Aaron Gerow is Associate Professor in the International Student Center at Yokohama National University and has published widely in English and Japanese on early and contemporary Japanese cinema. His essay on Kobayashi Yoshinori's *Sensōron* was published in *Sekai* in December 1998.

Laura Hein teaches Japanese history at Northwestern University. She and Mark Selden co-edited *Living with the Bomb: Japanese and American Cultural Conflicts in the Nuclear Age*. She is the author of *Fueling Growth: Energy and Economic Policy in Postwar Japan*. She is currently writing a book on the political goals of economists in twentieth-century Japan.

David Hunt is Professor of History at the University of Massachusetts at Boston. He has taught and written about the Vietnam War and about peasants and revolutions in Vietnam and elsewhere.

***Inokuchi* Hiromitsu** is associate professor of sociology at the University of East Asia, Shimonoseki, Japan. He received his Ph.D. from the University of Wisconsin-Madison. He has published articles in Japanese and English on Resident Koreans and Japanese educational politics, and is currently writing on the politics of compensation for Asian victims of World War II.

***Kimijima* Kazuhiko** is Professor of modern Japanese history at Tokyo Gakugei University. His books include *Kyōkasho no Shiso* (Ideology of Textbooks) and the coauthored *Chosen/Kankoku wa Nihon no Kyōkasho ni do Kakareteiruka* (How Japanese textbooks represent Korea). He is a specialist in the history of Japanese colonial rule of Korea and a longtime activist in support of Ienaga Saburō's textbook lawsuits.

James Loewen is the author of *Lies My Teacher Told Me: Everything Your American History Textbook Got Wrong* and *Lies across America: What our Historic Sites and Monuments Get Wrong*. He is a coauthor of *Mississippi: Conflict and Change*. Loewen is Professor of Sociology emeritus at the University of Vermont.

Kathleen Woods Masalski directs programs for teachers for the Five College Center for East Asian Studies at Smith College. A former high school teacher, she conducts summer study tours and institutes and develops curricula on East Asia for schools, including a widely used unit on Japan in World War II.

Gavan McCormack is Professor of Japanese History in the Research School of Pacific and Asian Studies, Australian national University. His recent books include *The Emptiness of Japanese Affluence*, which has appeared in Chinese, Japanese, and Korean editions, and the jointly edited volume *Japanese Multiculturalism: From Palaeolithic to post-Modern*.

***Nozaki* Yoshiko** recently accepted a Lecturer appointment in the Department of Educational Leadership and Social Policy Studies, Massey University, New Zealand. She studied educational anthropology and curriculum history at the University of Wisconsin-Madison. A former social studies teacher, she has published articles on feminist theory and education.

Mark Selden teaches sociology and history at Binghamton University. His recent books include *Living With the Bomb: American and Japanese Cultural Conflicts in the Nuclear Age* (with Laura Hein), *China in Revolution: The Yenan Way Revisited*, and *Chinese Society: Change, Conflict, and Resistance* (with Elizabeth Perry). He is completing a coauthored volume on "Revolution, Resistance and Reform in Rural China."

Yasemin Nuhoglu Soysal is Associate Professor of Sociology at Essex University. Her research focuses on historical origins andcontemporary reconfigurations of citizenship and the nation-state. Sheis the author of *Limits of Citizenship: Migrants and Postnational Membership in Europe*. Her current research explores the claims-making and mobilization by minority and regional groups on national education, and changing nation-state identities in postwar Europe as projected in history and civics curricula and textbooks.

Gregory Paul Wegner, Professor of Educational Policy at the University of Wisconsin-La Crosse, has written extensively on education and fascism in Germany and is presently completing a book, *Racial Anti-Semitism and Schooling Under the Third Reich*, exploring the interrelationship between Nazi race ideology and curriculum with special emphases on biology, history and literature. Wegner is also involved in establishing a new Institute for Shoah and Genocide Studies at La Crosse.

Index

A

Adenauer, Konrad, 30
Afanase'v, Aleksandr N., 113
African Americans, recognition of wartime
    contributions, 35, 36
After the Fact (Davidson and Lytle), 164
Aiuchi Toshikazu, 276, 277
Akiko Hashimoto, 30
Aktion Sühnezeichen, 239
Ali, Muhammad, 156, 157, 158
All the People (Hakim), 152-153, 155-156,
    158, 162, 165
All Under the Moon, 88
American Adventures (Peck, Jantzen, and
    Rosen), 152, 160
American Adventure, The, 152
American History (Garraty), 152
American Pageant, The (Bailey and
    Kennedy), 151, 152, 153, 155,
    156-158, 161, 162, 165, 168
American People, The, 152, 155, 158, 161,
    162, 165, 168-169
American Tradition, The (Green, Becker,
    and Coviello), 152
American Way, The (Bauer), 151
America Revised (FitzGerald), 168, 259
*America's Longest War: The United States
    and Vietnam* (Herring), 198
America in Vietnam (Lewy), 198
Andō Shōeki, 207
Antiwar movement, omission from textbook
    accounts, 37, 39, 40, 156-158, 159
Antlov, Hans, 4

Aoyama Shinji, 78-79, 80, 83
Apology
    to comfort women, 54, 56
    for complicity in Holocaust, 34
    German *vs* Japanese, 15
    for Japanese-American internment, 37
    Vietnamese claims for, 21-22
Apple, Michael, 3-4
Archeological digs, at Buchenwald youth
    program, 241-242, 245, 250, 251-252
Ariyoshi Kinokawa Sawako, 279
Asahi shinbun, 65, 102, 111
Asanuma Inejiro, 65
Asian regionalism
    and consumerism, 88-93
    obstacles to, 19-21
    opposed by Japanese nationalists, 69-70,
        78
    vs U.S.-Japan alliance, 18
Atarashii Shakai (New Society), 111
Auschwitz-Birkenau concentration camp,
    233, 239
Azegami, Chief Justice, 109

B

Bailey, Thomas A., 151, 155, 168
Bao Dai, 178
Barker, Eugene, 36
Battle of China, 279
Bauer, Nancy, 151
Becker, Laura L., 152
Bedürftig, Friedemann, 228, 232
Berkin, Carol, 151

Berlin, Holocaust memorial in, 229
Berman, Aaron, 270
Big turnip, A (Ōkina Kabu), 113
Billington, Ray A., 265
Bivins, Betty, 152
Bleyer, Wolfgang, 233
Bonhöffer, Dietrich, 241
Boorstin, Daniel J., 152, 155, 156, 158, 161,
    162-163, 165, 168
Bradley Commission on History in the
    Schools, 258
Britain, and Europeanization, 46n.20, 135
Broadcast Youth, 89
Browning, Christopher, 227
Bubis, Ignatz, 229
Buchenwald concentration camp, 31
  commemoration of liberation, 251
  Nazi victims at, 236
  oath of, 239, 250-251
  as Soviet prison camp, 236-237
  youth education program at, 236, 238-253
    contribution of, 252-253
    and east-west dialogue, 242-244,
        248-249
    emotional response to, 245-247
    enrollments in, 244, 249
    research projects in, 247-248, 249,
        250, 252
    teaching methods in, 238-242,
        244-245, 251-252
    and Weimar tour, 248

C

Calley, William, 168
Canada, Japanese-Canadian internment in,
    37
Catholic Church, 34
Challenge of Freedom, The (Sobel, LaRaus,
    De Leon, and Morris), 152, 156,
    163-164
Chang, Iris, 47n.25
Cheam Chapel massacre of 1919, 217
China
  and Asian regionalism, 20
  protest against Japanese textbook
      accounts, 113
  war remembrance of, 10, 43, 49-50n.54
Cho Hang-nae, 214
Chŏng Chae-jung, 209
Christian-Smith, Linda, 3-4
Citizens' Association for the Defense of
    Japan, 56
Citizens Commission of Inquiry, 173

Citizenship
  and multiculturalism, 31
  in textbook controversies, 23-39
  textbook modeling of, 3, 5, 284-285
City of Corpses (Ota), 269
Cloud over the hill (Shiba), 64
Cold War collapse
  and nationalist revival, 79
  and war remembrance, 14-21
Comfort women, 6-7
  apology to, 54, 56
  compensation of, 25, 54, 56
  nationalist case on, 60-62, 67
  protests by, 281
  silence about, 27
  testimony of, 27, 53-54
  textbook accounts of, 10, 11, 25
    gender and racial attitudes exposed by,
        27-29
    Korean, 218
    nationalist opposition to, 27, 57,
        59-60, 86
    response to social activist criticism,
        41-42
Commager, Henry Steele, 36
Committee to Write New History Text-
    books, 78
Compensation, 21-22, 25, 54, 56
Cook, Haruko Taya, 269
Cook, Theodore F., 269
Council of Europe, 143, 146
Course of Our Country, The, 100
Coviello, Robert E., 152
Cuban, Larry, 261
Curti, Merle, 152, 164, 167, 261

D

Davidson, James West, 151, 164
Day, Dorothy, 158
Debate over Vietnam (Levy), 163
De Fronzo, Jim, 169
De Leon, Linda Ann, 152
Diem, Ngo Dinh, 178, 179, 180, 182, 183
Diet Members League for a Bright Japan,
    56
Diet Members League for the Fiftieth
    Anniversary of the End of the War, 56
Diet Members League for the Passing on of
    a Correct History, 56
*Different Mirror, A: A History of
    Multicultural America* (Takaki), 276
Discovering American History (Kownslar
    and Frizzle), 152, 163, 165, 167, 168

Discredited wars
 vs defeats, 44n.5
 problems of teaching, 4-5
 repudiation of, 39
Dulles, John Foster, 160
Dürr, E., 244

E

Eagle Against the Sun (Spector), 270
Emperor, and nationalism, 70, 71
Enola Gay exhibit, 11, 79
Ettersberg Memorial, 238, 250
European Academy, 145
European Standing Conference of History
 Teachers Associations (EUROCLIO),
 145, 149n.37
European Union
 creation of, 149n.35
 education programs of, 143, 145, 146
 impact on education curriculum, 130, 132,
 134-136
 and national identity, 15-17, 32, 41,
 46n.20, 130-134, 139-141

F

Farben (I.G.), 233
Faulkner, William, 285
Faurisson, Robert, 67
Federal Center for Political Education,
 229-230, 232
Fest, Joachim, 226
Films and documentaries, 79, 80, 83, 84,
 87-92, 270, 279
Finn, Chester E., Jr., 259
Fire in the Lake (Fitzgerald), 158
FitzGerald, Frances, 36, 158, 168, 259
Five College Center for East Asian Studies,
 268-279
Forced labor
 compensation for, 25, 53
 prisoners of war, 47n.34, 62
 textbook accounts of, 29, 111, 233-235
Ford Motor Company, 234
France, apology for wartime stance, 34
Frizzle, Donald B., 152
Fujioka Nobukatsu, 274, 281
 comfort women case of, 60, 61, 62
 and "correct history," 26-27, 56, 57, 58, 68
 formation of Orthodox History Group, 26
 and history education, 25-26, 74, 84, 86
 intellectual development of, 19, 63-64,
 65-66

Fujioka Nobukatsu *(continued)*
 and national identity, 85-86, 92
 nationalist history of, 25, 74, 75-78
 rejection of Asian regionalism, 69-70, 78
 and social issues, 65
 supporters of, 56
 teachers questionnaire of, 274
 textbook campaign of, 25, 64-65, 274,
 276, 283
Fujisawa Hōei, 203-204
Fussell, Paul, 2

G

Galen, Clemens Graff von, 235
Garraty, John A., 152
General Motors, 234
Georg Eckert Institute for International
 Textbook Research, 143, 149n.33
*German Awareness of History: Responsibil-
 ity for War as Represented in
 Textbooks* (Fujisawa), 203-204
German nationalism
 and Europeanization, 17, 32, 41, 130-134
 and multiculturalism, 31-32
 and Neo-Nazi groups, 138-139, 227-229,
 232, 236
 reaction against war reappraisal, 32
 redefinition of national identity, 15-17, 32,
 41, 128-130
 revival of, 41, 129
German textbooks
 and corporatist/consensus-oriented
 production, 8, 129-130, 141, 142
 crossnational approaches to, 17, 25, 143,
 145
 East German, 31
 and Hessian reforms, 142
 multiculturalism in, 31, 136-139
 religious education, 142
 on resistance to Nazis, 235, 238
 response to foreign criticism, 10
 transnational dimension of, 130-136,
 139-141, 145-146
 See also Holocaust education
German war remembrance
 and anniversary events, 129, 251
 apology and compensation approach to,
 15
 and collective responsibility, 32, 33,
 45n.13
 and democratic education, 5
 East *vs* West German approach to, 31,
 232-235, 238

German war remembrance *(continued)*
memorials in, 12-13, 248, 253
and moral recovery concept, 30
and nationalist revival, 41
and occupation policy, 11
public attitude toward, 10, 13
repudiation of Nazi war, 39
right-wing critique of, 32
selective, 232, 238
See also German nationalism; German
textbooks; Holocaust; Holocaust
education
Gerow, Aaron, 19, 42, 74-95, 276
Geschichte 9, 233
Gluck, Carol, 270
Goldhagen, Daniel, 13, 226-227, 236
Good War: An Oral History of World War II
(Terkel), 269
Grave of the Fireflies, 273
Green, Robert, 152
Greer, Robynn, 152
Griffen, William, 163
Guilt, 10, 13

H

Habermas, Jürgen, 226
Hadaka no Gen, 278
Hagopian, Patrick, 153
Hakim, Joy, 152-153, 155-156, 158, 162,
165, 168
Happy People, 83
Harnischfeger, George, 242, 244
Hashimoto Ryūtarō, 57
Hass, Gerhard, 233
Hastings, Max, 177
Hata Ikuhiko, 26, 60-61
Hayashi Fusao, 57, 58, 79
Hayashi Hisako, 277
Hein, Laura, 3-44, 281
Hellfire, 279
Helpless, 79, 80, 83
Herf, Jeffrey, 249
Herring, George, 178, 179, 181, 182, 185,
188, 189, 191, 198, 199
Herzog, Roman, 128-129
Hess, Gary, 178, 179, 185, 189, 198, 199
Hidaka Rokurō, 124n.224
Hilgruber, Andreas, 226
Hirohito, Emperor, 79, 96
Hiroshima and Nagasaki bombings
challenge to traditional narrative, 278
and *Enola Gay* exhibit, 11, 79
museum, 281

Hiroshima and Nagasaki bombings *(continued)*
mythification of, 79
suppression of civilian perspective, 275
U.S. textbook accounts of, 266, 283-284
Hiroshima no Pika, 284
History Not Taught in Textbooks (Fujioka),
25, 74, 75-78, 93
History textbooks. *See* Textbook accounts;
specific countries (i.e., German
textbooks)
History of the United States, A (Boorstin
and Kelley), 152, 155, 156, 158, 161,
162-163, 165, 168
History of US, A (Hakim), 153
Hitler (Bedürftig), 228, 232
*Hitler's Willing Executioners: Ordinary
Germans and the Holocaust*
(Goldhagen), 226-227
Ho Chi Minh, 160, 161, 167, 178, 184, 186,
189
Holocaust
conservative reinterpretations of, 129, 226
denial, 45n.7, 63, 67, 129, 283
Goldhagen controversy over, 13, 226-227,
236
memorials and museums, 11-12, 229, 253
Holocaust education, 6, 7
in Buchenwald youth program, 236-253
contribution of, 252-253
and east-west dialogue, 242-244,
248-249
emotional response to, 245-247
enrollments in, 244, 249
research projects in, 247-248, 249,
250, 252
teaching methods of, 238-242,
244-245, 251-252
and Weimar tour, 248
cinematic, 24
and confrontation with past, 229
contemporary racism related to, 138, 240,
242, 249, 252
on corporate complicity, 233-235
democratic goal of, 5, 33-34, 232
experimental curriculum, 228, 229-232
ideological bias in, 245
in immediate postwar period, 29-30
and intercultural learning, 31-32, 39,
138-139, 242, 252
on resistance movements, 230, 241, 243,
246, 248, 250
response to foreign criticism, 41
reunification impact on, 229, 235,
248-250

Honda Katsuichi, 111
Honnecker, Erich, 241, 245
Hosokawa Morihiro, 57
Hotaru no Haka, 273, 286n.27
Hunt, David, 22, 173-200
Huntington, Samuel, 191, 193

I

Ienaga Saburō, 5, 10, 24, 74, 97, 99, 270,
    279, 280
  educational views of, 98
  as historian, 123n.11
  participation in state-authored textbooks,
    100
  screening of textbooks, 102, 107
  textbook lawsuits of, 107-111, 114-121,
    281, 284
Inokuchi Hiromitsu, 5, 96-126, 280-281
International Commission of Jurists, 54
Internment policy. *See* Japanese-American
    internment
Irving, David, 226
Isheda Takeshi, 68
Ishibashi Tanzan, 64
Ishii Kazutomo, 104, 113
Iwai Shunji, 87

J

Jäckel, Eberhard, 227
Jantzen, Steven, 152
Japan
  Constitution of 1947, 100, 104
  education law in, 100-101
  foreign nationals in, 81, 89, 219-220
  global mistrust of, 19
  and Gulf War, 19, 63, 79
  U.S. relations, 18-19, 68, 70, 78
  U.S. textbook accounts of, 263–266,
    280-281, 283
  youth culture in, 81-83, 88, 92
  See also Asian regionalism; Hiroshima
    and Nagasaki bombings; Japanese
    nationalism; Japanese textbooks;
    Japanese war remembrance
Japanese-American internment, 7, 24,
    36-37, 38, 39, 42
Japanese Canadians, 37, 270
Japanese Institute for Orthodox History
    Education. *See* Orthodox History
    Group
Japanese nationalism
  and Asian regionalism, 69-70, 78

Japanese nationalism *(continued)*
  and Cold War collapse, 79
  consumerist, 86-93
  and "correct history," 59, 68
  history education theory of, 83-86
  instability of, 70-71
  intellectuals' view of, 67-68
  intimidation and violence in, 64-65, 71
  postwar revival of, 104
  reaction against war reappraisal, 25-27,
    56-59
  and superpower aspirations, 65-66
  and threats to national identity, 78-83, 92
  and victim complex, 66-67, 68-69, 76-77
  war crimes denial of, 61-63, 67, 86
  See also Fujioka Nobukatsu; Orthodox
    History Group
Japanese textbooks
  American teachers' view of, 272-273
  blacked-out, 98, 123n.7
  challenges to government policy on,
    23-24, 25-26, 120-122, 279-281
  civilian-hardship emphasis in, 9, 103
  and comfort women issue, 10, 11, 25, 27,
    28-29, 41-42, 59-60, 86
  on critics of colonialism, 210-211
  and emperor-centered history, 96-97, 100,
    214-216
  foreign criticism of, 8, 10, 100, 113,
    203-217, 281
  Japan-South Korea Joint Study Group on,
    203-217
  on Korean conquest, 206-208
  Korean-Japanese, 220-222
  on Korean resistance to colonial rule,
    209-210, 212-214
  lawsuits against state screening, 107-111,
    114-121, 284
  on Nanjing massacre, 11, 19, 100, 107,
    111, 112, 116, 119
  nationalist campaign against, 25-27, 42,
    56-57, 64-65, 75-78, 83-86, 104,
    113, 274, 276, 283
  and nationalist curricula, 112
  occupation policy on, 7, 97, 101
  on origins of war, 208-209, 210
  recognition of aggression, 39, 41, 115-116
  response to foreign criticism, 10-11,
    41-42, 113-114, 141, 205-206
  sanitized version of war, 10, 12, 23, 74,
    114, 284
  state-authored, 98-102
  state control over, 8, 10, 104-105, 107,
    112-114, 216, 222, 280

Japanese war remembrance
apology and compensation approach to,
15, 25, 54, 56, 57, 69
broadening teachers' perspectives on,
272-279
and democratic education, 5
and historical documentation, 24, 25,
47n.25, 111
of home front, 276-277
memorials and museum exhibits, 13
nationalist opposition to reappraisal, 56-59
and occupation policy, 11, 57
public attitudes toward, 10, 13, 18, 39
public discussion of, 24-25
and war crime denial, 61-63
See also Comfort women; Japanese
textbooks
Japan in Modern History, 263
Japan's Decision for War, 270
Japan-South Korea Joint Study Group on
History Textbooks, 203-225
Japan Teachers Union, 24, 101
Japan at War: An Oral History (Cook and
Cook), 269
Jenkins, Brian, 188
Jikkyō Shuppan press, 217
Jinkō, Empress, 207
Joes, Anthony James, 177, 178, 179, 181,
183-184, 186, 188-189, 191, 193, 198,
199
Johnson, Lyndon, 156, 160, 180
Jugendbegegnungsstätte (JBS). *See*
Buchenwald concentration camp,
youth education program at
Jugendweihe, 251
Junk Food, 83, 84, 88
Just and Unjust Wars (Walzer), 63

K

Kades, Charles, 270
Kalenbach, Dieter, 228, 232
Kanghwa Island incident of 1875, 209
Karnow, Stanley, 178, 179, 182-183, 185,
186, 188, 189, 191, 194, 198
Katō Akira, 206-207
Kattago Siobhan, 13
Katzenstein, Peter, 17, 139, 140
Kelley, Brooks Mather, 152, 155, 156, 158,
161, 162-163, 165, 168
Kennedy, David M., 151, 155
Kennedy, John F., 160, 162
Kerry, John, 156
Kilpatrick, W.H., 247

"Kimigayo," 24, 85, 112
Kimijima Kazuhiko, 7, 29, 203-225
Kim, Richard, 270, 279
Kim Sŏng-il, 211, 220
King, Martin Luther, Jr., 156
Kinjō Shigeaki, 119
Kobayashi Yoshinori, 56, 57, 79, 81-83, 87
Kogawa, Joy, 270
Kohl, Helmut, 13, 232
Kolko, Gabriel, 196n.23
Korean Committee on Compiling National
History, 205
Koreans in Japan, 81, 89, 219-220
Korean textbooks
on Japanese aggression, 43, 218-219
Japanese-Korean, 220-222
state-authored, 217-218, 222
Korean war remembrance
criticism of Japanese textbook accounts,
113, 203-217
and Japanese critics of colonialism,
210-212, 214
of resistance to Japanese rule, 209-210,
211, 213, 219, 223-224n.10
Korean War, The (Hastings), 177
Kōtoku Shūsui, 210
Kownslar, Allan O., 152
Kraig, Bruce, 152
Kumazawa Banzan, 207
Kunihiro Masao, 68
Kurihara Sadako, 278
Kurosawa Akira, 264

L

Ladejinsky, Wolf, 182-183
Land of Promise (Berkin and Wood), 151
Lansdale, Edward, 189, 191
Lapham, Lewis, 171n.4
LaRaus, Roger, 152
League of Nations, 143
Lee Kwan Yew, 19
Lerner, Robert, 284
Levy, David, 163
Lewy, Guenter, 174-175, 177, 178-179,
180-181, 182, 184, 186, 188-189, 191,
193, 198, 199
Liberal Democratic Party (LDP), 54, 56, 57,
104, 112-113
Liberal View of History Study Group. *See*
Orthodox History Group
*Lies My Teacher Told Me: Everything Your
American History Textbook Got Wrong*
(Loewen), 151-152, 156, 260

Life and Liberty (Roden, Greer, Kraig, and Bivins), 152
Lipman, Jonathan, 270, 285n.1
Loewen, James, 22, 37, 39, 150-172, 260, 283
Lomperis, Timothy, 177, 178, 179, 181, 184, 186, 188, 189, 198, 199
Lost Names (Kim), 279
Love Letter, 87
Lu Xun, 270
Lytle, Mark H., 151, 164

M

Maastricht treaty, 143, 149n.35
McCormack, Gavan, 19, 53-71, 276, 281
Maclear, Michael, 178, 188, 189, 191, 198
McNeil, Linda, 150, 169
Mahathir Mohamad, 19
Mailer, Norman, 269
Makimura Hiroshi, 210
Map activities, 264, 265
Marciano, John, 163
Markovits, Andre S., 41
Maruki, Iri, 279
Maruki, Toshi, 279, 280
Maruyama Kunio, 99
Masalski, Kathleen Woods, 7, 258-285
Mason, Leslie, 270
Mayuzumi Toshiro, 56
Memorials and museum exhibits
  controversy over, 11-12
  German, 12-13, 229, 248, 250, 253
  Japanese, 13, 281
  U.S., 11, 79
Meyer, John, 139
Minear, Richard H., 63, 270, 272, 273-274, 276
Miyazawa Kiichi, 114, 205-206
Molding the Good Citizen: The Politics of High School History Texts (Lerner, Nagai, and Rothman), 284
Moral recovery concept, 30
Morris, Harry P., 152
Moss, George, 178, 179, 181, 184, 185, 186, 191, 198, 199
Multiculturalism, in Germany, 31-32, 39, 136-139
Museum exhibits. *See* Memorials and museum exhibits
My Lai massacre, 163, 164, 167, 168, 175, 283

N

Nagai, Althea, 284
Nagano Shigeo, 274

Nagasu Kazuii, 124n.22
Nakamura Masanori, 67
Nakasone Yasuhiro, 104, 114, 264
Naked and the Dead, The (Mailer), 269
Nanjing massacre
  public discussion of, 25
  textbook accounts of, 10, 11, 100, 107, 111, 116, 119
Narita Ryūichi, 84
Nationalism
  citizenship modeling in textbooks, 3, 4, 5, 284-285
  and foundational narratives, 43
  in U.S. textbooks, 265-266, 273-274, 280, 284-285
  See also German nationalism; Japanese nationalism
National Shrine Association, 56
Naumann, Michael, 229
Neo-Nazi groups
  attacks on foreigners, 227-229
  and Holocaust education, 232, 236, 242, 252
  textbook accounts of, 138-139
Neue Wache Museum, 12-13
Neumann, Klaus, 31
New Japanese history (Shin Nihonshi), 98, 102, 107, 108, 111, 114
New Society (Atarashii Shakai), 111
New York Times, 266
New York Times Magazine, 174
Nguyen Ngoc Loan, 155
Nishimura Yoshinori, 279
Nishio Kanji, 26, 56, 61-62
Nixon, Richard, 156-157, 168
Nobutaka Ike, 270
Nogi Maresuke, 64
Nolte, Ernst, 226
Nozaki Yoshiko, 5, 96-126, 280-281

O

Obasan (Kagawa), 270
Obsession, An, 83
O Buchenwald, 245
Occupation policy
  anticommunist focus in, 104
  on continuity of personnel, 11
  on prostitution, 47n.33
  on textbook accounts, 7, 98, 99, 101
  Tokyo Trials view of history, 57, 68
Oguma Eiji, 83
Okina Kabu (A big turnip), 113
Okinawa, Battle of, textbook account of, 116, 117-119

Okubo Toshikane, 100
Okuno Seisuke, 56
Olson, James, 178, 179, 181, 182, 184, 186-187, 191, 198, 199
Ōno, Chief Justice, 119
On war (Kobayashi), 81-83, 87
Orthodox History Group, 32, 42, 56
    and comfort women issue, 27, 59-63
    credentials as educators, 84
    education theory of, 83-86
    formation of, 26
    goals of, 26-27
    liberal self-image of, 86-87
    See also Fujioka Nobukatsu
Orwell, George, 96, 119
Ossietzky, Carl von, 230
Ōta Kōzō, 96-97
Ota Yoko, 269
Ōtomo Katsuhiro, 88
Ōtsuki Takahiro, 86-87
Ozawa Ichiro, 56
Ozawa Tatsuo, 56

P

Pacific War, The: 1931-1945 (Ienaga), 270
Pak Sŏng-su, 205, 214, 217, 220
Park Chung Hee, 217, 218
Pearl Harbor, 36, 270, 274, 278, 280, 283
Pearl Harbor: Surprise and Remembrance, 270
Peck, Ira, 152
Persian Gulf War, Japanese response to, 19, 63, 79
Polish war remembrance
    and anti-German feeling, 43
    and Europeanization, 17
    and Holocaust memorials, 11-12
Porno Star, 83
Prisoners of war, 47n.34, 55, 62
Professors for Peace Academy, 56
Promise of America (Cuban and Roden), 261

Q

Quang Duc, 155

R

Ravensbrück concentration camp, education program at, 253
Ravitch, Diane, 259
Red Cross, apology for wartime stance, 34

Reich, Simon, 41
Reise in die Vergangenheit, Die (Travels in the past), 136
Religious education, in Germany, 142
Reparations, 21-22, 25, 54, 56
Requiem for Battleship Yamato (Yoshida), 269
Rise of the American Nation, 152, 164, 167, 261
    See also Triumph of the American Nation
Rising sun flag, 24, 85
River Ki, The (Ariyoshi), 279
Roberts, Randy, 178, 179, 181, 184, 186-187, 191, 198, 199
Robertson, Jennifer, 91-92
Roden, Philip, 152, 261
Romanowski, Michael, 37
Rook, Helmut, 240, 245, 246, 251
Roosevelt, Franklin D., 160, 161, 269
Rosen, Daniel, 152
Rothman, Stanley, 284
Russo-Japanese War of 1904–1905, 209

S

Sachsenhausen concentration camp, education program at, 253
Saigō Takamori, 207
Sai Yōichi, 88
Sakai Toshiki, 220
Sakurai Yoshiko, 79, 86
Sankei shinbun, 25, 57
Sapio, 57
Sapporo seminar, 272, 273-277
Sarason, Seymour B., 150
Sasaki Masao, 279
Satō Manabu, 67, 86
Savio, Mario, 158
Sawa Hidekatsu, 83
Schneider, Paul, 243, 246
Schneider, Peter, 30, 33, 39
Second Indochina War, The (Turley), 198
Seicho No Ie, 56
Selden, Mark, 3-44, 281
Selected Readings from the Works of Mao Tsetung, 270
Selected Works (Lu Xun), 270
Service Civil International (SCI), 241, 242
Shady Grove, 83
Sheehan, Neil, 168, 174
Shiba Ryotaro, 57, 64
Shin Nihonshi (New Japanese history), 98, 102, 107, 108, 111, 114
Showakan Museum, 13

Siemens Corporation, 235
Sino-Japanese War of 1894–1895, 209
Smithsonian Institution, *Enola Gay* exhibit
    of, 11, 79
Sobel, Robert, 152
Social Education, 169, 263, 264
Sono Ayako, 119
Soysal, Yasemin Nuhoglu, 7, 15-16, 30,
    127-149
Spector, Ronald, 270
Stauffenberg Circle, 235, 238
Suga Hidemi, 87
Sugimoto, Chief Justice, 109
Supreme Command for the Allied Powers
    (SCAP). *See* Occupation policy
Suzuki, Chief Justice, 117
Suzuki Kōsuke, 83
Swallowtail Butterfly, 87-82
Switzerland, apology for wartime stance, 34
Syngman Rhee, 217

T

Taiwan war remembrance, 45n.8
Takaki, Ronald, 276
Takasaki Sōji, 210-211
Teaching the Vietnam War (Griffen and
    Marciano), 163
Ten Thousand Day War, The (Maclear), 198
Terkel, Studs, 269
Textbook accounts
  and democratic education, 5
  of discredited wars, 4-5
  Europeanization impact on, 130, 132,
    134-135
  and European Union programs, 143, 145
  foreign criticism of, 7-8, 10
  and globalization, 282
  international collaboration on, 143
  national myths in, 4, 130, 265-266
  as official history, 3-4
  response to foreign criticism, 10-11
  and social movements, 5-7
  teachers' reliance on, 150, 169, 259-260
  and vision of shared future, 42-44
  See also specific countries (i.e., German
    textbooks)
Thälmann, Ernst, 248, 253
Thieu, Nguyen Van, 178, 179, 180, 183
Time-line activity, 263
Times and people (Zeiten und Menschen),
    136
Todd, Paul Lewis, 152, 164, 261
Tokutake Toshio, 124n.22

Tokyo University, 67, 68, 84, 99
Tokyo War Crimes Trials, 27, 57, 120
  view of history, 57, 68
Tonnesson, Stein, 4
Toyoda Takeshi, 98-99
Toyoda Toshiaki, 83
Toyotomi Hideyoshi, 207
Travels in the past (Die Reise in die
    Vergangenheit), 136
Triumph of the American Nation (Todd and
    Curti), 152, 155, 161, 162, 164, 165,
    167
  See also Rise of the American Nation
Troop Sōmō, textbook account of, 117, 119
Truman, Harry, 160, 162
Turley, William, 178, 179, 183, 185, 187,
    188, 189, 191, 198, 199-200

U

Uchimura Kanz, 210
Ukai Tetsu, 79
Unification Church, 56
Unit 731, 25, 54, 62, 116, 119, 125n.41
United Nations Educational, Scientific, and
    Cultural Organization (UNESCO), 17,
    25, 143, 146, 222n.1
United Nations Human Rights Committee,
    54
United States
  and Asian economy, 20
  immigration "ban list," 54
  Japan relations, 18-19, 68, 70, 78
  See also Occupation policy; United States
    textbooks; United States war
    remembrance
United States textbooks
  on causes of war, 281, 283
  celebratory nature of, 22, 151
  decentralized control over, 8
  on Hiroshima and Nagasaki bombing,
    266, 283-284
  and inclusiveness issue, 8, 34-36
  on Japanese-American internment, 36-37,
    38, 39, 42
  lack of foreign criticism, 8, 281
  nationalistic bias in, 265-266, 280
  as national narrative, 273-274, 284-285
  national/state standards and guidelines,
    258, 259, 285n.9
  on Pacific War, 263–266, 280, 281, 283
  public debate over, 258-259
  publishers' response to past complaints
    about, 266-267

United States textbooks *(continued)*
  supplementation of, 37, 260, 268-272,
    273, 278-279
  teachers' reasons for using, 259-260
  and teaching strategies, 260-266
  See also Vietnam War textbook accounts
United States, The: A History of the
    Republic (Davidson and Lytle), 151,
    164
United States war remembrance
  broadening of teachers' perspectives,
    272-279
  Enola Gay exhibit, 11
  of racial segregation, 42
  response to foreign criticism, 21, 42, 44
  See also United States textbooks; Vietnam
    War remembrance; Vietnam War
    textbook accounts

V

Victim complex, in Japan, 66-67, 68-69,
    76-77
Victimhood, shared, in Germany, 13
Victor's Justice (Minear), 63
Viet Minh, 179, 184, 185
Vietnam: An American Ordeal (Moss), 198
Vietnam, A History (Karnow), 198
Vietnam and the United States: Origins and
    Legacy of War (Hess), 198
Vietnam Veterans Against the War (VVAW),
    40
Vietnam War remembrance
  and apology and compensation, 21-22
  response to foreign criticism, 13-14, 21
  schools' failure to teach, 169-171
  and winter soldiers' testimony, 173-174
  See also Vietnam War textbook accounts
Vietnam Wars, The (Young), 175, 198, 199
Vietnam War textbook accounts, 151-153
  of antiwar movement, 37, 39, 40, 156-158,
    159
  criticism of U.S. policy, 177, 182, 199
  exclusion/distortion of controversial
    issues, 158, 160-163, 283
  improvements in, 167-169
  and moral issues, 42, 163-167, 168,
    174-175
  neglect of Vietnamese society and people,
    22, 189-195
  of North Vietnamese, 185-189
  on origins of war, 158, 160-162, 167
  of Saigon government, 174-184, 199
  visual image selection in, 153-156

Visual images, of Vietnam War, 153-156

W

Walzer, Michael, 63
War Bereaved Families Association, 56
War crimes
  Japanese denial of, 59-62, 63, 67
  Japanese *vs* German, 62-63
  in Japanese textbook accounts, 111,
    116-119
  Tokyo Tribunal on, 27, 57, 68, 120
  in Vietnam War textbook accounts,
    163-167, 168, 174-175, 283
  and Vietnam War winter soldier hearings,
    173-174
  See also Comfort women; Holocaust;
    Holocaust education; Nanjing
    massacre
War Everyone Lost—and Won, The:
    America's Intervention in Viet Nam's
    Twin Struggles (Lomperis), 198
War remembrance. *See* Textbook accounts;
    World War II remembrance; *specific*
    countries (i.e., German textbooks,
    German war remembrance)
War for South Viet Nam, The (Joes), 198
Wartime: Understanding and Behavior in
    the Second World War (Fussell), 269
Wegner, Gregory, 5, 13, 30, 31, 34, 41,
    226-257
Weibelfeldschule, in Buchenwald education
    program, 236, 248-253
Weimar, Holocaust education program in,
    248
Westmoreland, William, 175
What Do Our 17-Year-Olds Know? (Ravitch
    and Finn), 259
When I Close My Eyes, 87
Where the Domino Fell: America and
    Vietnam (Olson and Roberts), 198
Williams, Raymond, 232
Wilson, Woodrow, 160, 161
Winter soldier investigation, 173-174
Wolf, Siegfried, 251
Women
  recognition of wartime contributions, 34,
    36, 271
  status in Japan, 81
  war memoirs of, 270, 276-277
  See also Comfort women
Wood, Leonard, 151
World Anti-Communist League, 56
World Apartment Horror, 88

World Trade Organization, 20
World War II remembrance
  binational, 272-279
  and collapse of Cold War, 14-21
  memorials and museum exhibits, 11-13,
    229, 248, 250, 253, 281
  selective, 232, 238
  See also Textbook accounts; *specific
    countries* (i.e., German textbooks,
    German war remembrance)

Y

Yamamoto Masashi, 83, 88
Yamashita Tomoyuki, 175
Yanagi Muneyoshi, 210

Yi Hyŏn-hee, 207
Yi T'ae-yŏng, 203-204
Yi Wŏn-sun, 211-212, 214,
  220
Yomota Inuhiko, 89
Yoshida Mitsuru, 269
Yoshimi Yoshiaki, 67
Young, Marilyn, 175, 178, 185, 186, 187,
  198, 199-200
Young Socialist Student Union, 142
Youth culture, in, Japan, 81-83, 88, 92

Z

Zeiten und Menschen (Times and people),
  136